The Business Literacy for HR Professionals Series

The Business Literacy for HR Professionals Series educates human resource professionals in the principles, practices, and processes of business and management. Developed in conjunction with the Society for Human Resource Management, these books provide a comprehensive overview of the concepts, skills, and tools HR professionals need to be influential partners in developing and executing organizational strategy. Drawing on rich content from Harvard Business School Publishing and the Society for Human Resource Management, each volume is closely reviewed by a content expert as well as by senior HR professionals. Whether you are aspiring to the executive level in your organization or already in a leadership position, these authoritative books provide the basic business knowledge you need to play a strategic role.

Other books in the series:

The Essentials of Corporate Communications and Public Relations
The Essentials of Finance and Budgeting
The Essentials of Managing Change and Transition
The Essentials of Negotiation
The Essentials of Power, Influence, and Persuasion
The Essentials of Project Management

BUSINESS LITERACY FOR HR PROFESSIONALS

The Essentials of
STRATEGY

Harvard Business School Press
Boston, Massachusetts

and

the Society for Human Resource Management
Alexandria, Virginia

ISBN-13: 978-1-59139-822-6

Library of Congress Cataloging-in-Publication Data forthcoming

Contents

Contents   xi

Introduction

This book is about strategy creation and implementation—and ways in which you, as an HR professional, can facilitate both in your company. A good strategy matched with outstanding implementation is every organization's best assurance of success. It is also an undeniable sign of good management. And HR practitioners can play a major role in shaping their company's strategy as well as ensuring that the strategy is carried out as planned.

Strategy creation is about *doing the right things* and is a primary concern of senior executives and business owners. Implementation is about *doing things right*, a very different set of activities. Both senior executives and lower-ranking managers must give implementation intense attention—because even a great strategy is worthless if people fail to carry it out properly. Oddly, many books and articles have been written about business strategy, but much less has been written about implementation. We hope to correct that problem in the chapters that follow.

What Is Strategy?

In its original sense, strategy (from the Greek word *strategos*) was a military term used to describe the art of the general. It refers to the general's plan for arraying and maneuvering his forces with the goal of defeating an enemy army. Carl von Clausewitz, the nineteenth-century theoretician of the art of war, described strategy as "concerned with drafting the plan of war and shaping the individual campaigns, and within these, deciding on the individual engagements."[1] More recently, in the era when nation states are pitted against each other, the concept of strategy has broadened. Historian Edward Mead Earle describes it as "the art of controlling and utilizing the resources of a nation—or a coalition of nations—including its armed forces, to the end that its vital interests shall be effectively promoted and secured."[2]

Businesspeople have always liked military analogies, so it is not surprising that they have embraced the notion of strategy. They, too, began to think of strategy as a plan for controlling and utilizing their resources (human, physical, and financial capital) to the end of promoting and securing their vital interests. Kenneth Andrews was the first to articulate these emerging ideas in his classic, *The Concept of Corporate Strategy,* which was first published in 1971. Andrews described a framework that remains useful today, of defining strategy in terms of what a business can do—that is, its strengths and weaknesses—and what possibilities are open to it—that is, the outer environment of opportunities and threats. A decade or so later, Harvard professor Michael Porter sharpened this definition, describing strategy as "a broad formula for how a business is going to compete."[3]

Bruce Henderson, founder of Boston Consulting Group and one of the tribal elders of corporate strategy, connected the notion of strategy with competitive advantage, perhaps borrowing a concept drawn from economics (comparative advantage). A *competitive advantage* is a function of strategy that puts a firm in a better position than rivals to create economic value for customers. Henderson wrote, "Strategy is a deliberate search for a plan of action that will develop a business's competitive advantage and compound it." Competitive advantage, he went on, is found in differences. "The differences between you and your competitors are the basis of your advantage."[4] Henderson believed that no two competitors could coexist if both sought to do business in the same way. They must differentiate themselves to survive. "Each must be different enough to have a unique advantage."

For example, two men's clothing stores on the same block—one featuring formal attire and the other focusing on leisure wear—could potentially survive and prosper. Their physical proximity might even create mutual benefits. However, if the same two stores were to sell the same things under the same terms, one or the other would perish. Faced with this situation, each would attempt to differentiate itself in ways most pleasing to customers—through price, product mix, or ambiance.

Michael Porter concurs with Henderson's idea of being different: "Competitive strategy is about being different. It means deliberately choosing a different set of activities to deliver a unique mix of value."[5] Consider these familiar examples:

- **Southwest Airlines** didn't become the most profitable air carrier in North America by copying its rivals. It differentiated itself with a strategy characterized by low fares, frequent departures, point-to-point service, and customer-pleasing service.

- **eBay** created a different way for people to sell and acquire goods: online auctions. Company founders aimed to serve the same purpose as classified ads, flea markets, and formal auctions, but made it simple, efficient, and wide reaching. Online auctions have differentiated the company's service from those of traditional competitors.

- **Toyota's** strategy in developing the hybrid engine Prius passenger car was to create a competitive advantage in the eyes of an important segment of auto buyers: people who want a vehicle that is either environmentally benign, cheap to operate, or the latest thing in auto engineering.

So far, these strategies have served their initiators very well and have provided competitive advantages over rivals. Southwest Air is the most profitable U.S. air carrier, eBay is the most successful Internet company ever, and, at this writing, Toyota has a four-month waiting list of customers for its hybrid car. Being different can take many forms. As we'll see later, even companies whose products are identical to competitors' can strategically set themselves apart by, for example, offering a better price or providing faster and more reliable delivery.

Being different, of course, does not in itself confer competitive advantage or ensure business success. A rocket car would be "different" but would be unlikely to attract enough customers to be successful. A hybrid (gasoline/electric)-powered car, in contrast, is different in a way that creates superior value for customers in terms of fuel economy and low emissions of air-fouling exhaust. Those are values for which customers will gladly pay.

So, what is strategy? *Strategy* is a plan that aims to give an enterprise a competitive advantage over rivals. Strategy is about understanding what you do, clearly defining what you want to become, and—most important—taking the right steps to get there. Likewise, it is about what you *don't* do. In this sense, it draws boundaries around the scope of your company's intentions. For example, suppose your company has discovered that outside vendors can manage its supply chain far more efficiently and cost effectively than it can. In this case, the company's strategy might well stipulate outsourcing supply chain logistics to ensure that its customers get the products they want, when they want them, and where they want them.

A sound strategy, skillfully implemented, identifies the goals and direction that managers and employees at every level need in order to define their work and make their organization successful. An organization without a clear strategy, in contrast, is rudderless. It flails about—dashing off in one direction after another as opportunities present themselves, but never achieving a great deal.

Strategy is formulated and executed at both corporate and operating unit levels. For example, General Electric consists of many divisions serving different industries: aircraft engines, home appliances, capital services, lighting, medical systems, plastics, power systems, and electrical distribution and control. GE even owns NBC, one of the major U.S. television networks. The people who run this vast enterprise have a strategy, as do the senior managers of each division. Because the divisions operate in very different industries and competitive environments, their strategies must be unique. But each must also align behind the larger corporate strategy.

In addition to the corporate and operating unit level, strategy must also be defined and implemented within each unit's major functions—such as human resources, marketing, finance, product development, and customer service. In each of these functions, leaders strive to ensure that their teams' activities and efforts support the higher-level strategy.

For example, suppose your company's strategy stipulates divesting one or more divisions that don't relate to the company's core competencies. Any company divesting an entity strives to get the highest possible purchase price for it. As HR leader, you can help add as much as 5 percent to the divested unit's selling price, as well as ensure a smooth transition after the divestiture, by taking the following actions in each phase of the divestiture process:[6]

- **Preshopping.** For the other members of your company's executive team, produce a clear-eyed assessment of the skills and competencies of the key talent at the unit being divested. Show how you'll keep your home talent while passing along enough to keep the divested piece attractive to potential buyers. Examine base salaries, benefits costs, and other costs to determine the unit's financial liability. Offer ideas for packaging the deal, such as including buyer responsibility for costly retiree benefits.

- **Shopping.** Formulate ideas for enhancing the purchase price as much as possible. For instance, one company brought in interim managers to run the division that would be sold. The people they selected knew there was a chance of going with the acquirer if they helped the transition unfold smoothly.

- **Shoring up.** To prevent sabotage, union unrest, and other damaging forces by people in the unit targeted for divestiture, implement a communication campaign. Tell the employees that the divestiture is the best thing that can happen: the unit needs to be owned by people who know the business and who have more money—or it may well go out of business. Coach the unit's managers to look sharp, so the acquirer will want to keep them on board.

Strategy Versus Business Model

Many people confuse strategy with a newly popular term: business model. *Business model* first came into popular use in the late 1980s, at a time when many people were gaining experience with personal computers and spreadsheet software. Thanks to these digital innovations, businesspeople found that they could easily "model" the costs and revenues associated with any proposed business. After the model was set up, it took only a few keystrokes to observe the impact of individual changes—for example, in unit price, profit margin, and supplier costs—on the bottom line. Pro forma financial statements were the primary documents of business modeling. By the time dot-com fever had become rampant, the term *business model* had become a popular buzzword. Still, many people were unable to articulate exactly what it meant.

Scholars define a business model as the economic underpinnings of a company's strategy. Management consultant Joan Magretta has provided a useful introduction to business models in "Why Business Models Matter," a 2002 *Harvard Business Review* article. In the article, she describes a business model as some variation of the value chain that supports every business. "Broadly speaking," she writes, "this chain has two parts. Part one includes all the activities associated with making something: designing it, purchasing raw materials, manufacturing, and so on. Part two includes all the activities associated with selling something: finding and reaching customers, transacting a sale, distributing the product or delivering the service."[7]

Thus, a business model is more about the mechanisms through which the entity produces and delivers a product or service, and less about what differentiates it in the eyes of customers and gives it competitive advantage. A business model answers these questions: How does this company work? What underlying economic logic explains how we can deliver value to customers at an appropriate cost?

Every viable organization is built on a sound business model. However, a business model isn't a strategy, even though many people use the terms interchangeably. Business models describe, as a system, how the pieces of a business fit together to produce a profit. But they don't factor in a critical dimension of performance: competition. That's the job of strategy.

Some of today's most powerful and profitable companies grew out of business models that were elegant and compelling in their logic and powerful in economic potential. Dell Computer is one of these and the most often cited example. eBay is another.

eBay, the online auction company, grew out of a very simple and traditional model. Like a long-distance telephone company, eBay created an infrastructure that allowed people to communicate; and, again like the long-distance provider, it picked up a modest fee from each use. Its Web-based infrastructure of software, servers, and rules of behavior allows a community of buyers and sellers to meet and conduct transactions for all manner of goods—from Elvis memorabilia to used Porsches. The company takes no part in the transactions, thereby avoiding many of the costs incurred by other businesses. Its only responsibilities are to maintain the integrity of the auction process and the information system that make its auctions possible.

As a mechanism for generating income, the eBay model is simple. It receives revenues from seller fees. Those revenues are reduced by the cost of building and maintaining the online infrastructure and by the usual marketing, product development, general, and administrative costs that keep the operation running and that attract buyers and sellers to the site. The net of these revenues and costs constitutes profits for eBay shareholders.

Aside from its simplicity, the great power of the eBay model is the fact that a small number of salaried employees and outsource partners can handle a huge and growing volume of business. Further, a doubling of transaction volume (and revenue) can be accommodated with relatively modest investments. Software and servers do the heavy lifting. This is much different from the company's stated strategy, which is to build and effectively support the world's most efficient and abundant Web-based marketplace—a marketplace in which anyone, anywhere, can buy or sell almost anything.

As this example should make clear, strategy and business models are different concepts, even though they are related. While strategy provides differentiation and competitive advantage, the business model explains the economics of how the business works and makes money.

The Strategy Process

Like most important things in business, strategy creation and its implementation should be approached as a process—that is, as a set of activities that transforms inputs into outputs. This process is described graphically in figure I-1. Here we see that strategy creation follows from the mission of the company, which defines its purpose and what it aims to do for customers and other stakeholders. Given the mission, senior management sets goals. These goals are tangible manifestations of the organization's mission and are used to measure progress. Goals, as shown in the figure, should be informed by a pragmatic understanding of both the external business/market environment and the internal capabilities of the organization.

Strategy creation typically begins with extensive research and analysis and a process through which senior management narrows in

FIGURE I-1

The strategy implementation process

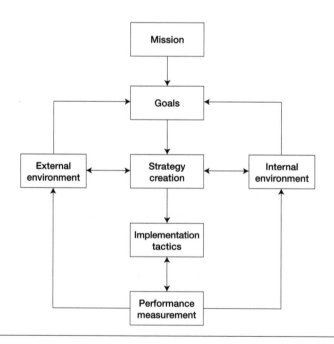

on the top-priority issues that the company needs to tackle to be successful in the long term. Priority issues related to human capital might include retention of talented managers and employees, leadership "bench strength," the spread of best practices throughout the organization, workforce productivity metrics, innovation in product development, turnaround of ailing business units, and so forth.[8]

For each priority issue, units, functions, and teams are asked to create high-level action plans. For instance, the HR group might create an action plan for improving leadership bench strength that includes longer-range succession planning and higher-quality recruiting processes. Once units and functions have developed their action plans, the company's high-level strategic objectives and direction statement are further clarified—as senior management weighs the various plans and further refines the company's priorities.

Formulating a high-level strategy takes time and requires a series of back-and-forth communications between senior management and the leaders of functions and operating units, whereby all parties examine, discuss, and refine the plan. As a result, various planning streams often happen in parallel. Involving functions and operating units in the strategic planning processes is crucial. The leaders of these entities house tremendous knowledge about their own capabilities and the competitive environments in which they operate. They can make informed recommendations about what the company should be doing and where it should be going. For example, when you're participating in strategy formulation at your company, you likely have information about what rival companies are doing to boost their workforces' productivity. You also know what competing firms' weaknesses are and how to exploit them to ensure that your company's productivity surpasses theirs. Your most important internal customer—senior management in your organization—needs that information to define the right strategy for your firm.

Furthermore, when functional and unit leaders are included in the planning process, they are more likely to support and implement the plans that are created. People, by nature, tend to embrace changes and projects they've had a hand in creating far more than efforts that have been imposed on them by others. Functions and units are the implementation centers of an organization. They have the leader-ship, people, and skills needed for effective execution. Organizations that fail to include them in the strategic planning process typically receive results inferior to those that do.

By undertaking the planning process together, senior management and unit and function leaders ensure that a company's strategies—cor-porate and unit—are tightly aligned and that successful implementa-tion can follow. The payoff for the organization? A sharply honed com-petitive edge that enables the company to leave rivals far behind, maintain its lead for years to come, and boost profits to new heights.

Playing an active role in shaping and implementing strategy—as well as aligning HR efforts behind the corporate strategy—pays big dividends for HR leaders as well. Consider these benefits of thinking and acting strategically:[9]

- You keep your job during layoffs.

- You get selected for cross-functional teams that increase your exposure to influential people and learning opportunities.

- Other executives seek out your ideas.

- You exert a significant impact on your company's profitability and success.

- You win more resources and larger budgets, because strategic actions generate a higher return than tactical actions.

- You get promoted faster.

- You earn more. (Indeed, many vice presidents of HR who demonstrate their strategic business impact bring in over $1 million per year.)

Clearly, it pays handsomely to be strategic.

What You'll Find in This Book

Strategic HR management has become more vital than ever—as the business arena grows ever more competitive and as companies increasingly look to their workforce to generate value. Chapter 1 defines strategic HR management and explains why it's so important today. It also describes HR's role as a strategic business partner and lays out the essential competencies you need to manage HR more strategically.

As you'll discover, strategy begins with goals, which naturally follow from the entity's mission. Goals, in turn, are influenced by an iterative sensing of the external environment and the organization's internal capabilities. The strategic choices available to a company likewise emerge from the process of looking outside and inside. Strategic planners refer to this activity as SWOT: strengths, weaknesses, opportunities, and threats. Chapter 2 helps you examine your company's external environment of opportunities and threats. Chapter 3 turns the focus inward, to the strengths and weaknesses of both your enterprise and your HR department. Knowledge of this inner world imparts a practical sense about which goals and strategies are most feasible and promising for your organization and department. The chapter emphasizes the most important areas in which you should evaluate strengths and weaknesses: core competencies and processes, financial condition, and management and culture.

Once you've gotten a clear sense of your company's and department's strengths and weaknesses, and the external environment in which you and the organization must operate, the question is, What type of strategy should our company pursue? There are many strategy "types" from which to choose. Chapter 4 describes four types and explains what it takes to succeed with each: low-cost leadership, product/service differentiation, customer relationship, and network effect. Chances are that one of these—or some variation—will be appropriate for your company and give it a defensible and profitable hold on some segment of the market.

Chapter 5 continues the discussion of strategy at the corporate level, indicating how companies can use their strategy to enter and build defensible positions in the marketplace. This chapter explores a number of potential strategic "moves": creating a market beachhead, using innovation to overcome barriers to entry, applying the principles of *judo strategy*, and others.

Defining a sound competitive strategy is only part of the challenge for your company. You and other executives must give equal or greater attention to implementation: the effort to translate strategic intent into actions that produce the intended results. Successful implementation begins with figuring out whether your company has the right people, processes, structures, and culture in place to carry out the high-level strategy. If so, your organization is what we call *aligned*—ready to execute the strategy the executive team has defined. In chapter 6, you'll learn more about how to assess these aspects of your company.

Not only does your entire organization need to align with the corporate strategy; every part of the company must do so as well by developing supportive strategies of their own. Chapter 7 shifts the focus to how you can define an HR strategy that aligns behind your company's strategy. You'll discover how the HR strategy alignment process works, how to develop a sound, aligned HR strategy, and how to structure your department to enable execution of your strategy. And you'll learn how to make a compelling case for your HR strategy to the rest of your executive team.

Once you've defined an HR strategy, you develop action plans to help you implement the strategy. Chapter 8 segments the action planning process into a number of key steps. It also contains an example of one company's formal HR action plan.

Chapter 9 explores ways to keep your action plan on track. HR professionals cannot simply issue a set of instructions and expect flawless implementation. Instead, they must support their plans with consistent behaviors, training, and other supportive structures. And they must communicate relentlessly with respect to the nature of the HR strategy and its benefits to everyone in the company.

People are the most important ingredient in the implementation of any strategy. Harnessing their energy and commitment to strategic change is often an HR professional's greatest challenge. Employees and managers must feel that they've had something to say about the plans they are told to implement. They must know that success is important. They must be motivated to do the right things well. And they must see real incentives for all their hard work. Chapter 10 addresses each of these requirements.

In chapter 11, we take a closer look at ways to successfully implement HR initiatives—the programs, projects, and policies laid out in your strategic action plan. The chapter explores human capital initiatives in several key HR areas: workforce planning, recruiting, retention, compensation, and training and development. You'll also find a section on how to evaluate your HR initiatives' strategic impact.

No strategy, even a great one, remains effective forever. Something in the environment eventually changes, rendering the strategy ineffective or unprofitable. You and other leaders throughout your company must be alert to these changes—so you can make the appropriate midcourse corrections in the high-level strategy or your HR strategy. Chapter 12 explains how to assess the effectiveness of your company's and department's current strategies and recognize when it's time to change them. It offers tips on how to monitor the performance of your strategies and identify areas where intervention may be necessary.

Thinking and acting strategically is an ongoing learning process. Chapter 13 sums up the advantages of developing a strategic mind-set in HR and explains how to strengthen that mind-set. You'll also find guidelines for assessing your HR department's ability to exert a strategic impact in your company.

That's it for the book's chapters. But the end matter contains material you may also find useful. First, you'll find an appendix containing the following items:

- **SWOT analysis worksheet.** As described in chapters 2 and 3, HR professionals use SWOT analysis to identify the strengths, weaknesses, opportunities, and threats facing their company or department. This worksheet (figure A-1) helps you systematically think about and evaluate these internal and external factors—for your company overall or for your HR department specifically.

- **Work breakdown structure (WBS) worksheet.** Borrowed from the art and science of project management, work breakdown structure is a potent implementation tool. This worksheet (figure A-2) helps you deconstruct large HR initiatives into their component parts and estimate the time needed to complete them.

- **Project progress report.** This form (figure A–3) helps you assess the progress of an HR initiative, present the information to others, and think through next steps.

The worksheet appendix is followed by a glossary of terms particular to strategy creation and implementation. Every business activity has its special vocabulary, and this one is no different. When you see a term in italics, that's your cue it's included in the glossary.

Finally, a "For Further Reading" section identifies readily available books and articles that can tell you more about the topics covered in this book. Because this volume focuses on essentials, it cannot cover everything you might want to know about strategy creation and implementation. So, if you want to know more, refer to the publications listed in this section.

The content of this book draws heavily on the strategy scholarship published in books and articles over the past twenty-four years. Many of these first appeared as articles in the *Harvard Business Review* and in *HR Magazine*. We've also drawn from numerous white papers published by the Society for Human Resource Management, as well as from material in the "Implementing Strategy" module of Harvard ManageMentor®, an online service of Harvard Business School Publishing. All other sources are noted with standard endnote citations.

CHAPTER ONE

Strategy and the HR Professional

Why Strategic HR Management Is Vital

Key Topics Covered in This Chapter

- *What strategic HR management is*
- *HR's role as a strategic business partner*
- *Trends in HR's strategic role*
- *Competencies you need to be a strategic business partner*
- *Self-assessment of your current understanding about strategic HR management*

A s you read in the introduction to this book, companies formulate and execute high-level strategies to remain competitive in a rapidly changing business arena. And this is no easy task. Businesses are under constant pressure not only to adapt to change but also to extract strategic value out of it. Whether change takes the form of new technologies, new markets, shifts in competitors' actions, emerging workforce demographics, or some other dimension of business, companies must constantly seek ways to carve out a unique position for themselves in the competitive field and generate value for their customers. An enterprise's corporate strategy aims to do just that.

Strategic HR management—a phrase often used interchangeably with *HR strategy*—plays a vital role in helping companies define and carry out their competitive strategy. In this chapter, you'll learn what strategic HR management is, why it's a crucial activity for any business, and what competencies you'll need to acquire or strengthen in order to manage HR strategy in your organization. You'll also see a detailed case study of an HR leader who successfully served as a strategic business partner. The chapter concludes with a self-assessment tool to help you take stock of your current knowledge about HR and strategy.

What Is Strategic HR Management?

The phrase *strategic HR management* or *strategic HRM* is on more and more executives' lips these days. But what does it really mean? There's no single short, snappy definition of the term. Instead, many people find it easier to understand what strategic HRM is by envisioning what it looks like in action. When you manage HR strategically in your firm, you do the following:[1]

- Anticipate important potential changes outside and within your company that will exert a significant impact on its ability to compete.

- Help shape high-level strategy by contributing your insights about the company's most daunting competitive challenges and valuable new opportunities.

- Define the skills, knowledge, behaviors, and attitudes your firm's workforce needs to acquire or strengthen in order to move the organization toward its strategic goals.

- Develop HR-related programs and initiatives that enable the company to execute its high-level strategy, sustain its competitive edge, and create economic value in the form of increased share price, revenues, and profitability.

- Shape an organizational culture that encourages and enables executives, managers, and employees to embrace, thrive on, and learn from change.

- Integrate the many different HR-related efforts taking place across the organization into one overarching strategic effort that supports the company's long-term goals.

To achieve all of this, many experts recommend that companies develop their HR strategy as an integral part of formulating the high-level corporate strategy—rather than developing it in parallel with or after the corporate strategy. In this sense, strategic HRM bridges corporate-level strategy and HR management—tightly integrating HR with the business. Moreover, the most effective HR strategies are much more sharply focused on their company's future than on remedial, short-term initiatives. Savvy HR strategists also leverage technology to free up energy and time to focus on adding value instead of handling routine processes. For example, many employee questions about compensation, health insurance claims processing, and retirement accounts can now be answered through Web-based self-service HR systems.

What are the most important levers you can use to manage HR strategically in your organization? They run a wide gamut:[2]

- Defining the roles and responsibilities that need to be filled throughout the company in order for the firm to execute its strategy

- Attracting, hiring, and retaining talented employees to fill those roles and shoulder those responsibilities

- Ensuring adequate leadership bench strength

- Developing communication strategies to convey the importance of strategic initiatives and motivate the workforce to embrace change

- Leveraging the power of teamwork through flexible job design

- Using training and professional development programs to encourage learning and growth throughout the company

- Designing and implementing effective performance management systems—including performance metrics, compensation, and monetary and nonmonetary incentives

- Integrating complementary "bundles" of HR practices so that, collectively, they support the company's high-level strategy

- Using your powers of influence and persuasion to "sell" HR initiatives to line managers throughout your organization

- Translating your organization's needs into business language and helping other executives see what must be done with regard to people if your company's competitive strategy is to be achieved

- Being willing to engage in ongoing dialogue with line managers, stand firm on the importance of strategic change, and challenge other executives' ideas—as well as being open to having your ideas challenged

Why is strategic HRM so crucial in today's business world? One reason is that, with the shift from a manufacturing to a knowledge-based economy, many companies' competitive advantages now stem more from their human assets (skills, knowledge, behavior, and attitudes) than from their physical assets (such as manufacturing plants, equipment, and land). Still, even in the most automated factory, skilled, motivated employees are needed to operate machinery. Nowadays, the assets embodied in an enterprise's workforce can make or break that organization's ability to fulfill its mission—whether the mission entails innovating profitable new products and services (in the case of for-profit companies) or fulfilling a social mandate (in the case of not-for-profit organizations). Skillfully implemented, strategic HRM translates human assets into shareholder value, profitability, and value for an organization's customers. It gets everyone in the organization working toward the same high-level objectives and understanding how their everyday efforts contribute to their company's future success.

Another reason that strategic HRM is important has to do with the benefits it generates for both a company's workforce and its HR team. When people understand what their company is trying to do and how their work contributes to those efforts, their dedication, focus, and job satisfaction increase. And when HR professionals adopt a strategic mind-set and serve as strategic partners, their standing in the company improves. Why? They begin building a track record of measurable results for their organization—demonstrating that they can help the company create significant value. In an age when many companies are outsourcing some or all of their HR function, those human resource practitioners who can help their companies define and carry out high-level strategy will be much more likely to keep their jobs, earn handsome salaries, and win the trust and appreciation of their bosses and colleagues.

Finally, strategic HRM creates a competitive advantage that is difficult for your company's rivals to copy. Unlike a new product feature, the ways in which your organization manages its human capital are difficult for competitors to discern. Thus it's much harder for rivals to co-opt your HR strategy for their own advantage.

See "HR in Action: HR Steers Strategic Change at General Motors" for an example of one human resources leader who played a vital strategic role at a large, established company.

HR in Action: HR Steers Strategic Change at General Motors

Despite the business boom resounding through the United States in the 1990s, American automakers were struggling to sustain market share in the face of stiff competition from overseas. General Motors was no exception. Rick Wagoner, who became GM's president and COO in 1998, defined a bold new corporate strategy that entailed radical new approaches to manufacturing and selling cars, as well as a major internal reorganization. He also created the Automotive Strategies Board, which comprised GM's top-level executives.

Knowing that hiring, training, and retaining the best possible workforce would be a crucial ingredient of the new strategy, Wagoner promoted Kathleen Barclay—vice president of global human resources—to the Strategies Board. Her title became chief human resource officer, and she reported directly to Wagoner.

Barclay formulated an HR strategy—called 3Ts: technology, talent, and transformation—that aligned strongly behind GM's high-level strategy. In the *technology* phase of the strategy, most of GM's HR-related activities were placed online in a new HR portal. The online employee service center cut out HR as the "middleman" and freed up the human resources staff's time to work on more strategic aspects of the business, such as developing and retaining talent.

Talent, indeed, was the second phase of the strategy. During this phase, most of the training courses offered at GM University were moved online as well. One course, "HR Skills for Success," became required training for GM's three thousand HR professionals.

In the third phase of Barclay's HR strategy, *transformation*, the company standardized training across its geographically far-flung plants and offices. Barclay also built a strong global network of HR professionals to combat the "siloed syndrome" that had characterized GM's corporate HR function in earlier years. Barclay's intimate knowledge of GM's HR function, gained through her employment there in 1978–1981 and 1985–1998, helped her standardize HR processes across GM's many separate HR departments, each of which had operated independently.

Barclay's 3T strategy for HR yielded important benefits for GM. For one thing, the company began showing market-share gains in a slumping economy and competitive global marketplace. In addition, HR personnel in GM's overseas subsidiaries feel more a part of the global team. Communication between headquarters and subsidiaries has improved markedly, as Detroit actively asks for suggestions and input from HR on strategic issues and projects.

What factors enabled HR to play a strategic role at GM? Barclay's extensive knowledge of GM and the HR field helped her establish credibility among the rest of the executive team. She was also able to identify points of resistance to change among middle managers and work to win their support. Equally important, she was willing to make personnel changes—including redeploying change-resistant managers to other parts of the company if necessary—to overcome resistance. Senior executives' support also helped: Wagoner and other high-level executives saw the importance of including HR in high-level strategy formulation and execution. By including Barclay in the Strategies Board and drawing on her experience and knowledge, upper management sent a strong message to the rest of the company about the strategic importance of HR. Barclay's capacity to think and act strategically—to see the long-term impact of changes she proposed, and to demonstrate the causal links between the three parts of her HR strategy—further enhanced HR's strategic impact at GM.

SOURCE: Bill Leonard, "GM Drives HR to the Next Level," *HR Magazine*, March 2002.

HR's Role as a Strategic Business Partner

In serving as a strategic business partner, you might be involved in formulating and executing strategy at numerous levels in your organization. These levels go significantly beyond the activities that historically have been associated with the human resources function—namely, handling daily HR transactions such as new hires and benefits, and creating and maintaining HR policies. In increasingly strategic importance, these strategic-business-partner levels can be thought of in the following terms:[3]

- **Enhancing workforce productivity.** At this level, you develop initiatives that increase the dollar value of employee output while maintaining or reducing the average labor cost per unit of your company's products or services.

  To enhance workforce productivity, you need to know what behaviors lead to productivity, which metrics will enable you to measure changes in productivity, and which resources are required to support continual boosting of productivity. Additional productivity-related HR activities include retention of key employees, redeployment of employees from areas of low business impact to high, nonmonetary motivation and recognition, and the spread of best practices within the organization.

- **Boosting your company's people management competitive advantage.** At this level, you compare each key HR program and service in your organization directly to those of rival firms. You thus shift your strategic focus from inside to outside your enterprise. Moreover, rather than merely tracking what your company's rivals are doing, you identify their weaknesses and suggest ways to exploit them—all with an eye toward ensuring that your company's productivity exceeds your competitors'.

  To operate at this level, you must know how to obtain and analyze extensive information about rival companies' "people programs," as well as use that information to form ideas for improving on those programs. Your goal isn't to copy competitors' approaches to leveraging their human capital; it's to come up with better approaches that suit your organization. Additional skills needed for this level include workforce forecasting and planning, as well as employment "branding"—by which you ensure that talented job seekers view your company as "an employer of choice."

- **Attacking strategic business problems and opportunities.** At this level—which we can think of as the holy grail of strategic HRM—you help your company address its most strategic problems. These problems might be related to product development, quality, customer service, or business-unit performance—or some combination of any of these. To operate at this level, you need to know how to assemble business-unit or problem-product turnaround teams, enhance speed and innovation in product development, build a companywide culture that emphasizes performance, identify merger and acquisition targets based on the talent housed by those entities, and help your company get the best price for any divested units.

Clearly, serving as a strategic business partner differs markedly from providing the more transaction-related offerings traditionally associated with HR. See table 1-1 for more information about how the HR role is changing—and how HR is increasingly being perceived as a major force in creating strategic value for organizations.

TABLE 1-1

Trends in HR's strategic role

Businesspeople are increasingly recognizing HR's value as a strategic partner. In one survey of HR professionals, respondents were asked to indicate their level of agreement with several statements about perceptions of HR's strategic value.* Here's a sampling of how they responded to some of the statements listed in the survey:

Statement	Agreed (%)	Disagreed (%)
"HR's body of knowledge and skills is recognized as a profession by society in general."	58.6	9.7
"Employees recognize that HR practitioners have specific knowledge and skills that add to the value of the organization."	56.5	10.1

continued

TABLE 1-1 *continued*

Trends in HR's strategic role

"Line managers recognize that HR practitioners have specific knowledge and skills that add to the value of the organization."	60.1	9.6
"Non-HR business executives recognize that HR practitioners have specific knowledge and skills that add value to the organization."	53.2	12.4
"Overall, HR professionals are held in high esteem in organizations today."	36.6	21.4
"HR professionals feel they are being regarded as a business partner by the leaders of the senior management group."	42.6	20.7

According to another study of 740 corporations, firms with the greatest intensity of HR practices that reinforce performance—often a key component of high-level corporate strategy—had the highest market value per employee.[†] This finding suggests that investors are also beginning to understand HR's strategic value.

Another study compared the percentage of time spent on various HR activities from the late 1980s to the early 2000s.[‡] According to this research, HR practitioners in 2001 spent 23.2 percent of their time on management-team activities (strategic HR planning, organizational design, and strategic change), up from only 9.1 percent five to seven years previously. During those same years, their time spent on more transactional activities, such as maintaining records and ensuring compliance to internal operations and regulations, decreased significantly.

*Source: Lisbeth Claus and Jessica Collison, *The Maturing Profession of Human Resources in the United States of America Survey Report* (SHRM/SHRM Global Forum, January 2004), 5.

†*Source:* Edward E. Lawler and Susan Albers Mohrman, *Creating a Strategic Human Resources Organization: An Assessment of Trends and New Directions* (Stanford, CA: Stanford University Press, 2003), 3–4.

‡Ibid., 22.

Essential Competencies

To serve as a strategic business partner, HR professionals must demonstrate a distinctive set of competencies. One expert lists the following skills as particularly essential:[4]

- Understand your company's business—particularly its strategic challenges and new opportunities.

- Be able to translate business strategies into their human resource implications.

- Know how to involve line managers in the designing of initiatives that will affect how people are managed, developed, and rewarded.

- Help other executives understand what must be done with regard to people if the company's competitive strategy is to be achieved.

- Sense the issues that count, and be ready to send tough messages to management about what needs to be done.

- Win commitment and buy-in for strategic change throughout your organization.

Other experts emphasize culture management, change leadership, strategic decision making, and marketplace understanding as essential competencies for strategic HR management.[5] Let's examine each of these in turn.

Managing culture strategically means defining the specific behaviors and attitudes—such as risk taking and entrepreneurship—needed to carry out the company's business strategy. Once you've defined these behaviors and attitudes, you create HR practices (for example, incentive programs) that encourage them. You'll also want to design ways to measure progress toward the desired culture—such as surveys that enable you to assess workforce morale or strategic understanding, or metrics that reveal changes in willingness to take risks or master new skills.

In addition to managing culture, facilitating rapid change is another vital competency for strategic HRM. Competitive strategies are implemented through strategic initiatives—small- or large-scale programs or projects aimed at improving customer-service processes, updating information technologies, adopting a new performance management methodology, and so forth. Many strategic initiatives require people throughout the organization not only to alter the way they do their work but also to reexamine their beliefs and attitudes. Thus, not surprisingly, such initiatives often encounter resistance from managers and employees who prefer the status quo.

(See *The Essentials of Managing Change and Transition* in this series for more information on how HR professionals can surmount the challenges of leading change.)

To lead rapid change, you need to facilitate efficient decision making among executives and managers in your firm, as well as identify lessons from previous change efforts and apply them to new efforts. Additional change-leadership skills include ensuring the availability of resources (money, information, people) that enable change, and monitoring the progress of existing change efforts.

Facilitating strategic decision making is another key competency demonstrated by HR practitioners who serve as strategic business partners in their organizations. This competency entails providing alternative insights on business issues, clarifying business goals, and understanding the company's vision for its future. You must also know how to apply intellectual rigor and critical thinking to business decisions, forecast potential obstacles to success, and identify the problems the corporate strategy is seeking to solve and the opportunities it aims to leverage. Lending your knowledge and input to the formulation of high-level strategy is equally important for this competency.

Finally, to manage HR strategy, you need to know how to amplify important signals from your company's market—for instance, customer information—and disseminate these signals throughout your company. By sharpening awareness of market changes in your workforce, you enable people to see why the company's competitive strategy is important. When managers and employees understand the strategy's importance, they're more likely to embrace the changes needed to execute the strategy.

There are many ways to express this market-amplification competency. For example, some companies' HR departments have established a practice of using cross-functional employee teams to conduct in-person or over-the-phone market research. Employees and managers who participate in such teams hear valuable information directly from customers. Thus they're more likely to give that information serious consideration. And many customers are more willing to provide thoughtful and accurate feedback to credible company employees than to faceless representatives of a market research consultancy.

Clearly, managing HR strategically is no small feat. It requires radically different skills and mind-sets from those needed to fulfill the more transaction-based, administrative activities previously associated with the human resource function. By reading this book, you've taken an important step in familiarizing yourself with the principles and practices of strategic HR management. To gauge your current understanding of strategic HRM before you proceed with the following chapters, see assessment tool 1-1. In the next chapter, we'll examine a key component of strategic HRM: assessing your company's external threats and opportunities.

Assessment Tool 1-1
Test Your Understanding of Strategic
HR Management

To gauge your understanding of the concepts in this book, take the following multiple-choice test. Then review the answer key that follows, which points you to particular chapters for more information on specific aspects of strategic HR management.

1. **Which of the following statements about SWOT analysis is false?**
   A. A SWOT analysis is an assessment of a company's or an HR department's strengths, weaknesses, opportunities, and threats.
   B. A SWOT analysis can be done at every level within an organization—companywide, division, unit, department, and team.
   C. A SWOT analysis focuses on a company's primary financial strengths, weaknesses, opportunities, and threats.
   D. A SWOT analysis is a key step in formulating strategy.

continued

2. Which of the following is *not* an aspect of a company or an HR department that you should evaluate while assessing strengths and weaknesses during a SWOT analysis?

   A. Core competencies
   B. Competitors' position
   C. Management and culture
   D. Financial strength

3. There are numerous types of strategies a company can define. What does the "differentiation" strategy emphasize?

   A. Becoming the low-cost leader in the market
   B. Providing unique advantages that customers value
   C. Providing unparalleled customer service
   D. Leveraging the impact of networks of customers

4. What is a "strategic move"?

   A. A procedure by which a company anticipates possible trends in competitors' behavior and selects the one most potent strategy to respond to those trends
   B. The process by which a company takes stock of the range of strategies most appropriate for it to adopt
   C. The method by which a company changes its strategy based on emerging developments in the business arena
   D. A tactic by which a company uses its competitive strategy to enter the marketplace and build defensible positions there

5. In determining whether your company overall is aligned behind the corporate strategy, which of the following aspects are the *most* important to evaluate?

   A. Whether your company's workforce has the right skills, attitudes, and resources needed to make the strategy succeed
   B. Whether unrelated activities throughout your company reinforce one another and the corporate strategy

   C. Whether your company is structured in the right way and has the right culture and quality of leadership to execute the strategy

   D. All of the above

6. **To be successful, which criteria must your HR strategy meet?**

   A. The companywide business plan and budget can accommodate the initiatives laid out in the HR strategy.

   B. The HR strategy calls for an extensive revision of existing HR programs, projects, and policies based on the corporate strategy.

   C. The HR strategy can be implemented in your organization, and it strongly supports the corporate strategy.

   D. The HR strategy has the support of the CEO, CFO, and other members of the executive team.

7. **In developing an action plan for implementing your HR strategy, you need to determine interlocks. What are interlocks?**

   A. The work you owe other units and the work they owe you in order to carry out the plan

   B. Programs in your plan that can't be executed successfully until other programs have been implemented first

   C. Strategic information that cannot be shared widely throughout the organization

   D. Sections of your plan that are reflected in line items in the company's overall business plan

8. **Which of the following is the *most* common cause behind failed implementation of a company's or an HR department's action plan for implementing its strategy?**

   A. The action plan is expanded and people resist change.

   B. The action is trimmed and interlocks fail.

   C. Resources are inadequate.

   D. All of the above.

continued

9. While getting the right people on board to implement your HR strategy, you need to develop enabling structures. Which of the following is *not* an example of an enabling structure?

    A. A pilot program that lets you and your implementation team experiment with and debug initiatives before rolling them out more broadly

    B. A celebration recognizing the success of your implementation team as soon as they've reached the first important milestone in your strategic plan

    C. A training program that gives people the skills needed to carry out the initiatives defined in your strategic plan

    D. An incentive program that rewards the behaviors and performance you want your plan's implementers to demonstrate

10. Which of the following statements is true about strategic HR initiatives?

    A. Their strategic impact is virtually impossible to measure.

    B. They should emphasize workforce training and development.

    C. They are the programs, projects, and policies laid out in your plan for implementing your HR strategy.

    D. They focus primarily on retention and recruiting.

11. Which of the following is *not* a method for evaluating how well your HR strategy is working?

    A. Analysis of competitors' moves

    B. Your HR scorecard

    C. Financial analysis

    D. Market analysis

12. In determining whether your HR department exerts a significant strategic impact, you can ask yourself whether the department meets certain criteria. Which of the following are examples of these criteria?

A. HR focuses specifically on improving workforce pro-ductivity by adding innovative HR programs to its suite of existing programs.

B. HR has a global approach and focuses on fulfilling the company's immediate strategic objectives.

C. HR uses extensive anecdotal evidence to make strategic decisions and leverages technology.

D. HR is future focused and coordinates its internal efforts.

Answer Key

1. **C. A SWOT analysis focuses on a company's primary financial strengths, weaknesses, opportunities, and threats.**
   Chapter 2: SWOT Analysis I: Looking Outside for Opportunities and Threats

2. **B. Competitors' position**
   Chapter 3: SWOT Analysis II: Looking Inside for Strengths and Weaknesses

3. **B. Providing unique advantages that customers value**
   Chapter 4: Types of Strategy: Which Fits Your Business?

4. **D. A tactic by which a company uses its competitive strategy to enter the marketplace and build defensible positions there**
   Chapter 5: Strategic Moves: The Mechanisms of Success

5. **D. All of the above**
   Chapter 6: From Strategy to Implementation: Seeking Alignment

6. **C. The HR strategy can be implemented in your organization, and it strongly supports the corporate strategy.**
   Chapter 7: Aligning Your HR Strategy: Key Practices

7. **A. The work you owe other units and the work they owe you in order to carry out the plan**
   Chapter 8: Action Plans: The Architecture of Implementation

continued

8. D. All of the above.
   Chapter 9: How to Stay on Course: Sensing and Responding to Deviations from Plan

9. B. A celebration recognizing the success of your implementation team as soon as they've reached the first important milestone in your strategic plan
   Chapter 10: The People Side of Implementation: Getting the Right People on Board

10. C. They are the programs, projects, and policies laid out in your plan for implementing your HR strategy.
    Chapter 11: Implementing Human Capital Initiatives: The Rubber Meets the Road

11. A. Analysis of competitors' moves
    Chapter 12: Strategy as Work in Progress: Keep Looking Ahead

12. D. HR is future focused and coordinates its internal efforts.
    Chapter 13: Developing and Leveraging Your Strategic Mind-set

Summing Up

In this chapter, you learned that:

- Strategic HR management is a complex activity that more and more companies are encouraging. At its heart, it consists of using your knowledge about human capital to shape your company's high-level competitive strategy and to design HR-related programs that support the corporate strategy.

- Strategic HR management often involves activities related to improving workforce productivity, increasing your company's people management competitive advantage, and directly attacking strategic business problems (such as declining business-unit performance) and opportunities (for example, staking a claim in emerging markets).

- Studies suggest that HR professionals are increasingly spending more time on strategy-related activities than on transactional or administrative activities, and that executives, line managers, and employees are increasingly acknowledging the strategic value that HR brings to their organizations.

- To serve as a strategic business partner, HR professionals must enhance and demonstrate a distinctive set of competencies, including shaping their organization's culture, leading rapid change, facilitating strategic decision making, and amplifying market signals throughout your company.

Leveraging Chapter Insights: Critical Questions

- What percentage of your time is devoted to strategy-related activities versus transactional or administrative activities? If you've worked in HR at your company for more than a few years, has that ratio changed at all? If so, how?

- Of the different levels of strategic HR involvement described in this chapter—improving workforce productivity, enhancing your company's people management competitive position, and attacking strategic business problems and opportunities—at which level do you operate most frequently as a strategic business partner? Cite examples.

- Of the essential competencies needed to serve as a strategic business partner, which do you already demonstrate? Which do you need to strengthen? What steps might you take to strengthen weaker competencies?

CHAPTER TWO

SWOT Analysis I

Looking Outside for Opportunities and Threats

Key Topics Covered in This Chapter

- *Identifying threats and opportunities in the external environment*

- *The world of workplace and lifestyle trends that can affect your business*

- *Assessing customers*

- *Changes in the competitive arena*

- *Porter's five forces framework*

Y our company's high-level strategy begins with goals, which naturally follow from the organization's mission. But business leaders don't develop goals in isolation. Instead, they constantly assess their enterprise's external environment (new threats and opportunities) and its internal realities (strengths and weaknesses). Practical executives form goals based on what is feasible, given the environment in which they must operate and their existing resources and capabilities.

For example, 3M Corporation has committed itself to annual numerical goals: 10 percent earnings growth or better, 27 percent return on employed capital, and so forth. 3M's executive team didn't pull those specific goals out of a hat; they developed them based on their understanding of the markets 3M serves and the capabilities of the company. They looked outside and inside to determine those goals.

As shown in figure 2-1, the strategic choices available to an enterprise emerge from the process of looking outside and inside. Among strategic planners, this activity goes by the acronym SWOT: strengths, weaknesses, opportunities, and threats.

- *Strengths* are capabilities that enable your company or unit to perform well—capabilities that it must leverage in order to carry out its strategy.

- *Weaknesses* are characteristics that prohibit your company or unit from performing well and that must be addressed.

- *Opportunities* are trends, forces, events, and ideas that your company or unit can capitalize on.

FIGURE 2-1

External and internal analysis

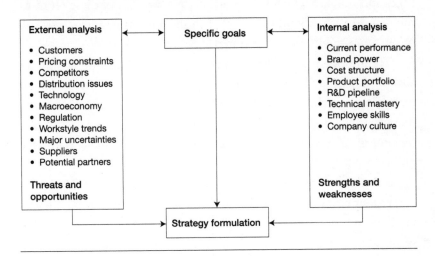

- *Threats* are possible events or forces, outside of your control, that your company or unit needs to anticipate and decide how to mitigate.

    In developing strategic goals for your company and for HR, it's vital to consider both external and internal factors. Why? These factors clarify the world in which your business and your department operate. By assessing these factors, you can better envision your company's and unit's desired future. In this chapter, we'll focus on the first of these challenges: external analysis. We'll take up internal analysis in the next chapter.

Spotlight on External Analysis

"The essence of formulating competitive strategy," writes scholar Michael Porter, "is relating a company to its environment."[1] Every company's environment—as well as every department's environment—is populated with customers, competitors, suppliers, and, in most enterprises' cases, regulators. And all have an impact on the organization's profit potential or the unit's cost-effectiveness and value to the larger enterprise. There are both current and potential customers, each with requirements for product/service quality, features, and utility. Savvy business leaders ask, Are any of these requirements unserved? There is also a set of current competitors and still others who might enter the arena.

Technology is also part of the competitive environment, and it's always changing. Is there something developing in the world of technology that could alter your company's competitive environment, perhaps making its products or services obsolete? Is there a technological innovation that might enable you to make certain HR processes more efficient or strategic?

Substitutes represent another form of threat in a company's external environment. For example, in the early 1980s, newly developed word processing software for personal computers represented a substitute for the typewriter. The substitution rate was so rapid that typewriters largely gave way to word processors within just ten years. The current popularity of cell phones with digital imaging capabilities likewise has created a substitute for cameras and film. Strategy-minded businesspeople ask, What are the potential substitutes for our company's products? Do any of our products have substitute potential in other markets? HR professionals who think and act strategically ask, What are possible substitutes for the services our group provides?

By analyzing the external factors listed in the left-hand box of figure 2-1, you and other executives can uncover threats and opportunities that may shed light on your company's strategic options. Note, however, that this list is by no means exhaustive. You will likely think of other factors that pertain to your company's industry.

Because detailed coverage of each item in figure 2-1 is beyond the scope of this book, we will address just a handful here. We will also discuss Michael Porter's "five forces" approach to analyzing competition in an industry—a conceptualization that has proved its value to businesspeople for more than twenty-five years.

Note: for a more complete discussion of external analysis, see the texts listed in the "For Further Reading" section at the back of this book. In particular, refer to Michael E. Porter, *Competitive Strategy* and David Aaker, *Developing Business Strategies*.

Workstyle and Lifestyle Trends

No matter what industry your company operates in, workstyle and lifestyle trends will likely affect its future. Consider this statistic: according to IDC, a private research firm, the number of U.S. employees working from the road (that is, while traveling for business) increased to 40 percent in 2004 and may rise to 66 percent by the end of 2006. Depending on your company's business, that raw statistic should provoke a number of questions.

- How will these millions of people travel?

- Where and what will they eat?

- Where will they spend the night, and what special accommodations would make evenings on the road more tolerable?

- How will they keep in touch with their families, offices, and clients while traveling?

- What can be done to reduce the cost of so much travel?

- How can wasted travel time be turned into productive time?

Executives in the travel, restaurant, hospitality, and mobile computing and telecommunications industries should be particularly interested in seeking answers to these questions. Moreover, this trend will present threats for some industries and opportunities for others. For example, IDC's projection of increasing business travel is good news for airlines and hotels that cater to this segment of travelers. It's also good news for companies that provide effective travel substitutes, such as Web conferencing and videoconferencing products and services. But the success of these substitutes poses a direct threat to those same airlines and hotels. Why should businesses spend piles of money and eat up productive time flying people to meetings when they could have employees meet online or use videoconferencing facilities near home?

The growth in business travel is just one of many workstyle and lifestyle changes happening right under our noses. Each represents some combination of threat and opportunity to companies in a range of industries. Consider these additional developments and their possible implications for your company's HR strategy:

- **Telecommuting.** More and more people are working from home offices. These people rely heavily on telecommunications, PCs, and Internet connectivity. Their office-bound managers are not sure how to supervise them. How will these facts affect your company or provide opportunities for new business? If such work arrangements would benefit your company or its employees, what new HR policies and programs should you develop to extract those benefits as well as effectively manage employees who work from home? For example, should you emphasize the opportunity to telecommute while recruiting talented job seekers who might value this option? Should you develop a telecommuting policy that lays out how such employees' work will be evaluated?

- **The Internet.** The Internet has made recruiting, shopping, research, travel arranging, and money management faster and more convenient. Will this trend kill your company's current business or open new opportunities to serve its customers profitably and manage its workforce more efficiently? How might you use the Internet to improve your recruiting processes? How might it help you automate additional HR processes so that you and your team have more time to focus on high-level strategic matters? What are the implications for training in your company?

- **Health concerns.** U.S. officials have declared obesity a national health epidemic, and European Union citizens are also getting more portly. What does this declaration portend for your company? For example, what might it mean for the cost of the medical benefits your organization provides workers?

- **Rising real-estate prices.** The price of new and older homes has exploded along the East and West Coasts of the United States, putting home ownership out of reach for a growing number of people, and there is no relief in sight. What does this mean for your firm? If your company operates on either coast, might this trend make it harder to find talented employees who are willing to pay the high prices for housing? If the organization is located in the Midwest, do you have an opportunity to snap up some of the valuable professionals who are migrating away from the coasts in search of more affordable housing?

- **Aging populations.** In several nations, the populations are aging, and women of childbearing age are having few children. What are the implications for your company's workforce—today and in the future? For example, will a larger component of your workforce consist of retirees seeking to work part-time? Will your company have to compete harder against rival organizations to recruit talented younger workers? What might this mean for your firm's retirement and pension systems? Transitions like these present ominous threats for some companies and tremendous opportunities for others. How might HR reduce any threat and seize advantage of any opportunity?

These are just a few of the many developments that are reshaping the world of business and HR. Each trend is forcing companies to reformulate their high-level and HR strategies. How to keep abreast of such changes? Regularly review reports from think tanks, from IDC, Forrester Research, government agencies, and other investigative organizations. Scan many papers and periodicals. Conduct your own research into trends that may affect your business and form the basis of a new strategy. Pay particular attention to any area in which significant change is under way. And cast your net wide; the changes that affect your company the most may been brewing far outside its industry. See "Workplace Trendspotting" for additional insights into the importance of monitoring workplace trends.

Workplace Trendspotting

How can you help your company mitigate any threats posed by workstyle and lifestyle trends and leverage any opportunities offered by such trends? Consider these tips:

- **Pay special attention to the trends that pose the greatest potential threats and opportunities.** For instance, many experts emphasize the rising cost of providing health-care coverage for employees, the use of technology, electronic learning, safety and security, and demographic changes.

- **Think about ways to address a trend's impact on work-force skills.** For example, with aging populations and an exodus out of high-cost-of-living regions, many companies are investing more in training and succession planning.

- **Be willing to closely examine and question your own beliefs about key trends and the future of work.** Ask others for their perspectives on how changes might affect your company and its HR strategy. Invite people to brain-storm with you and to challenge one another's interpretations of the changes you're seeing in the business arena.

- **Use scenario planning.** With other strategic planners, come up with several possible scenarios of what the future may hold for your business—given the trends you're detecting. Plan for the most likely scenarios, but also remain flexible enough to respond quickly to the unexpected.

SOURCE: Jennifer Schramm, "Top Trends Facing HR," *HR Magazine*, October 2004.

Customers

A business, as Peter Drucker once wrote, has no higher requirement than to create customers. In the absence of customers, the many things that businesses do—product development, manufacturing, shipping, and so forth—are utterly pointless. Thus, business leaders who are ana-

lyzing external factors important to their enterprise generally begin
with a study of customers:

- Who are they?

- How sensitive are they to price?

- How can they be reached?

- How are they currently using a particular product or service?

- Which of their needs are poorly served—or unserved?

- What level of loyalty do they have to their current vendors?

- Do they seek an arm's-length transaction or a long-term
  relationship?

Since potential questions about customers are so numerous, it's
useful to segment customers into groups that have common features. *Market segmentation* comes directly from the marketer's tool kit;
it is a technique for dividing a large heterogeneous group of customers into smaller segments with homogeneous features. Companies define those homogeneous features in any number of ways.
Here are some examples:

- **Age**—senior citizens, teenagers, college students, and so forth

- **Gender**—women, foreign-born men

- **Geographic location**—suburban families north and west of
  New York

- **Type of users**—heavy users of voice messaging, lead users, and
  so forth

- **Income**—households with total incomes between $100,000
  and $200,000

- **Behavior**—people who shop regularly via the Internet

Defining and analyzing customer segments offers many benefits
for strategists. Segmentation makes it easier to identify the needs,
price sensitivity, accessibility, loyalty, and unmet requirements of

identifiable customers. It can also help you identify which customers are the most profitable to serve. For example, during the early days of the cell-phone era, research by one telecom firm uncovered several distinct customer segments:

- **People (mostly women) who subscribed at the minimum level and mostly for personal safety reasons.** This segment bought the lowest-price service and was unprofitable to serve. Turnover in the segment was extremely high, as these customers switched service providers in response to special, low-priced deals offered periodically by rivals.

- **Occasional users.** These customers made only a few calls each week. The cell-phone company broke even on this group.

- **Business professionals.** These people used their cell phones regularly and subscribed to the premium services. They were also loyal and relatively insensitive to price. Most of the company's profits came from this segment.

These findings helped the telecom company develop an effective strategy for the future.

Take a few minutes to think about the customers in your industry—both the ones your company currently serves and the ones you'd like to see it recruit. How much does your company really know about these people and their needs? Has it segmented them into homogeneous groups that reveal key facts for strategic planners? Are any important and potentially profitable segments not served by your organization or its competitors?

Also think about your HR department's internal customers. How might you segment them, identify their needs, and create strategies for serving those needs? For example, your primary customer is your CEO, but additional customer segments include line managers and employees. Each segment needs something different from you—and you need something different from each in order to provide HR programs that support the company's overall strategy.

Price Sensitivity and Elasticity of Demand

Among the external factors that you and other strategists in your company must analyze is the price sensitivity of customers. Whether a company intends to offer customers a new disk drive, a low-carbohydrate family of snack foods, or a novel drug therapy, it must have an informed awareness of the relationship between price and customer demand.

A basic tenet of economics in a free market is that people will buy more of a product or service when the price goes down, and less as the price goes up—all other factors being equal. This is both intuitively obvious and easily substantiated. Rational consumers are sensitive to price. Figure 2-2 shows the elasticity of demand for two products. The sharp slope in the demand curve (D) indicates a high sensitivity to a price increase; customers will make many fewer purchases as the price increases. Product B, in contrast, demonstrates much less sensitivity to a price increase; customers reduce their purchase only slightly in the face of rising prices; as economists would say, demand in this case is relatively inelastic.

Some goods and services demonstrate relatively low price sensitivity—at least in the short term. Consider automobile fuel. The 30 percent rise in U.S. gasoline prices in the fall of 2004, when crude oil skyrocketed to $54 per barrel, caused only a 2–3 percent drop in U.S. gasoline consumption. Why? People were so locked into vacation

FIGURE 2-2

Sensitivity to price changes

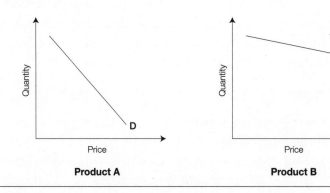

Product A   Product B

plans and commuting routines that the increase caused little more than a ripple in demand. If that level of pricing (or rising prices) were to persist for a long time, however, consumption might well drop substantially as people stopped buying gas-guzzling SUVs, opted to use public transportation, began carpooling to work, and so forth. As if to confirm this long-term effect, OPEC, the cartel of oil-producing countries, intimated that it wanted to set crude prices to return to the $22- to $25-per-barrel range. Though the spurt in prices yielded a huge windfall for OPEC members, they knew that sustained high prices would induce their customers to find substitutes for petroleum and to invest seriously in alternative energy sources—hurting the oil producers in the long run.

Many products and services exhibit a much more immediate and dramatic response to price changes, usually because the offering is nonessential, or because it has many available substitutes. Beef is one example. Every time the price of beef has increased sharply, demand has declined immediately and almost as dramatically. Shoppers look at the price and say, "I think we'll have chicken for dinner tonight."

Economists use the term *price elasticity of demand* to quantify the impact of price changes on customer demand. If you've taken micro-economics, you're probably familiar with this concept. You calculate price elasticity of demand as follows:

Percentage increase in price/Percentage decrease in quantity = Price elasticity of demand

Thus, if a company raised the price of one of its products from $100 to $120, the price increase would be 20 percent. If that increase caused the quantity of the product sold to drop from 600 units to 550 units, the percentage decrease would be 8.3 percent. Following our formula, the price elasticity of demand would be:

20/8.3 = 2.4

The *higher* the final number in this calculation, the *more sensitive* customers are to price changes.

Executives can often get insights into how customers will re-spond to a price change by conducting focus groups, sending out questionnaires and surveys to customers, and experimenting with price changes in local markets. For example, the producer of a breakfast cereal sold throughout the United States might raise its price in one major city and observe the impact on unit sales.

To complete this analysis, however, strategists must calculate the anticipated impact of a price change on *total* revenue. Why? People may be buying fewer items at a higher price. For the example just

Price Elasticity of Demand: Implications for Strategic HR Management

Price elasticity of demand can have significant implications for HR activities. Consider these examples:

- **Compensation practices.** What happens to your workforce if people's compensation is raised, lowered, or frozen? How long can you freeze wages before talented employees start leaving? By what percentage must your company's salaries be higher than rival companies' in order for you to recruit the talent you need?

- **Benefits.** How does your workforce respond to changes in benefits—for instance, a rise in the percentage of health-care costs that employees must cover?

- **Program funding.** How sensitive to "price" is your CEO and other executives as they're reviewing proposals for new HR initiatives and considering whether to approve funding? Do these decision makers tend to opt for the least expensive initiatives?

- **Use of outside vendors.** In negotiating contracts with outside vendors, such as staffing agencies or benefits administrators, how sensitive are *you* to price?

given, suppose the company had been selling 600 units of the product at \$100 each, generating revenues of \$60,000. Under its new scenario, it expects to sell 550 units at \$120 each, resulting in total revenue of \$66,000. The company's strategists would need to conduct further analysis to determine whether that higher revenue figure would translate into higher or lower gross profits. See *The Essentials of Finance and Budgeting* volume in this series for more information on interpreting financial measures such as revenue and gross profit. Also see "Price Elasticity of Demand: Implications for Strategic HR Management" for insights into how elasticity of demand may affect HR strategy.

The Competitive Arena

As George Day, a professor at the Wharton School, has perceptively written, "One of the primary issues facing managers in formulating competitive strategy is defining the arena of competition. Where are you competing? Who are your competitors? How attractive is the competitive arena?"[2] No examination of your company's and unit's external environment is complete without thoughtful analysis of competitors and the competitive arena. You surely know who your company's competitors are. They are the ones your sales force wrestles with every day in closing key sales. They are the companies that aim to steal your firm's best customers. Yes, you know who they are, but how much do you know *about* these rivals—in particular, their strengths and weaknesses? Are you aware of emerging arenas of competition? And what about the new competitors who will appear in the months and years ahead?

Some arenas of competition are relatively static, particularly in mature, capital-intensive industries. The steel industry up until the 1970s could be defined as static. A handful of large competitors were slugging it out, each trying to lower unit production costs and capture a larger slice of the market at the expense of its rivals. Other industries are more dynamic. The entertainment industry is a prime example. Twenty years ago, people could watch three or four network television stations, go to a movie theater, or attend a live performance. Today, TV viewers can still watch network channels, but can also access hundreds of cable channels. The movie theaters are still there, but thousands of movies are now available through VHS, DVD, and pay-per-view outlets. Because many of these entertainment services are vulnerable to substitution by others, vendors are scratching their heads and asking, "What strategy will help us carve out a profitable niche in this dynamic marketplace? And what's coming next?"

The hallmarks of a dynamic market include:

- Many different products or services addressing a similar need (e.g., landline phones, cell phones, instant messaging, and e-mail)

- A diversity of competitors (e.g., TV networks, cable companies, video rental shops, live venues)

- Few insurmountable barriers to entry into the competitive arena

- Market fragmentation

How well do you understand competition in the market your company and your unit aim to serve? And what are the possible implications of that competition for your HR strategy? For example, who's competing for the skilled job seekers in your industry or region? Who's poaching valued employees from your company? And are there individuals or organizations competing to provide the same kinds of services your HR team supplies in your company? See "Who Are Your Company's Labor Competitors?" for one example of how understanding competition is vital for HR practitioners.

Who Are Your Company's Labor Competitors?

Your company's competitors for skilled workers and managers include more than rival firms in the same industry. These competing companies may operate outside your industry and may be located elsewhere in your country or in another nation entirely. By knowing who they are, you can develop a strategy for offsetting the severe labor shortages that analysts predict for the coming years. To

continued

determine who's competing with your company for labor, ask yourself which outside organizations offer the following:

- Better compensation than your company does—including signing bonuses, higher wages, more frequent and larger pay raises, and performance-based bonuses

- More attractive benefits—including more desirable health insurance programs, lower health-care costs borne by employees, tuition reimbursement, and paid assistance for new hires who must relocate

- Richer career-development opportunities—such as on-the-job training, apprenticeships, career counseling, clear career paths through skills development and promotions, and mentoring programs

- More opportunities to achieve work/life balance—for example, flextime, telecommuting, job sharing and part-time work, on-site daycare, and paid sabbaticals

- More job security in the form of a stable workplace or a policy that stipulates avoiding layoffs as much as possible

- More opportunities for high school and college students to participate in internships, job shadowing, and other business-related experiences that groom them for employment later

- Easier access to cultural or community activities that employees value, such as proximity to theaters or the ballet, churches or synagogues with active memberships, or museums and historical sites

- Higher prestige, based on the companies' standing in their industry

To win the talent wars, you have several HR strategies available to you. These include offering attractive compensation and benefits, strengthening your company's employment "brand," engaging in creative recruiting (such as importing immigrant labor), and partnering with labor "suppliers" such as schools. For example, business/education partnering—in the form of internships, cooperative education programs, school-to-career initiatives, and job shadowing—can help future employees develop job skills and positive attitudes toward work and learning. Your reward? A pool of talented potential workers you can draw from as the need arises in the future.

SOURCES: Haig R. Nalbantian et al., *Play to Your Strengths: Managing Your Internal Labor Markets for Lasting Competitive Advantage* (New York: McGraw-Hill, 2004), chapter 5; and Phyllis G. Hartman, "Strategic Recruiting by Partnering with Suppliers: The Business/Education Connection," SHRM white paper, June 2002.

Emerging Technology

Technology is a major driver of the modern economy. Intel, Cisco Systems, Siemens, and Genzyme have made their way in the world by creating and harnessing new or improved technologies. eBay, Amazon.com, Google, Cingular, and Yahoo! wouldn't even exist if computers and Internet technologies had not been developed. Even your local grocery store, a very traditional business, relies on technology to speed checkout lines, reduce errors, track sales by category, and manage its inventory.

Technology represents both a threat and an opportunity. It is a threat in the sense that a new technology may undermine your company's existing business—just as word processing software and PCs torpedoed the typewriter industry, and just as digital imaging is currently undermining the photographic film/film processing business today. Putting the shoe on the other foot, we know that technology can present powerful new opportunities to companies that commercialize it in ways that create clear benefits and value to customers.

As you consider the possible impact of technological advances on your company and your HR strategy, view technology as a double-edged sword. Think of ways to leverage the opportunities technology presents, while also mitigating any threat that it poses.

Porter's Five Forces Framework

No discussion of the competitive environment would be complete without some discussion of Michael Porter's five forces framework. First articulated in 1979 in the award-winning *Harvard Business Review* article "How Competitive Forces Shape Strategy," Porter's framework remains a useful tool for getting an analytical grasp on the state of competition and the underlying economics within an industry. This framework also encourages you to look outside the small circle of current competing rivals to other factors and influences that determine your company's profitability and growth. Porter identified the following forces as governing industry competition (see figure 2-3):

- The threat of new entrants

- The threat of substitute products

FIGURE 2-3

Forces governing competition in an industry

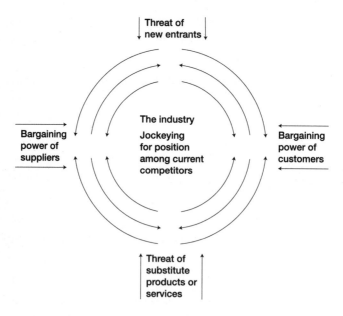

Source: Reproduced from Michael E. Porter, "How Competitive Forces Shape Strategy," *Harvard Business Review*, March–April 1979, 141, reproduced with permission.

- The bargaining power of suppliers

- The bargaining power of customers

- Tactical jockeying for position among current competitors

"The collective strength of these forces," Porter writes, "determines the ultimate profit potential of an industry." Owing to these factors, the profit potential will vary from industry to industry. Today, for example, sectors of the telecommunications industry are facing weak profit potential because so many factors conspire against existing providers: industry participants are continually fighting to grab their rivals' customers, often by cutting prices and extending services; customers can switch suppliers easily; and many communications substitutes are available, such as landlines, cell phones, e-mail, instant messaging, and Internet phone. Meanwhile, the rapid pace of technical change is forcing the existing players to spend royally to remain on the cutting edge. Participants in other industries, in contrast, confront a much more favorable combination of the five forces.

The key to growth and survival, according to Porter, is to use your knowledge of these five forces to "stake out a position that is less vulnerable to attack from head-to-head opponents, whether established or new, and less vulnerable to erosion from the direction of buyers, suppliers, and substitute goods." Companies can gain such a position, he argues, by solidifying relationships with profitable customers, differentiating their products and services (either through redesign or marketing), integrating operations, or gaining technical leadership.[3]

A complete discussion of Porter's five forces framework is beyond the scope of this chapter. We encourage you to obtain the article and think about how its concepts apply to your own company's industry.

Looking outside for threats and opportunities is one step in the preparation you must do before you even discuss your company's and your HR department's strategic plans. Leaders of great companies do this analysis continually. They send their technical people to professional conferences and subscribe to key academic journals.

They are always in touch with current and potential customers via focus groups and interviews with *lead users*—that is, companies and individuals whose needs are far ahead of typical users'. Some HR executives even set up special "intelligence" units to scan newspapers and technical journals, keep an eye on proposed regulations, and so forth. These leaders are constantly sensing the outer world for threats and opportunities that could affect them. Your company should do the same.

Summing Up

In this chapter, you discovered that:

- Workstyle and lifestyle trends will powerfully shape your company's future workforce needs.

- Market segmentation can help your company divide a large heterogeneous group of customers into smaller segments with homogeneous features. By analyzing these segments, you can deepen your understanding of which customers your firm can serve most profitably. Segmentation also enables you to identify customers' needs, price sensitivity, accessibility, loyalty, and unmet requirements.

- By determining the "price elasticity of demand" for HR practices (such as how sensitive potential new hires are to salaries and signing bonuses), you can quantify the impact of compensation and HR changes on "customers'" (that is, job candidates' and employees') demand.

- Porter's framework encourages strategists to examine five industry forces to assess the competitive arena: the threat of new entrants, the threat of substitute products, the bargaining power of suppliers, the bargaining power of customers, and tactical jockeying for position among current competitors.

Leveraging Chapter Insights: Critical Questions

- What workstyle and lifestyle trends pose the greatest possible threats and opportunities for your company?

- What changes in your company's customer base present threats and opportunities? What about changes in your internal customers—such as your CEO, line managers, and employees?

- What are your organization's competitors doing to gain market share or achieve some other edge in the industry? How might their actions pose important threats or opportunities for your company?

- What emerging technologies might introduce major threats or opportunities for your organization?

- Consider all the threats and opportunities you identified in the previous questions. What HR strategies might you develop to mitigate those threats and help your company take advantage of the opportunities?

CHAPTER THREE

SWOT Analysis II

Looking Inside for Strengths and Weaknesses

Key Topics Covered in This Chapter

- *Identifying and assessing core competencies*

- *Understanding your company's and unit's financial capacity for undertaking a new strategy*

- *Evaluating the strategic readiness of your company's and unit's management and culture*

- *A nine-step method for evaluating strengths and weaknesses*

H AVING TESTED the outer world for threats and opportunities, HR professionals must look inward and evaluate their company's and department's strengths and weaknesses in order to develop a sound HR strategy. As with the outer world, knowledge of the inner world helps you identify what company goals are most feasible and promising, and which HR strategies would best support those goals.

What are a company's or unit's strengths and weaknesses? The cost structure of its operations is one place to look for answers. Another is the company's brands or a unit's reputation within the organization. The business acumen and skills embodied in the employees of your organization or department can also generate valuable insights for your internal assessment of strengths and weaknesses. Because you help shape your company's high-level strategy as well as develop its HR strategy, it's important to evaluate the strengths and weaknesses not only of your company overall but also of the HR department specifically.

Conducting this internal analysis takes considerable thought and the ability to analyze extensive information. In this chapter, we'll address three of the most important areas to explore: core competencies and processes, financial condition, and management and culture. We'll then turn to a method that can help you conduct your evaluations.

Core Competencies

A core competence can serve as a foundation for any new or revised strategy that an organization or a unit devises. The term *core competence* refers to a company's or unit's expertise or skills in key areas that directly drive superior performance. Let's consider corporate-level examples: one of Sony's core competencies, for instance, is its ability to unite microelectronics and innovative design in a stream of useful consumer products. Corning, on the other hand, has enormous competencies in the area of glass and ceramic materials. It has used those competencies strategically over the years to produce successful product lines—from Pyrex ovenware and television tubes to fiber optics and the innards of catalytic converters.

What are your company's core competencies? Don't answer this by simply stating what your company does: "We make lighting fixtures." Instead, determine what the organization is uniquely good at—better than others—and what customers value most about it. In some cases, what your firm is good at may be a core process—that is, a key activity that turns inputs into outputs. Like core competencies, these processes are the ones that make or break your business. 3M, for example, has a reputation for being able to turn out dozens of innovative, customer-pleasing products every year. Over the years, it has learned much better than most how to generate promising ideas—many in the area of adhesives—and convert the best of these into real solutions for consumer and industrial problems. For USAA, the member-owned financial services company, its processes for handling customer transactions is a core activity, and one that it does particularly well.

Just as companies have core competencies, so do units. To illustrate, your organization's HR group may be highly effective at communicating the importance of large-scale change initiatives to the entire workforce. Or perhaps your department knows how to extract more value out of technology than most other HR departments.

One warning: being exceptionally good at something does not in itself confer a strategic advantage. Your company and your department must be exceptionally good at something valued by its *customers*—whether those customers are the people who buy the company's products, or the executives, managers, and employees whom your department serves. This might seem obvious, but some executives overlook it. In addition, your organization and unit must be better than others at a particular activity in order to deem it a core competence or process. See "Is Your Unique Competence a Sound Basis for an Effective Strategy?" for additional criteria to consider while assessing core competencies.

Is Your Unique Competence a Sound Basis for an Effective Strategy?

To form the basis for an effective strategy, a particular core competence or resource must be valued by your company's or unit's customers. But it must also pass the following tests, according to David Collis and Cynthia Montgomery:

- **Inimitability.** The competence must be hard to copy. Don't try to base a long-term strategy on something your competitors can quickly copy.

- **Durability.** Durability refers to the continuing value of the competence or resource. Some brand names, like Disney's or Coca-Cola's, have enduring value. Some technologies, however, have commercial value for only a few years; they are swept aside by new and better technologies.

- **Appropriability.** This test determines who captures the value created by your competence or unique resource. In some industries, the lion's share of profits goes to retailers, not to the companies whose ingenuity developed and produced the actual products.

- **Sustainability.** Can your special resource be trumped by a substitute?

- **Competitive superiority.** Is your special competence or resource truly superior to those of competitors? As Collis and Montgomery warn, "Perhaps the greatest mistake managers make when evaluating their companies' resources is that they do not assess them relative to competitors'." So always rate your strength against the best of your rivals.

SOURCE: David J. Collis and Cynthia A. Montgomery, "Competing on Resources," *Harvard Business Review,* July–August 1995, 118–128.

One way to assess the relative power of a company's or unit's core competencies and processes is through benchmarking. *Benchmarking* is an objective method for rating one entity's activities against similar activities performed by organizations recognized for best practice. In addition to rating your unit or company, you can identify opportunities for process improvement through benchmarking. The benchmark target may very well be in another industry. For example, when Xerox discovered problems in its parts and components logistics operation, it sent a team of people to Freeport, Maine, to study how L.L. Bean, the successful direct-mail apparel and equipment retailer, managed its picking and packing of individual customer orders. The Xerox team then used what it learned to improve its own handling of customer orders.

Remember: a competence is meaningful only when you compare it with that of rival firms or units. Here is one example of a method you can use to systematically assess the strength of your company's core competencies relative to those of rivals. The hypothetical company in this illustration is Gizmo Products, Inc., which designs and manufactures high-end cookware. In its benchmarking analysis, Gizmo has compared its competencies in critical areas with those of Company A and Company B—both serious competitors (see table 3-1). Notice that Gizmo has identified areas of primary and secondary competitive performance.

Ratings like the ones shown in table 3-1 can help managers and executives identify strengths and weaknesses in the areas that matter most. How to obtain such ratings? Some companies encourage groups of managers and employees to brainstorm them. But some employees may have difficulty looking at their company's competencies through an objective lens and may lack the knowledge required to assess rival firms' competencies. So, if you adopt this method, be sure to also bring in the voices of salespeople, defectors from rival companies, and consultants who know the industry well. In addition, make use of any data from surveys your company's marketing research group has conducted on customers and distributors. Look also to quality and repair incidences compiled by objective

TABLE 3-1

Comparing core competencies and resources

5 = very strong; 1 = very weak

	Gizmo	Company A	Company B
Competencies			
Primary importance			
New-product time-to-market	5	2	3
Product quality	4	4	5
Dealer service	4	2	5
Satisfaction of final customers	5	2	4
Developing and attracting human talent	4	2	4
Flexible manufacturing	4	2	3
Secondary importance			
Project management skills	4	?	3
Cost control	4	3	5
IT systems	3	?	4
Critical assets			
Brand power	3	1	4
Supply chain power	5	1	4
Physical plant	4	2	4
Strategic partnerships	3	2	5
Distribution network	4	3	5

third parties. What you want is an unvarnished assessment of where your company is strong and weak relative to key competitors.

The same suggestions apply to comparing a unit's core competencies against those of counterpart units in rival companies. For instance, to objectively compare your HR department's core competencies with those of HR functions in other organizations, consider gathering input from HR consultants, experts you've met through networking and participation in professional associations, and books and periodicals that provide case studies of HR organizations.

The method of assessment illustrated in table 3-1 differs from the traditional benchmarking exercise in that it examines many key aspects of company competence, not just one. And like benchmarking, it has a methodological weakness: it provides a snapshot of where

TABLE 3-2

Evaluating competencies with trajectory

Arrows indicate the trajectory of relative strength or weakness

	Gizmo	Company A	Company B
Flexible manufacturing	4 ↓	2 →	3 ↑

different companies stand at one point in time. But it's the trajectory of competence that matters for the future.

For example, in table 3-1 Gizmo appears stronger than Company B in terms of flexible manufacturing—a key competence. Gizmo rates a 4 versus Company B's 3 on this important measure. However, owing to changes in workforce skills or use of technology, Gizmo may be losing relative strength in this area, while Company B may be improving rapidly from year to year. Thus, next year, Gizmo may have lost its lead in flexible manufacturing. For these reasons, it's useful to add a sense of trajectory to your assessments, as shown in table 3-2. This table indicates that Gizmo is declining in flexible manufacturing, Company A is on a plateau, and Company B is improving this competence.

Financial Strength

If formulating a new strategy is the purpose of your internal analysis of strengths and weaknesses, you'll need to assess the current financial strength of your organization and unit. After all, a new strategy may be costly to implement, especially if it requires the purchase of assets or the acquisition of some other operating company or unit. So when you're considering high-level corporate strategy, ask the CFO to provide a full report that includes the following:

- **Cash flows.** To what extent are cash flows from the company's current operations sufficient to support a major new strategic initiative? A fast-growing company usually gobbles up cash flow from operations and then has to go hunting for outside capital to finance growth. In contrast, a mature, low-growth company can often finance a new initiative with cash flow from current operations.

- **Access to outside capital.** If cash flow is insufficient to finance a new strategy, your company will have to look to outside creditors and/or investors. So determine the company's (1) borrowing capacity, (2) ability to float bonds at a reasonable rate of interest, and (3) in the event of a major initiative, ability to attract equity capital through a sale of company stock.

- **Other scheduled capital-spending plans.** Your company may have already approved other capital-spending projects. If it has, those might absorb all available capital. Get a list of these scheduled projects and determine the extent to which they will compete for resources with any new strategy.

- **The hurdle rate required of new projects.** The *hurdle rate* is the minimum rate of return expected from new projects that require substantial capital investments. It is usually calculated as the enterprise's cost of capital plus some expectation of profit.

Also ask the CFO for information on the financial performance of current operations. In particular, you'll want to know the company's return on invested capital and its return on assets. You should also discern whether these return figures are trending upward or downward or are stable. Why bother learning about these returns? They are measures of profitability, and any new strategy you're considering must be able to improve on them. These returns represent baselines against which executives will need to compare the contribution of any new strategy. For example, if your company's current return on invested capital is 12 percent—and stable—any new strategy would have to improve that measure of profitability. For more information on cash flow and other financial measures, see *The Essentials of Finance and Budgeting* volume in this series.

Just as you assess your company's financial status to help shape strategy, you need to take stock of the HR department's financial condition while developing your HR strategy. That is, consider which initiatives are already in the works, which efforts require funding, which programs might be cut to free up investments in more strategic projects. Take a close look at your HR budget: can it accommodate the important initiatives you know are essential to supporting your company's competitive strategy? If not, what changes must be made to align the budget with the high-level strategy?

Management and Culture

Some companies can recognize when a shift in direction is necessary, and they have both the management competence and organizational culture required for successful change. Others cannot. It took many years, for example, for the management of General Motors (GM) to recognize the seriousness of the threat posed by Asian competitors. Once those executives were alert to the danger, their well-intended plans for change were hobbled by a vast organization, installed plants, and labor contracts that made change difficult and painfully slow. Employees and critics alike joked that GM stood for "glacial movement."

Like General Motors, every established enterprise faces constraints on its flexibility and adaptability. Not surprisingly, years of practice mold managerial thinking and organizational systems to the requirements of the existing strategy. That is a virtue so long as the strategy makes sense, but a handicap when it doesn't. So, as you look for your organization's internal strengths and weaknesses, ask, Is the company "change ready"? A change-ready company is prepared to discard what is not working and define and implement strategies capable of generating better results. A change-ready company has these characteristics:

- Managers are respected and effective.

- People feel personally motivated to change.

- The organization is nonhierarchical in its reporting and decision-making structure.

- People are accustomed to collaborative work.

- People are accountable for results.

- Performance is rewarded.

Companies with these characteristics are in a good position to implement a new strategy. As explained in *The Essentials of Managing Change and Transition* volume in this series, HR professionals can—and must—play a key role in helping their organizations become change-ready. Powerful practices for shaping a change-ready culture include the following:[1]

- **Help managers assess their units' change-readiness.** Some units may be more change-ready than others—with effective leaders and collaborative work styles. Identify these units and use them as test beds for strategy-related change initiatives.

- **Encourage managers to demonstrate participative approaches to everyday business.** Model and encourage participative work. Assess how much managers and executives share information, listen as well as talk, invite input from employees while making decisions, and exhibit other participative behaviors. Provide coaching and training for managers who need help mastering these behavioral changes.

- **Assess complacency in your organization.** Look for symptoms of complacency, such as lack of a highly visible crisis, a focus on narrow functional goals versus broad business performance, finger-pointing when performance problems arise, and leaders' unwillingness to acknowledge companywide weaknesses. Discuss your findings with other executives and convey the importance of nipping complacency in the bud when implementing high-level corporate strategy.

By shaping a change-ready culture in your organization, as well as enlightening executives and line managers to the importance of change-readiness, you lay the groundwork for your organization to embrace and implement a new corporate strategy.

A Method for Evaluating Internal Strengths and Weaknesses

While some company strengths and weaknesses can be easily quantified (e.g., return on assets, net income, number of new accounts), many others cannot. For example, consider the question of whether your company rewards performance—an important strength for an organization seeking to carry out a new strategy. Some people may believe that the company rewards performance. "We all got merit increases last year," they'll say. But others may believe just the opposite: "We get bonuses for individual accomplishments, but not for team accomplishments." Clearly, the notion of rewarding performance is quite subjective: How does a company carry out this practice, exactly? And how can it figure out how well or consistently it's rewarding performance?

To address such questions, you need a method that accommodates many perceptive people representing different functions within the organization. Their collective judgment is bound to provide a fuller, more accurate picture than that of one or two bright individuals who see things from their narrow viewpoints. As James Surowiecki noted in his interesting book *The Wisdom of Crowds*, "If you put together a big enough and diverse enough group of people and ask them to 'make decisions affecting matters of general interest,' that group's decisions will, over time, be 'intellectually superior to the isolated individual,' no matter how smart or well-informed he is."[2] As an HR leader, you can—and should—play a central role in organizing this collective intelligence about your organization's strengths and weaknesses. Where to begin? The following nine steps can help.[3]

Step 1: Select an Individual to Facilitate the Analysis

The person facilitating an analysis of your company's internal strengths and weaknesses should be someone whom people trust and respect. He or she should also be viewed as objective and not aligned with any particular "camp" within the company. As an HR professional, you may well possess these qualities. If your schedule doesn't permit taking on this role, list other individuals in your organization who have unassailable credibility in the eyes of their colleagues. Who seems to always have the company's best interests at heart, rather than his or her own "turf"? Who is skilled at eliciting creative, forthright input from others? At managing group dynamics? Some organizations also choose to hire a consult to facilitate such analyses.

If you've decided that someone else in your company would best serve as the facilitator, broach the subject with him or her of leading an analysis of your company's internal strengths and weaknesses. If the person claims to be too busy to take on this role, exert your powers of influence: explain the importance of the assessment to the company's future and its ability to formulate and execute a powerful competitive strategy. Express your appreciation for the skills that he or she will bring to the process. Offer your assistance, if that would make it easier for the person to accept the role.

Step 2: Create a Strengths and Weaknesses Assessment Team

Like the facilitator, members of this team should be trusted and respected by their peers and have reputations for objectivity and "truth telling." They should also come from different functional areas of the company. To identify potential members, interview functional leaders throughout your firm (or ask your facilitator to do so). Explain the goals of the assessment project and the personal qualities that the assessment team members must demonstrate. Ask your interviewees whom they would recommend as members, and suggest that they nominate managers as well as individual contributors.

Step 3: Invite the Team to Brainstorm the Company's Strengths

Once you've gathered the members of your assessment team, have the facilitator go around the room and solicit everyone's ideas about what strengths the company possesses. Be sure to consider your company's core competencies, its financial condition, management, and organizational culture, as described earlier. Also encourage team members to give some attention to your company's leadership and decision-making abilities, innovation, speed, productivity, quality, service, efficiency, and use of technology. You or the facilitator should ensure that all members have a chance to offer input.

Step 4: Record All Suggestions on a Flip Chart

Have the facilitator or a team member take responsibility for recording suggested strengths on a flip chart. Put all entries under headings. For instance, under the heading "Organizational Culture," you might list entries such as "Willingness to take risks" and "An entrepreneurial spirit." Use as many flip-chart pages as necessary to document all the input offered by team members, and try to avoid making duplicate entries.

Also make it clear that you will also be talking about weaknesses later in the meeting. Explain that the assessment may reveal that the company has both strengths and weaknesses in specific areas. For example, your company may enjoy some strengths in customer service, but suffer from certain weaknesses in that area as well. At this point, your goal is to capture on paper as many ideas about strengths as possible, without evaluating them just yet.

Step 5: Consolidate Ideas

Post all flip-chart pages on a wall. Though the recorder may have made every effort to avoid duplicate entries, you will likely see some overlap. For instance, perhaps the "Management" category has the entry "Encourages participation in decision making," and the "Organizational Culture" category has the entry "Everyone feels comfortable providing their input on important decisions." In this case, you could consolidate these two entries under either heading.

Consolidate such duplicate points by asking the group which items can be combined under which heading. But resist the temptation to overconsolidate—lumping lots of ideas under one subject.

Often, this results in a lack of focus. A good rule of thumb in making any list is that more than ten items can make it difficult for people to understand the list.

Step 6: Clarify Ideas

Go down the consolidated lists item by item, and discuss any strengths that participants have questions about. It's helpful to reiterate the meaning of each item before discussing it. Stick to defining strengths. Restrain any urge to talk about possible solutions to problems or to propose high-level strategies at this point in the process.

Step 7: Identify the Top Three Strengths

Of all the strengths the team has generated, which are the top three? Ask the group for input. Sometimes the top three strengths are obvious. In that case, you or the facilitator simply tests for consensus. Otherwise, give participants a few minutes to pick their top issues and vote on them. Allow each team member to cast three to five votes (three if the list of issues is ten items or fewer, five if it is longer). Identify the top three items. If there are ties or the first vote is inconclusive, discuss the highly rated items from the first vote and vote again.

Step 8: Summarize Company Strengths

Once the team has identified what it considers the company's top three strengths, summarize them on a single flip-chart page.

Step 9: Repeat Steps 2–8 for Company Weaknesses

Now that you've identified your company's most important strengths, use the same steps to identify its top three weaknesses. Like strengths, a company's weaknesses can fall into the categories of core competencies, finances, management, culture, leadership abilities, decision-making abilities, speed, innovation, productivity, quality, service, efficiency, and use of technology. As you or the facilitator elicits team members' input about weaknesses, make sure that everyone knows that it's safe to provide honest suggestions—even if it's painful to do so. It's especially important to make this point if some people in the room report to others on the assessment team—and are describing weaknesses in that manager's or executive's department.

Note: you can use this same process to tap collective insights on external threats and opportunities, as described in the preceding chapter. If you do so, however, you might want to expand the assessment team to include people from outside the company: a supplier who knows the industry intimately and with whom your firm works regularly, a consultant with broad industry experience, and so forth.

Once you have completed the nine steps, suggest that your assessment team compile its findings in a formal report for the benefit of top management, strategic planners, and other interested parties. And if you've done the same for external analysis, your company will be ready to move on to the business of creating a strategy.

By participating in or leading a SWOT analysis for your company, you increase your value to the organization. Why? As you work with your assessment team to identify strengths and weaknesses, you arm yourself with critical insights that can help you suggest an effective high-level strategy for your company during strategy-formulation sessions with other executives.

Keep in mind, too, that you can use this same SWOT analysis method for your HR department in the initial phase of developing an HR strategy. By conducting a SWOT analysis for the HR function, you boost your chances of leveraging the department's strengths in ways that support the corporate strategy. You also improve your HR department's "strategic readiness"—a topic that we turn to in the following section.

Evaluating Your HR Department's Strategic Readiness

Strategically ready HR departments exhibit a kind of maturity that some experts maintain is achieved through a company's evolution through the following stages:[4]

1. **No conscious personnel management.** In this stage, no one at the company thinks about managing the organization's human resources. For example, a small catering business recruits workers for occasional events. It pays them in cash when the event is over, and it keeps no personnel records.

2. **Personnel administration.** The company manages its personnel in accordance with the law and establishes a payroll system. It creates reports of the number of people employed and their pay histories. But leadership views people management as merely managing "bodies"—controlling staff, making sure tasks are completed, and grappling with disciplinary problems.

3. **Professional practice.** Company leaders recognize that, to get the best performance from the organization's workforce, they must do more than just manage bodies. They begin using personnel records to record basic performance comments from each employee's supervisor. In the catering company example earlier, managers might use these records to again recruit previous workers who did a high-quality job during a catering event. However, the company does not have an HR department.

4. **Effective HR management.** Company leaders notice that competing organizations are winning more business based on price. So they decide to improve efficiency and lower costs in their own organization. They realize that supervisors need training in these areas and that the company needs to learn how to assess managers' skills, so they hire an HR professional to tackle these efforts. That professional offers ideas for bringing in new leaders, modifying compensation to attract more skilled managers, and establishing structured training programs.

    As a result, business picks up. Moreover, long-standing managers begin to demonstrate more effective people management skills. A new, formal performance management system takes shape—including formal performance assessments, and severing of employment relationships with workers who don't reach the required standards. A performance culture begins to emerge.

5. **HR management integral to operations.** The company links its budgeting and management information systems to workforce performance. For example, leaders approve budgets that provide funds for training and on-the-job coaching. The company defines and uses a set of metrics for measuring performance and making personnel decisions based on those measurements. For instance, someone measures project lead times and identifies who was running the best and worst project teams. Managers use this information while selecting team leaders for new projects. Finally, line managers have moved beyond valuing HR management expertise: they now can't do their jobs effectively without it. And they've adopted the mind-set of actively developing and coaching their staff to meet the needs of the business. However, company leaders are still more focused on current business objectives and targets than future strategic goals.

6. **Shift from operational HR to strategic HR.** The focus shifts from meeting existing business objectives to delivering even better performance in the future. For example, HR encourages production managers to look beyond reducing wastage today, and to consider ways to redesign production processes to achieve entirely new levels of performance tomorrow. Reporting structures loosen: even though the organization chart shows a distinct hierarchy, individual managers aren't required to get approval from their own boss to help out another department or project team.

7. **HR and the organization as a whole system.** HR and the rest of the company work together organically to continually define and execute strategy. Though people have nominal bosses, they work with one another on an ad hoc or regular basis to address strategic challenges and carry out strategic initiatives as necessary. People feel free to come up with new ideas constantly, and they don't take it personally if their idea isn't implemented: they conclude that the choice was made for a good reason. An ad hoc SWOT assessment, conducted by a

broad and deep cross-section of people in the organization and guided by HR, is a good indicator that a company is reaching this level of maturity.

To diagnose where your company fits along this HR maturity spectrum, try your hand at assessment tool 3-1.

Assessment Tool 3-1
Diagnose Your HR Department's Maturity Level

For each statement below, check whether you agree or disagree. Then see the instructions for interpreting your score.

In my organization . . .

1. No one makes a conscious effort to conduct personnel management.

   Agree   Disagree

2. Only senior managers make decisions and are accountable for the company's performance.

   Agree   Disagree

3. A command-and-control mind-set exists.

   Agree   Disagree

4. People blame one another for the company's problems.

   Agree   Disagree

5. Those of us in HR acknowledge that we could be making better personnel decisions in the company.

   Agree   Disagree

6. We conduct perfunctory performance reviews.

   Agree   Disagree

7. We conduct formal performance appraisals and use the information to make personnel decisions and project assignments.

Agree   Disagree

8. We've established systems for providing feedback on employees' and managers' performance.

Agree   Disagree

9. We have a performance management system that includes clear business-related metrics.

Agree   Disagree

10. People throughout the organization are accountable for the company's performance.

Agree   Disagree

11. We develop tailored solutions for addressing under-performance.

Agree   Disagree

12. Our performance measurement systems cross functional boundaries.

Agree   Disagree

13. Reporting lines are clear but flexible.

Agree   Disagree

14. We've put structures in place to maximize customer satisfaction.

Agree   Disagree

15. Our training and development efforts focus on the importance of continual learning.

Agree   Disagree

continued

16. There's a clear line of sight between all activities and the company's strategic objectives.

    Agree   Disagree

17. All employees feel a sense of ownership of the company's strategic objectives.

    Agree   Disagree

18. People take responsibility for performance problems, rather than pointing fingers at others.

    Agree   Disagree

19. The culture is characterized by a widespread obsession with continual improvement.

    Agree   Disagree

20. Bosses and employees trust one another to have the company's best interests at heart.

    Agree   Disagree

Total:

Interpreting your score

If you answered "Agree" to most of statements 1–8 and "Disagree" to most of statements 9–20, your HR department is not strategically ready. If you answered "Disagree" to most of statements 1–8 and "Agree" to most of statements 9–20, your HR department appears to be on its way to being strategically ready.

SOURCE: Adapted from Paul Kearns, *HR Strategy: Business Focused, Individually Centred* (Burlington, MA: Butterworth-Heinemann, 2003), 45.

Summing Up

In this chapter, you learned that:

- A core competence is a potential foundation for any new or revised strategy.

- A competence is only meaningful when compared with that of rivals.

- It's vital to assess the current financial strength of your organization or unit before thinking about how to define a corporate-level or HR strategy. A new strategy may be costly to implement, especially if it involves the purchase of assets or the acquisition of some other business.

- Management competence and the right organizational culture are required for successful strategic change.

- It's helpful to determine whether your company is ready to execute major strategy-related change by looking for the following characteristics: managers are respected and effective; people feel personally motivated to change; the organization is nonhierarchical; people are accustomed to collaborative work; there is a culture of accountability for results; and performance is rewarded.

- It's best not to rely on one or two people to do an analysis of your company's internal strengths and weaknesses. Instead, bring together a small group of objective, respected people who represent different activities in the organization. Have them use the nine-step process offered earlier to identify strengths and weaknesses. They can also use the same process to clarify external threats and opportunities.

- Conducting a SWOT analysis is one step toward becoming a strategically ready HR department. Strategic HR management is marked by the ability of an HR department and an organization to work together as one system to anticipate, define, and execute strategic change.

Leveraging Chapter Insights: Critical Questions

- What do you see as your company's core competencies? Your HR department's core competencies? Why?

- How would you define your company's and HR department's financial readiness to carry out strategy?

- How well positioned are your company's management and culture to define and execute high-level strategy? Which characteristics need strengthening? What steps might you take to strengthen them?

- Which individuals in your organization would be best qualified to facilitate and participate in a team to assess the company's internal strengths and weaknesses? How might you best enlist them for the job?

- Given your understanding of how HR organizations mature over time, where do you see your HR department fitting along the maturity spectrum? What steps might you take to move it further along the spectrum toward a strategically ready HR department?

CHAPTER FOUR

Types of Strategy

Which Fits Your Business?

Key Topics Covered in This Chapter

- *Low-cost leadership strategy, and how to make it work*

- *Differentiating a product or service—even a commodity—in ways that create real value for customers*

- *Customer relationship strategy, and six approaches for making it valuable for customers*

- *The network effect strategy: winner-take-all*

- *Determining which strategic approach is right for your company*

- *Selecting a business strategy: implications for HR*

L OOK AT THE MANY BOOKS on business strategy, and you'll find a cornucopia of strategy frameworks: low-cost leadership, diversification, merger-acquisition, global, customer focus, product leadership, vertical integration, flexibility, product/service differentiation, and so forth. What are these strategies, exactly? And now that you understand your company's and your unit's threats and opportunities, along with strengths and weaknesses, how can you determine which strategy is most appropriate for your company? And what are the implications of this choice for your HR strategy?

At bottom, every for-profit entity aims for the same goal: to identify and pursue a strategy that will give it a defensible and profitable hold on some segment of the marketplace. That market segment, by choice, may be large or small. And it may produce, by choice, high profits on a small number of transactions or low profits on every one of millions of sales. It may involve superficial relationships with many customers or long-term and deep relationships with just a few. No matter which strategies they follow, for-profit companies will also try to increase the range of profitability—that is, the difference between what customers are willing to pay and the company's cost of providing its goods or services.

This chapter describes four basic strategies: low-cost leadership, product/service differentiation, customer relationship, and network effect. It is difficult to find a business strategy that is not one of these or some variation. And each one has different implications for HR strategy.

Low-Cost Leadership

Low-cost leadership has paved the road to success for many companies. Discount retailers in the United States such as E.J. Korvette and later Kmart grabbed significant chunks of the retail market away from traditional department stores and specialty stores when they first appeared in the 1950s and 1960s. Their success derived from their ability to deliver goods at lower prices, and they developed that ability by keeping their cost structures much lower than those of traditional competitors. These early discounters were displaced, in turn, by Wal-Mart and Target, which proved even more effective in executing the low-cost strategy.

In this strategy, the company's offerings are usually the same as the products or services offered by rivals. They may be commodities, such as rolled steel or household electrical wire, or they may be something readily available through other vendors. Items sold by Wal-Mart, for example, can be obtained at many other locations—some just down the street. Duracell batteries, Minolta binoculars, Canon cameras, Kodak photographic film, Wrangler jeans, Hanes underwear, Gillette razor blades, Bic pens. So why do so many people in North America head to Wal-Mart and Target to buy these items, often driving past rival vendor locations? Because they believe they will get the same items for less money. And they usually do. Wal-Mart in particular was built with this low-cost advantage as a key part of its overall strategy.

The key to success with the low-cost strategy is to deliver the customer's expected level of value at a cost that ensures the company an adequate level of profitability. Consider figure 4-1, which is adapted from a model first advanced by Adam Brandenberger and Gus Stuart. The vertical distance between the willingness of customers to pay (top line) and the cost of providing the product itself (bottom) represents the range of pricing within which every company must operate. It also represents the value added by the company, as perceived by customers. For commodity or undifferentiated products, the spread between these lines is narrow. And the top line—what customers are willing to pay—is generally fixed. So, to enhance profitability, the company must push the cost-of-providing line lower. It will generally attempt to do

FIGURE 4-1

Expected value

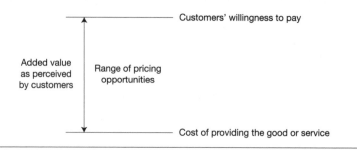

Customers' willingness to pay

Added value as perceived by customers | Range of pricing opportunities

Cost of providing the good or service

this through operational efficiency—for example, pressuring suppliers for lower prices. This is the game that Wal-Mart has been playing and winning for many years. It has squeezed more costs out of its supply chain than has any other major retailer.

It's easy to assume that the low-cost leadership strategy applies solely to physical products: jeans, paint, tons of steel, and so forth. However, we can find many examples of low-cost strategy in the service sector. Consider The Vanguard Group, a leading investment management company. Started in 1975, the company provides a broad array of mutual funds and a very high level of client service. There is nothing particularly fancy about Vanguard or its funds. While some of its actively managed funds have been top performers over the long term, many are index funds that purposely aim to replicate the return of the market, not "beat" it. In most years, these passive index funds actually outperform the average managed fund.

What really sets Vanguard apart from other fund families is its no-commission policy and the fact that it has the lowest average expense ratio among fund families. In 2003, for example, Vanguard's average expense ratio was a tiny 0.25 percent of assets—less than one-fifth of the mutual fund industry's average expense ratio of 1.38 percent. Results? Vanguard's clients get a 1.13 percent greater annual return on their money (all else being equal). By keeping management and transaction costs low, Vanguard helps ensure that more of a client's money is actually invested and reinvested. And that produces better returns over time. Vanguard's success with this strategy has earned it accolades among individual investors and made it one of the largest fund families in the United States.

Making the Low-Cost Strategy Work

As we saw earlier, the key to retaining low-cost leadership is keeping the cost of providing goods or services lower than other companies do. This is a constant challenge, because you can be certain that rivals will work hard to drive their costs lower than yours. But it can be achieved through several means. Consider these four:

- **Continuous improvement in operating efficiency.** The Japanese developed the philosophy of *kaizen*, or continuous process improvement, to gain their well-known lead in manufacturing. Kaizen encourages everyone, from the chief executive to the loading dock guy, to seek out ways to incrementally improve what they are doing. A 1 percent improvement here and a 2 percent improvement there quickly add up over time, giving the firm a notable cost advantage. The concept of *process reengineering* aims for a similar result. But whereas kaizen aims for incremental improvements to the existing work, process reengineering aims for large breakthrough change—either through wholesale transformation or the total elimination of existing activities. Both kaizen and process reengineering have exerted profound impacts on operating efficiency in both manufacturing and services.

- **Exploitation of the experience curve.** Production managers know that people learn to do the same job more quickly and with fewer errors the more frequently they do the job. Thus, a heart operation that once took eight hours to complete can be done successfully in four hours as a surgical team gains experience with the procedure. And before long, the team may have it done in just two or three hours. The same phenomenon occurs in manufacturing settings where managers and employees focus on learning.

The *experience curve* concept holds that the cost of doing a repetitive task decreases by some percentage each time the cumulative volume of production doubles. Thus, a company that gets onto the experience curve sooner than an imitator can theoretically maintain a cost advantage. Consider the two cost curves in figure 4-2. Both companies A and B begin at the same cost level and learn at the same rate. They compete primarily on price. But A got into the business first and, consequently, is farther down the cost curve than rival B, maintaining its cost advantage at every point in time. At time T, for instance, that advantage is C. Company B must either learn at a much faster rate, accept a permanent cost disadvantage (and smaller profit margin), or exit the market.

- **An unbeatable supply chain.** Everyone is familiar with the Dell business model. Dell sells its personal computers directly to consumers, skipping the middleman. It also builds those PCs to order, thus eliminating the costly finished goods inventory problem that plagues rivals who operate with traditional business models. Dell has no finished goods idling on a shelf and becoming more and more technologically obsolete by the day.

  What people often overlook about Dell is the efficiency and effectiveness of its supply chain. That chain includes component suppliers, assemblers, and the logistical services of United Parcel Service. All are digitally linked so that order information is immediately translated into production and delivery schedules. The ability of this supply chain to deliver a customized PC to a customer's door in a week or so makes it possible to eliminate middlemen and inventory costs—giving the company cost leadership in its field. Wal-Mart provides yet another example of a company that commands cost leadership through the power of its supply chain.

- **Product redesign.** Companies can sometimes achieve huge cost reductions through product redesign. For example, back in the 1970s, Black & Decker (B&D), a manufacturer of consumer power tools, found itself going head-to-head with low-cost

Asian competitors. It had a serious cost disadvantage that could not be cured by simply being more thrifty and efficient. Something more dramatic was required. B&D responded by re-designing its entire family of consumer power tools *and* the process for making them. At the heart of its product-line makeover was a single electric motor that could be inexpensively altered to provide power for any number of different hand tools. That innovation eliminated dozens of different motor types and the need to make and store hundreds of different components. The core product platform's simplicity and "manufacturability" enabled B&D to produce the new family of tools with 85 percent fewer labor costs. Inventory and other related costs tumbled by similar percentages.

Société Micromécanique et Horlogère accomplished similar results with its Swatch watch, which was based on the company's development of a reliable, plastic, quartz timekeeper that could be mass produced for a tiny fraction of the cost of traditional watchworks. This design breakthrough enabled the Swiss company to compete and prosper in a market dominated by low-cost Asian competitors.

FIGURE 4-2

The experience curve

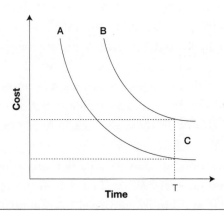

Operational excellence is an important part of the low-cost leadership strategy, but only a part. As we'll see later, becoming the low-cost leader involves more than pinching pennies and squeezing the fat out of business processes. Above all, it entails a thoughtful plan for structuring the enterprise. Consider this analogy: if you want to be the fastest sailboat in your area, you don't simply wax the hull and train your crew to get the most out of the floating bathtub you call your boat. Instead, you build a craft that is designed for speed from the keel up. The business equivalent is to structure the organization to deliver low-cost leadership.

Is a low-cost strategy feasible for your company? If it is, what would have to happen to make it work?

Differentiation

Every successful strategy—even the low-cost leadership strategy—is about *differentiation*. "We can fly you to Geneva for less than our competitors." "At Auto City Sales, we will not be underpriced." But for most companies, differentiation is expressed in some qualitative way that customers value. For example, when Thomas Edison first began to market his system of electric incandescent lighting, his principal rivals were local gas companies. Both methods of illumination were effective, but Edison's approach had clear differences that most customers favored. Unlike gas lamps, electric lighting didn't noticeably heat up people's living rooms on hot summer nights. It was more convenient, requiring just a flick of the switch to turn it on and off. And it eliminated a serious fire hazard in many applications. Edison played on these qualitative differences as he attacked and eliminated the gas companies' dominance of urban lighting in the late 1800s.

Companies today likewise adopt differentiation strategies. Consider the auto industry. To set itself apart, Volvo touts the crashworthiness of its vehicles. Toyota plays up its reputation for quality and high resale value; more recently, it has differentiated its Prius model with hybrid engine technology. The MINI Cooper practically screams, "I'm cute and I'm fun to drive!" to potential buyers. Sports carmaker Porsche has also differentiated itself by concentrating on the development of high-performance vehicles. While GM may offer a vehicle for every household budget, and Toyota may claim a high level of quality and reliability, neither has much appeal for the small number of drivers who hunger for speed, agility, and the sense that they could handle the raceway circuit at Le Mans. That is what Porsche aims to deliver through its strategy of differentiation.

Differentiating a Commodity Product

Even among commodity products, business strategists have uncovered and exploited opportunities to differentiate themselves. Even when price and product features are identical, it is still possible to differentiate on the basis of service. The cement business provides an example. Cement is cement, right? That's the situation that Mexico-based Cemex, the world's third-largest provider of cement, faces. Cement is a commodity product. Nevertheless, Cemex has developed a strategy of fast and reliable delivery that qualitatively differentiates the company from its many rivals. As described by David Bovet and Joseph Martha in their book on supply chain excellence, Cemex has become a major power in many markets because it adopted a production and high-tech logistics strategy that achieves on-time delivery 98 percent of the time. Compare that to most competitors' 34 percent record of on-time delivery. Construction companies operating on tight schedules prize that reliability, especially when a late delivery means that dozens of highly paid crew members will be standing around doing nothing. "This super reliability," write Bovet and Martha, "allows Cemex to charge a premium in most markets, contributing to profit levels 50 percent higher than those of its key competitors."[1] In this case, super reliability has effectively differentiated a commodity product. Companies can achieve similar feats by offering superior customer support.

Effective Differentiation

Is your company following a strategy of differentiation? If it is, what sets the organization's offerings apart from rivals' products and services?

Whatever the answer, remember that differentiation matters only to the extent that *customers value* the difference—maybe not all customers, but the ones you've targeted. If these customers truly value that which sets your product or service apart, they will either (1) select your offering over those of others, (2) be willing to pay a premium for what you offer, or (3) some combination of 1 and 2. How to determine whether customers will value your difference? Many companies use customer and market research.

Customer Relationship

Everyone knows that you can buy a camera or wide-angle lens for less at Wal-Mart, Best Buy, or one of the other discount stores. Film and film processing are cheaper at these stores as well. But many people still patronize small, independently owned photography shops when they purchase cameras, accessories, and film. Likewise, Fantastic Sam's, a national franchise, provides great hairstyling services at low prices. Yet many—if not most—women will pay more to go to the stylist who has been serving them for the past many years. Many women, in fact, can claim a longer-term relationship with their hairstylists than with their husbands! In the words of one, "A husband is replaceable—a good hairdresser isn't." And consider the quip "Only her hairdresser knows for sure"—which stems from the widespread tendency of women to hold lengthy personal conversations with their hairdressers while at the salon.

What's going on here? Why do so many customers pay more to patronize local camera shops, hairdressers, corner bookstores, neighborhood meat markets and bakeries, and many other vendors of goods and services when they could get a cheaper deal elsewhere? The reason is that they *value* the personal connection they experience while doing business with these companies, their owners, and their employees. That relationship can take many forms: doing business with a familiar face; the fact that the other person knows them and their needs; the vendor's willingness to explain what the product is, how to use it, and what the pros and cons are of different purchase choices. These are services and qualities you cannot find online, in a direct mail catalog, or at most "big box" stores. Those vendors provide a transaction, but not a relationship.

Relationship Strategy at Work: USAA

While big companies face a disadvantage in building and executing a customer relationship strategy, it is not impossible. Consider the case of USAA (United States Automobile Association). You may not have heard of this *Fortune* 500 financial services company, even though it has $71 billion under management. That's because it caters exclusively to a very thin slice of the total U.S. population: active-duty military personnel, National Guard and Reserve enlisted personnel, officers and officer candidates, and their dependents.

The people in USAA's target market, however, know the company very well, and a large percentage of them patronize its banking, insurance, and credit card services. Among active-duty officers, participation is 90–95 percent. And because USAA is a mutual company, customers are also part owners.

After decades of serving this population, USAA understands its customers' unique banking, insurance, and retirement needs. And it knows how to deal with the fact that military officers are transferred from post to post and around the world with great frequency. USAA expresses its understanding of customers in many ways that people appreciate. For example, when customers are deployed overseas or to a war zone, they often put their autos in storage for one or more years; in these cases, USAA urges them to request elimination of the costly liability component of their auto insurance policies. No other auto insurer would think to do that. And unlike other life insurers, USAA's policies have no war clause provision. USAA customers know that full policy death benefits will be paid if they die for *any* reason, including wartime service.

USAA's close relationship with its military clientele and its understanding of their unique lifestyle have roots stretching back to the company's founding in 1922 by twenty-five army officers who encountered difficulties—owing to their profession and mobility—in obtaining auto insurance. Even today, a substantial number of USAA executives and employees are former military people, and customer-serving employees are given extensive training on the unique financial needs of military personnel.[2] Personal service is these employees' highest priority.

USAA focuses on a much narrower market segment than just about any other *Fortune* 500 company, but that focus and attention to customer relationships has paid off in terms of revenue growth, profitability, and customer satisfaction. In 2004, a poll of affluent investors put USAA at the top, with a satisfaction score 8 percent higher than TIAA-CREF (which also serves a focused market group) and 73 percent higher than Fidelity (which serves the general public). That same year, a survey conducted by Forrester Research put the company at the top among financial services companies for customer advocacy. According to that study, customer advocacy is customers' perception that a company is doing what's best for them and not just for the company's profitability. "USAA scored highest in our ranking" explained the researchers at Forrester, "in part because of its focus on simplifying customers' lives through efficient call center experiences. Many large banks, on the other hand, are at the bottom of our ranking because many of their customers feel nickel-and-dimed."[3]

Making the Customer Relationship Strategy Work

Companies like USAA succeed to the extent that the relationships they build with people add real value—as perceived by customers. That value can take many forms:

- **Simplifying customers' lives or work.** A USAA auto insurance holder does not have to obtain a new insurance policy every time he or she is transferred to another state.

- **Ongoing benefits.** Microsoft gains relationship points by notifying software users of critical updates, which customers can download without charge.

- **Personalized service.** Many top-tier hotels have developed personalized approaches to handling repeat visitors by storing check-in information and customer preferences in their companywide databases. This practice enables express check-in, gives customers the service they want, and adds a personal touch: "Welcome back to XYZ Hotels, Mr. Jones. We have a nonsmoking room for you. Do you still prefer having the *Wall Street Journal* delivered with your continental breakfast?"

- **Customized solutions.** Most companies continue to sell one-size-fits-all products and services. Thus, if you can economically customize your offering to individual customers' unique requirements, you'll build a stronger personal connection to them as well as boost profits.

- **Personal contact.** Instead of channeling incoming customer calls to whichever service rep is available, give every established customer an account representative. This lends a personal voice to what would otherwise be an impersonal transaction.

- **Continuous learning.** Many companies have adopted customer relationship management (CRM) techniques and technologies to better understand and serve their most loyal and profitable customers. CRM identifies contact points between customers and the company, and enables the organization to use each "touch point" to learn more about customer needs.

A strategy based on customer relationships can produce powerful results and strong customer loyalty. The danger, of course, is that many people profess a strong affinity for the personal touch but turn to the low-cost provider when large sums are at stake. As one homeowner put it, "I usually patronize the small hardware store in my neighborhood. The owner knows me, and I can count on him for advice when I have to repair a leaky faucet, install ceramic tile, or do some other job. But when it comes to big purchases—expensive power tools or something of that nature—I end up at Home Depot. I can't afford not to." The vendor's challenge in these cases is to keep control of major purchases.

See "Focus Strategy—What's Different?" for another perspective on the customer relationship strategy.

Focus Strategy—What's Different?

As described by Michael Porter in his landmark book *Competitive Strategy*, a *focus strategy* is "built around serving a particular target very well, and each functional policy is developed with this in mind."[a] In many respects, the focus strategy and customer relationship strategy go hand in hand. It is next to impossible to develop serious relationships with anything but a highly focused, clearly targeted customer segment, as in the USAA example.

On the other hand, a focus strategy can exist independently of customer relationships. Consider the case of Cracker Barrel Old Country Stores. This nationwide chain of restaurant/gift shops focuses on travelers—particularly motorists on the U.S. interstate highway system—who like traditional foods. Cracker Barrel offers country-style meals and gift items in each of its locations. To encourage repeat visits, the company Web site includes a "trip planner" that identifies the locations of all Cracker Barrel outlets along any "to-from" driving route. It is doubtful that many travelers perceive any relationship benefits from their visits to Cracker Barrel, but they do seem to appreciate the consistency of the food, ambience, and shopping opportunities it provides. Repeat customers know exactly what to expect from these facilities, which makes the choice of where to stop for a meal easy for people on long driving trips.

a. Michael E. Porter, *Competitive Strategy: Techniques for Analyzing Industries and Competitors* (New York: Free Press, 1980), 38.

Network Effect

When the first telephones were sold in the late nineteenth century, they weren't particularly useful. After all, a person could call only one of the few other owners of the new gadget. But the telephone's utility grew as more and more homes, stores, and offices joined the telephone "network." This phenomenon is called the *network effect*.

Through this effect, the value of a product increases as more units are sold.

As a strategy, the network effect is fairly new. Perhaps its most obvious practitioner and beneficiary is eBay, the online auction company. eBay began as a hobby business of its founder, Pierre Omidyar, who developed software and an online system that enabled individuals to list new and used items of all types for auction. His wasn't the first online auction site, but it was the first to become widely popular. And that popularity sent the network effect into high gear. Buyers flocked to eBay instead of to other sites because it had the most sellers. Sellers listed their items on eBay because it attracted the most buyers. This virtuous circle quickly established eBay as the dominant online auction site, and it continues to fuel eBay's remarkable growth.

There is no evidence that Omidyar and his colleagues set out with an implicit network effect strategy. It simply happened. However, early success encouraged them to use their rising tide of revenue to keep up the momentum, which they did through heavy investments in site development, customer service, brand recognition, and strategic acquisitions.

To succeed using a network effect strategy, a company must stake a claim in the emerging market and become the dominant provider. By getting out in front of potential rivals, the organization leaves very little space available for challengers, which is why some call this a *winner-take-all strategy*. eBay quickly dominated its industry by taking this tack. Microsoft did the same with its Windows operating system. True, most experienced computer users agree that the user-friendly Macintosh operating system developed by Apple is superior to Windows. Nevertheless, Windows dominates the industry because it achieved the most widely installed base—early. Since most PCs operated with Windows, most new software was developed for Windows machines. And because most software was Windows-based, more people bought PCs equipped with the Windows operating system. To date, no one has managed to break this virtuous circle.

The Trade-offs of Selecting a Strategy

Each of the four general strategies you've just read about has been a winning ticket for numerous companies. Chances are that one or another—or some variation—would be appropriate for your company. But which one? Look for the answer in your company's mission, its goals, and your SWOT analysis, as described in figure 4-3. Think of the mission as setting the boundaries within which your organization may seek a new strategy. The company's goals set the bar of achievement that the strategy must be capable of attaining. Then use your SWOT analysis to identify threats and opportunities as well as the current capabilities of the organization. These three factors—in consultation with people who know and understand the many facets of your industry—will guide you and the rest of your company's executive team to define the most appropriate high-level strategy.

But keep in mind that any strategic choice involves trade-offs. If your company opts to focus on a narrow set of customers, as in the USAA example, you and other leaders will have to give up the idea of serving the broad general market. As Michael Porter has warned, "Companies that try to be all things to all customers . . . risk confusion in the trenches as employees attempt to make day-to-day operating decisions without a clear framework."[4] Thus, if your firm

FIGURE 4-3

Which strategy is best?

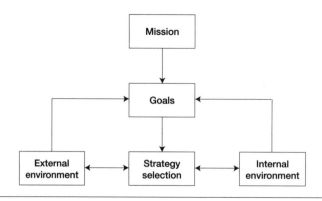

wants to be the low-cost retailer in its field, it shouldn't try to set up a special boutique chain of stores to cater to high-end customers. That will only confuse customers and employees—ultimately eroding your company's profits.

Above all, make sure that your choice of strategy is aligned with the primary market segment you plan to serve. This may be the most critical factor in strategy creation. Keep your chosen customers in your sights at all times, and make sure your colleagues do the same. Alignment between strategy and customers is absolutely essential to successfully executing any strategy.

Selecting a Business Strategy: Implications for HR

Regardless of which type of strategy you and the rest of the executive team select for your organization, your choice will have important implications for your HR strategy. Unless your HR practices, programs, and policies align behind the high-level strategy, your company will find it difficult—if not impossible—to carry out the strategy successfully.

The overarching question you must ask yourself while helping your company select a strategy type is, "What kinds of people will this company need in order to pursue this strategy?" This question, in turn, raises numerous additional queries: What skills should your company's people possess? What attitudes and behaviors should they demonstrate? What ratio of permanent to contingent workers should you aim for? How much should you invest in training? What compensation systems should you use? What qualities and goals should you emphasize during performance appraisals? Which units or teams in the company should receive the most resources? How will you handle the units or teams from which resources are taken away? What changes might you need to make in how your HR department is structured? What new skills will the HR professionals in your organization need to acquire? See "New Business Strategy, New HR" for an example of how one company developed a new HR strategy in response to major shifts in the corporate-level strategy.

New Business Strategy, New HR

In the late 1980s, Amoco—the global oil firm—decided that emerging developments in the industry called for a new competitive strategy. Facing new competitors, falling demand for its products, and declining productivity, Amoco defined an ambitious corporate-level strategy characterized by an overall focus on improving customer relationships. The new strategy emphasized building better connections with customers, managing supply and demand cycles more effectively, reducing costs, increasing investment outside North America, and using joint ventures and acquisitions to bolster assets and enhance operating efficiency.

Amoco executives agreed that optimizing the productivity and creativity of the company's workforce was critical to achieving long-term competitive success through the new strategy. To that end, the company defined an aggressive HR strategy to support the newly defined overarching strategy. The traditional HR strategy had been based on establishing uniform policies for managing people, viewing people as costs versus investments, expecting a lifetime employment commitment, and being in the middle of the "oil company pack" in terms of pay, benefits, and employment policies. The new HR strategy emphasized flexibility, a focus on value created by employees, global collaboration, downward delegation, trust, collaboration, and a more aggressive HR function.

To fuel these shifts, the revised HR strategy contained the following major components:

- **New HR initiatives.** The company redesigned its performance appraisal system to set new standards, establish professional development activities, give feedback on performance, and allocate rewards based on performance. It also overhauled its reward systems to link incentives more closely to extraordinary performance. And it adopted new recruiting strategies to focus on hiring for newly defined skills and values.

- **New HR task forces.** A task force composed of HR and line managers formed to develop new people strategies.

These strategies included building an organizational-capability assessment process into the strategic planning process for all business units, developing action plans to build and maintain required organizational capabilities, and developing and communicating a global vision. Another new HR group was also created to help business units define and assess required capabilities and create action plans to develop capabilities.

- **New HR organization.** Much of Amoco's HR function was moved into Shared Services, which helped unify the formerly decentralized function. (Previously, the HR function had consisted of three parts: corporate HR, operating company HR, and business unit HR.) Performance standards for HR professionals were made clear and aggressive, and HR professionals shouldered greater accountability for meeting those standards. In addition, some HR activities (such as medical-plan administration and certain surveys) were outsourced to generate major cost savings for Amoco.

- **New HR competencies.** To carry out the new HR strategy, the HR professionals within Amoco needed to master new competencies. They did so by participating in workshops where they learned more about change management, team-based work, customer service, and diversity. Additional workshops focused on understanding how HR work fit with business strategy, what the financial implications of people strategies were, and how to create a personal action plan for implementing new people strategies in the organization.

By defining and implementing a new HR strategy, Amoco's HR function played an integral role in helping the company put its new competitive strategy into action. As a result, the HR function added more value than ever to the business, and the company was able to position itself to respond to new challenges emerging in the business landscape.

SOURCE: Dave Ulrich, *Human Resource Champions: The Next Agenda for Adding Value and Delivering Results* (Boston: Harvard Business School Press, 1997), 219–228.

With each strategy type described earlier in this chapter, your answers to these questions will differ. The result? A unique HR strategy. Some experts have suggested that each strategy type indicates the following corresponding HR strategies:[5]

- **Low-cost leadership.** If your company has adopted a low-cost leadership strategy, you'll want employees to focus on the short term, avoid risks, generate predictable results, and focus on measurable business results rather than processes. Thus your performance appraisal system will likely emphasize short-term achievements. You may also want to define specialized jobs and narrow career paths, as well as continually track wage rates in the labor market.

  Many companies that use this strategy also emphasize in-house development of talent—hiring people at entry level, developing them through training, and filling higher-level vacancies by promotions from within. These companies "make" rather than "buy" talent and strive for long employment periods and low turnover.

- **Differentiation.** Has your company chosen a differentiation strategy? If so, you'll need a highly creative, innovative, and collaborative workforce comprising managers and employees who are oriented toward the long term, who take risks, and who are comfortable with uncertainty. Your performance appraisal system will likely emphasize group achievements reached over the long term. In your training and development efforts, you may also aim for generalized skill enhancement and broad career paths. Your compensation systems will likely be flexible and include stock ownership.

  Numerous organizations that use a differentiation strategy invest in training that helps employees acquire skills that apply beyond their present jobs. Such firms bring in talent at any level—taking a "buy" approach. However, they may develop such employees through rapid assignment changes and opportunities to work with ever-changing teams. Often, such companies must accept that skilled employees will come and go as they take jobs with other companies to further develop their skills and enhance their compensation, responsibility, and professional stature.

- **Customer relationship.** If your organization has selected a customer relationship strategy, your HR strategy will look a bit like something in between low-cost leadership and differentiation. For example, you'll likely want to put substantial emphasis on internal development of talent, though you may want to hire some outsiders to fill higher-level positions. That is, your firm will probably both "make" and "buy" its human resources.

   Many such companies also offer extensive career paths within the organization, and emphasize processes rather than quantifiable results in their performance appraisal systems. The processes that are evaluated will likely include analysis of market segments and customer preferences, as well as use of new CRM technologies.

- **Network effect.** If your company has opted to use a network effect strategy, you'll need a workforce dominated by managers and employees who know how to excel at getting as many people to buy your product as possible—and as quickly as possible. After all, unless your company can get more and more people to use its product, it stands little chance of activating the network effect. Remember how the network effect works: The more people who use your product, the more value the product has in the eyes of consumers.

   To excel at carrying out this strategy, employees will need performance metrics related to quality of service and speed of sales. Why? The faster your company can get people using your product, the more quickly it will activate the network effect. Examples of such metrics might include "Number of units sold per month," "Length of time required to solve callers' technical problems," and "Number of product returns." Since successful implementation of the network effect strategy hinges on speedy saturation of the market with your product, your compensation systems might feature hefty sales bonuses and other policies that support the strategy. And your training and development efforts might emphasize the technical skills required to fix problems and keep consumers happy with—and using— your product.

As we've seen, each strategy type has distinct implications for your HR strategy. But all four strategies also have some shared implications. For example, no matter which type of strategy your company selects, you and other executives may also decide to outsource certain activities to third-party providers. Why outsource? This practice can support an overall low-cost leadership strategy if you outsource activities to vendors that can handle them at lower costs and in less time. Outsourcing can also be helpful with a differentiation strategy—for instance, if your firm hires a consultancy to develop innovative product features that will set your offerings apart from those of rivals.

Whatever your reason for outsourcing, the decision to outsource has significant implications for your HR strategy.[6] Specifically, you'll want to ensure that your company has some employees who are good at negotiating vendor contracts and managing vendor performance. You'll also need to develop a workforce that has a lower ratio of permanent to contingent employees. And you'll want to invest heavily in training your permanent core of highly skilled managers and workers.

In addition to leading to decisions to outsource some activities, your company's selection of a strategy type can have major implications for allocation of resources. In particular, once your company has chosen a strategy, you'll want to concentrate resources on those few activities that most support that strategy. Often that means taking resources from parts of the company that offer few strategic opportunities and lack the capabilities most needed to carry out the strategy—and reallocating those resources to parts that have the opportunities and strengths most needed to successfully execute the strategy.

Whenever you reallocate resources in this way, you need to keep in mind that the parts of the company that are losing resources are likely still critical to the functioning of your firm—at least in the short run. Thus it's vital to treat the employees in those parts of the organization in ways that maintain morale and enable successful implementation of the overall strategy. For example, how you handle redeployment of workers or layoffs can make or break your company's execution of its strategy.

Summing Up

In this chapter, you discovered the following:

- As a strategy, low-cost leadership is most appropriate in industries in which competitors offer similar products or services.

- To achieve low-cost leadership, companies can use continuous improvement in operating efficiency, process reengineering, exploitation of the experience curve, supply chain power, and product redesign.

- A differentiation strategy sets a company's product or service apart from those of rivals in a qualitative way that customers value.

- Companies can differentiate commodity products—those with standard features, quality, and price—by providing faster, more reliable delivery and/or superior customer support.

- Product or service differentiation works well only when the difference is something that customers truly value.

- Companies can use strong customer relationships to retain customers who would otherwise gravitate toward lower-cost providers.

- To be effective, a customer relationship strategy must provide something that customers value—for example, a product feature that simplifies their lives or work, ongoing benefits, personalized service, or customized solutions to their unique problems.

- Through the network effect, the value of a product increases as more units are sold. Companies that pursue this strategy (or benefit from it) succeed to the extent that they can stake a claim in the emerging market early and become the dominant provider of some enabling product or service. eBay's online auction site and Microsoft's Windows operating system are two well-known examples.

- Whichever strategy type your company considers, you and other leaders must always look for alignment between the strategy and your target market.

Leveraging Chapter Insights: Crucial Questions

- What type of corporate strategy has your organization been pursuing—low-cost leadership? Differentiation? Customer relationship? Network effect? Some variation on one or more of these?

- What have been the implications of this choice for your HR strategy? For example, how was the HR function structured to support the current choice of high-level strategy? What HR policies, programs, and projects were put in place to support the strategy? What skills did HR professionals in your organization need to strengthen or acquire in order to support the existing strategy?

- Have SWOT analyses conducted by you and other executives revealed the need for a change in the corporate strategy? If so, in what respects might the high-level strategy be changed to better position the company to compete? For example, would the organization be more competitive if it focused its strategy more on customer relationships and less on low-cost leadership?

- If the corporate strategy changes substantially, what might that mean for your HR strategy? Consider strategic dimensions such as HR policies and programs, structure of the HR function, new skills required of HR professionals, and so forth.

CHAPTER FIVE

Strategic Moves

The Mechanisms of Success

Key Topics Covered in This Chapter

- *Gaining a beachhead in occupied market terrain*

- *Using innovation to overcome barriers to market entry*

- *Applying the principles of "judo strategy"*

- *Using product differentiation to expand into a market*

- *Creating and then dominating a new market*

- *Bypassing entry barriers through strategic acquisition*

I N CHAPTER 4, you read about the most common types of
corporate strategy: low-cost leadership, product/service differentiation, customer relationship (and focus), and network
effect. You also discovered tactics for assessing a selected corporate
strategy's implications for your HR strategy. Of course, there's much
more to strategy than deciding which version or variant of these
strategies is best for your company and which HR policies and programs will most support the selected high-level strategy. This chapter continues the discussion by introducing the notion of strategic
moves—the ways by which companies can use their competitive
strategy to enter the marketplace and build defensible positions
there. We explore a number of potential strategic moves in the chapter. These moves are selective, owing to the "essentials" nature of this
book. But they should help you begin thinking about what your
company might accomplish with its corporate strategy, and how
your HR department can help.

Gaining a Market Beachhead

In his classic book on military strategy, Carl von Clausewitz told his
nineteenth-century readers, "Where absolute superiority is not
attainable, you must produce a relative one at the decisive point by
making skillful use of what you have."[1] Von Clausewitz's advice
reminds us that business and HR strategists must reckon with the
realities of the market and the existence of competing firms—some

of which will have greater market power and financial resources. Thus an organization must strike in an area where a competitor is weak, where it is unlikely to fight back, or where it can't fight back effectively. The selected strategy, then, must take these possibilities into account.

Consider the case of the U.S. auto industry during the 1960s and 1970s. None of the domestic carmakers of the time were skilled at producing small, fuel-efficient vehicles. This didn't stem entirely from engineering ineptitude; there simply wasn't strong demand for small cars in the United States. Fuel prices relative to incomes were very low, and most consumers liked roomy vehicles. Also, profits on the few small cars made or sold in America—in terms of both margin and absolute dollars—were skimpy compared with those obtained from larger vehicles. Detroit automakers said, "Why bother?" to the notion of developing small cars. Nevertheless, a small segment of the market gravitated to small, affordable, fuel-efficient vehicles. The Volkswagen (VW) Beetle had already become something of a statement among students, the thrifty, and antiestablishment types.

Before long, foreign carmakers such as Datsun, Fiat, and Renault had joined VW in bringing their small, economical vehicles to the low end of the huge U.S. market. In that market, they had relative superiority (in Clausewitzian terms), and they faced little opposition from domestic producers. Toyota, Mitsubishi, Honda, and others followed suit and successfully established themselves. The fuel shortages and price spikes of the 1970s gave these small-car makers a huge boost and positioned them to move upstream into larger, more profitable segments. Figure 5-1 shows how foreign producers, particularly from Asia, moved strategically from their initial beachheads into different (mostly mid-range) market segments. By the 1990s, some of these producers had also begun introducing cars like the Lexus to challenge the high-end, profit-rich sedan segment. They did the same in the fast-growing light-truck category as well.

Asian watchmakers followed a similar approach in the early 1970s when they entered the low end of the "personal timekeeper" market. In that market, unit sales were potentially large but profits were small, and opposition from the dominant companies proved weak. Precision

FIGURE 5-1

Moving beyond the beachhead

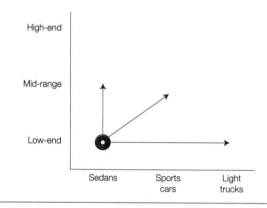

watchmakers were unwilling to contest the Asian companies in those
low-margin markets, but were content to retreat into the upper-
end/high-profit segments of the market. Once the Asian firms had
established a beachhead, however, they developed products for those
high-profit segments as well. This move forced established producers
based in Europe and North America to compete head-to-head with
the Asian rivals or fold.

The lesson in both of these examples is to follow Clausewitz's
timeless advice: aim the sharp end of your strategic spear where
rivals are weak or uninterested in what you're doing. That advice applies in just about every industry. Sam Walton, for example, did not
initially launch a frontal assault on Sears or JC Penny—the retail
giants of his day. Instead, he located his new Wal-Mart stores in small
towns that those formidable rivals had ignored.

Think for a moment about the market segments in your company's
industry. Draw a graph similar to that shown in figure 5-1. Which
are the undefended segments where your organization could establish a beachhead? Once the firm has established a beachhead, what
would it take to expand into more profitable adjacent segments?

Entering a New Market Through Process Innovation

Some barriers to entry into a particular market cannot be circumvented as recommended earlier; your company must confront them directly. Doing so can be costly and dangerous if an organization plays the same game as the established competitors, because copying rivals' strategic tactics only weakens both attacker and defender. The better approach is to bring an innovation to the market—something that will turn entrenched rivals' strengths into weaknesses.

For example, when Nucor Corporation first began thinking about entering the rolled steel market, it faced huge incumbents that had already invested billions in the massive plants needed to produce rolled steel at competitive rates. Nucor couldn't make those same kinds of investments and still make money. Its solution? Develop an entirely new, more cost-effective approach to producing the same product. More specifically, Nucor licensed an unproven German technology for "continuous casting," the holy grail of steelmaking for over one hundred years. More important, Nucor made that technology work. Next, the company decided to use scrap steel as its raw material. By contrast, the big producers were vertically integrated: they dug raw iron ore from the earth, then shipped it to blast furnaces that used it to pour and form mattress-sized blocks of steel. These blocks were run through miles of milling machines and reheating furnaces that gradually reduced them to long, thin ribbons of steel. Nucor skipped all those highly capitalized and labor-intensive steps in favor of an electric furnace that could melt scrap into molten steel on the spot as needed.

In the end, newcomer Nucor was able to produce the same quality steel at a lower cost through the power of process innovation. That edge made Nucor both successful and profitable. Thanks to its innovative "mini-mills," it has become the largest U.S. steel producer and consistently generates handsome profits in an industry plagued by wide swings in customer demand. Its return on invested capital is a stunning 25 percent. "Big Steel," in contrast, discovered that its renowned strengths—huge plants and labor forces, extensive mining operations, and so forth—had now become weaknesses.

Nucor is not alone among companies that have used process innovation to muscle business away from bigger, more established rivals. Nor is this strategy reserved for small upstarts. Pilkington Glass, for example, became the dominant player in the plate glass industry by developing the "float glass" process. Like Nucor, it found a method for continual casting that reduced manufacturing time and costs by orders of magnitude.

Whether your company sells products or services, process innovation can be its ticket to entering or gaining dominance in a target market. Have you or anyone else in your company given this approach any thought?

Applying Judo Strategy

Judo masters use bodily movement, balance, and leverage to defeat more powerful opponents. David Yoffie and Mary Kwak have incorporated these principles in a strategic business mechanism that they term *judo strategy*. They argue that businesspeople can also use movement, balance, and leverage to confront larger and stronger competitors. As they tell their readers, "Movement throws your competitors off balance and neutralizes their initial advantages. Balance helps you engage with the competition and survive an attack. And leverage can enable you to bring your opponents down. When used together, these three principles will help you defeat rivals of any size."[2] Consider these examples of Yoffie and Kwak's three principles at work, as described in their book.

Principle 1: Movement

Through the principal of movement, a company avoids actions, such as a direct challenge or publicly visible marketing initiatives, that would invite an attack from more powerful rivals. Capital One, the seventh-largest credit card issuer in the United States, is one example. The company employed what Yoffie and Kwak describe as the "Puppy Dog Ploy."[3] Through this movement strategy, it staved off

attacks from rivals by quietly developing its business in ways that
didn't attract unwanted attention.

For example, Capital One collected detailed information on customers and tested thousands of offerings on consumers who fit various profiles. It then identified new customer segments and customized new offerings in ways that minimized its risks. To prevent
industry giants from matching its moves, Capital One avoided eye-
catching advertising campaigns and public announcements of its successes. Its market researchers used telephone solicitation and direct
mail instead. Competitors that came across the mailings couldn't see
the strategy underlying the products described in the mailings.

Strategists can also use the movement principal to address opportunities to which "muscle-bound," slower opponents can't respond.
Large firms, like Big Steel in the Nucor case, have amassed substantial
physical assets, entrenched production methods, complex labor contracts, and long-standing customer relationships. These established assets
make change difficult, because organizations can't simply walk away
from them. The consequence? A lack of flexibility. Of course, small,
young firms lack the muscle of these larger competitors. However, they
can usually move more rapidly to address new market opportunities and
adopt new processes. Through these means, they avoid head-on con-
frontation with powerful rivals—a contest they can't hope to win.

Principle 2: Balance

Success through movement will eventually bring a firm into con-
frontation with a larger opponent. In these cases, Yoffie and Kwak
recommend avoiding a situation in which you simply trade punches.
That's a loser's game for the less powerful firm. When your company
is attacked by rivals suddenly aware of the danger your firm poses, it's
best to use the attacker's own strength to advance your position.

Consider the example of Drypers, a company that was striving to
establish itself as a maker of infant diapers. The industry Goliath, Proc-
ter & Gamble, struck at Drypers by blanketing Texas with coupons to
squelch the upstart's introduction in that important market. "Unable
to match P&G's promotional campaign . . . Drypers just accepted its

rival's coupons. The more coupons P&G distributed, the more diapers Drypers sold."[4] Thus Drypers became the beneficiary of its rival's costly promotion program.

Principle 3: Leverage

Per Yoffie and Kwak, the judo business strategist applies leverage by turning an opponent's strengths into weaknesses. Your company can accomplish this by spawning conflict among a competitor and its allies—causing them to fight among themselves instead of battling you. Your organization can also transform a rival's assets into handicaps. Take Freeserve, the leading Internet service provider in the United Kingdom. Freeserve faced dire competition from AOL, which had invested heavily in brand, content, and customer service. Using a very different business model that involved partnering with Energis, a British telecommunications carrier, to split fees the carrier received from the British Telecom, Freeserve was able to offer free Internet access. As Yoffie and Kwak note, "[This move] forced AOL to make a painful decision: whether to match Freeserve, thereby killings its high-margin, high-cost core business, or stick to its strategy and see its market share fall."[5]

Are the principles of judo strategy appropriate for your company? If your organization is small and new, or if it's moving into territory dominated by a powerful rival, movement, balance, and leverage can probably help. But before you and other executives recommend judo strategy, make sure you familiarize yourself with its principles and application tactics. Yoffie and Kwak's book is an excellent start.

Entering a New Market Through Product Differentiation

As another strategic move, your company can use product differentiation to gain a market foothold. Inventor Edwin Land and the company he founded, Polaroid, did this in the photographic imaging business. During the 1950s, when Land was developing his technology, the photography business was already mature. Kodak dominated that business and many of its niches. Land knew he would never make headway by producing his own brand of traditional films and cameras; that market was already well served. So he differentiated his product, creating a film capable of developing itself in just one minute. This was new. It was different. And it set Polaroid's products apart. Instant photography scored a big hit with many consumers— so big that Land's company flourished for several decades.

To use product differentiation successfully, your company must ensure that its targeted customers value the unique characteristics of the new offering. That's fairly obvious. But your firm also has to protect its innovation through patents or other proprietary methods that prevent rivals from duplicating the product. Unfortunately, many innovators have overlooked this crucial aspect of product differentiation. George Eastman, founder of Kodak, knew better than to ignore it. Eastman hit the mother lode with his innovation of photographic film on a roll of cellulose. But he went a step further. Understanding how easily other companies could duplicate his product, he protected it and the equipment developed to manufacture it with an impenetrable thicket of patents. Thanks to this foresight, his company could stake out and dominate the photographic film business for generations.

Eastman's level of success is difficult to replicate. Most product differentiators are lucky if they can capture more than a two- or three-year monopoly once they've launched their innovation. Consider the experience of Minnetonka Corporation, a small, Minnesota-based firm that introduced a product called Softsoap to a mature market dominated by huge national corporations. Softsoap came in a small plastic bottle with a handy pump. At first blush, this innovation doesn't seem all that impressive: after all, liquid hand soap isn't rocket science. Anyone with a small laboratory and rudimentary knowledge of chemistry could develop a marketable version of it. In fact, the first liquid soap developed in the United States had received its patent way back in 1865.

But over a century later, in 1980, Minnetonka introduced and branded its own version, which scored a big hit. Any one of the big soap producer-distributors—companies that controlled shelf space in retail stores across the continent—could have introduced a rival version and smothered the upstart innovator under a tidal wave of promotions and store incentives. However, Minnetonka had taken steps to protect itself in the short term by buying up the entire supply of plastic pumps needed for the liquid soap dispensers. That move held the competition at bay for a while. Eventually, in 1987, Minnetonka Corporation sold its liquid soap business to the Colgate-Palmolive Company, which has extended the brand with many product variations.

Creating and Dominating a New Market

Is your company struggling to match or outperform its rivals on cost, quality, or features? If so, that might be a loser's game. A better approach might be to invent an entirely new market where no competitor has yet ventured. And if your firm blankets key niches of that new market with valued products or services, it will achieve a level of dominance that makes it that much more difficult for rival organizations to enter the market you've created.

Consider Sony, which conceived of the personal portable stereo market and created the ideal product for tapping it: the Walkman. First introduced in 1979, the Walkman gave consumers great sound at a low price and in a small package that could be carried in a coat pocket or briefcase or attached to a jogger's waistband. No boom box could rival it. Millions of commuters, music buffs, joggers, and people stuck in office cubicles from nine to five o'clock bought them. To serve the many customer segments of this new market—and thereby achieve dominance—Sony introduced different versions of the Walkman, including a more rugged sports version, a version that included AM/FM radio, and so forth. Yet almost all of these versions were based on the same successful product platform. And though rivals soon entered the market with versions of their own, Sony maintained its dominance and continued to introduce new models.

What Sony accomplished decades ago has today been leap-frogged by the Apple iPod, a pocket-sized digital sound system capable of storing thousands of music files. The iPod is fast becoming a "must-have" item for music lovers of all persuasions. Between the product's market launch in October 2001 and late 2004, consumers snapped up 5.7 million units. "It's one of the most in-demand electronics gifts for the holidays," declared a spokesperson for Best Buy, a major electronics retailer, in December 2004.

Like Sony before it, Apple has begun offering iPod variants for different market segments, all based on the same basic product platform. By late 2004, these included iPod Photo, a device capable of storing thousand of photo *and* music files, and the special-edition iPod U2, which comes preloaded with every tune recorded by that popular rock group.

Breaking Free of the Old Formula

Success often becomes a barrier to market innovation because it enforces a formula that hamstrings innovation and change. For example, back in the late 1970s, the computing world was dominated by powerful mainframe computers, and IBM dominated that business. So, when personal computers began to appear, few people within IBM showed a lot of interest in the new market. The individuals with the most clout at IBM were mainframers who understood how to make big computers and distribute them through corporate leases. Desktop computing and the selling of small, inexpensive machines to individuals were alien ideas within "Big Blue." The only way the company could get its first PC into the market was through a *skunkworks* of engineers that it set up in Boca Raton, Florida—far from the company's center of power.

Sometimes the best way to break free of the old formula and address a new market is for your company to establish a new subsidiary or new operating unit—and then give it substantial autonomy to generate fresh ideas and bring them to market.

How to help your company create a new market? Shift your thinking from building and making products to something more basic: satisfying customers' most pressing needs in new ways. Ask, "What could we offer customers if we forgot everything we know about our industry's current rules and traditions? How might we combine the advantages of several industries' offerings to provide new value for buyers?"

Throwing away the rule book and starting with a clean slate isn't easy—especially if your company has had success using the old rules. Nevertheless, it's the only way to think your way to new, competition-free markets. See "Breaking Free of the Old Formula" for more on this.

Buying Your Way In

Sometimes the quickest and surest way for a company to enter a new market or expand substantially in an existing one is through a strategic acquisition, merger, or joint venture partnership. Consider this example.

A U.K.-based manufacturer saw expansion opportunities in several industrialized Asian countries. It sent people from London to Japan, South Korea, and China to open up sales, but all came back empty handed. Then it tried to set up sales and distribution agreements with local companies. Yet these initiatives, too, produced no results. Eventually, the firm's executives decided that the most fruitful approach would be to form a new company with an Asian partner. That partner knew the market, had an established distribution network, and understood the cultural requirements for business success in the target market. Under the terms of the joint venture, the U.K. company would provide two-thirds of the required capital and ship its goods to a warehouse owned by the partners in Hong Kong. The Asian partner would then distribute those goods, along with its own products, and be credited for every U.K. product sale. In turn, it would ship some of its Asian-made products to the U.K. partner, which would distribute them on a best-effort basis, taking a cut of all sales.

A joint venture arrangement is just one of many ways to break into a market. Each partner brings something the other needs to the venture, and each aims to extract a share of the benefits. As a means of entering an unfamiliar market, engaging in a joint venture is almost always faster than going it alone. These arrangements also provide valuable learning opportunities for both partners.

In addition to forging joint venture partnerships, your company can simply buy another company that makes a product or serves a market that fits your strategic plan. Fleet Bank, for instance, expanded its operation in the northeastern United States during the 1990s and the opening years of the new century through an aggressive strategy of acquisitions. It in turn was gobbled up by Charlotte, North Carolina–based Bank of America, which had the same goal. On a different front, eBay acquired the live auction house Butterfield & Butterfield as part of its strategy of rapidly consolidating as much of the auction "space" as possible. It then bought Kruse International, a leading vendor of collector-quality automobiles, for that same purpose.

Strategists in these cases face the classic build-versus-buy decision. And maybe your company does, too. Buying may be the fastest route to your company's goal, but success is by no means ensured. In fact, most research on acquisitions indicates a very high level of disappointment—if not outright failure. While researching his book *Good to Great*, author Jim Collins asked an associate to determine the role of large mergers and acquisitions in creating exceptional business results. As Collins described to readers of his column in *Time* magazine, "While you can buy your way to growth, you cannot buy your way to greatness." Worse, "Two big mediocrities joined together never make one great company."[6]

While mediocre companies made no headway toward greatness through mergers and acquisitions, good companies (in Collins's definition), have found that their best acquisitions met three litmus tests: (1) the acquisition accentuated what the company already did better than all other companies; (2) the acquisition enhanced a powerful preexisting economic engine; and (3) the acquisition "fit the driving passions of the company's people."[7]

Clearly, your company can choose from a number of different strategic moves to enter existing markets or create new ones and then dominate them. The total universe of these approaches is limited only by your and other executives' imagination. However, keep in mind that the range of strategic possibilities is limited by practical constraints. For example, as described earlier, Sony and Apple successfully created new markets and filled key niches with imaginative products—but few business organizations have the creative talent, customer knowledge, financial capital, and technical wherewithal to do the same. Likewise, a strategic move based on a joint venture assumes that the instigator has something special to offer the venture partner. Not every firm fits this criterion.

So consider the strategic moves described here, but think also about your company's ability to adopt any one of them. What are the constraints on your organization's ability to make a particular strategic move? What HR policies, programs, and projects might help relax those constraints?

For example, suppose your company is contemplating making a strategic acquisition or engaging in a merger. In this case, what steps can you take now to lay the groundwork for a successful blending of two previously separate workforces and organizational cultures? How might you help your company assess the value of a potential acquisition's human resources? If the acquisition or merger is going to entail some job losses, what policies can you put in place now to ensure smooth downsizing or restructuring and sustain morale in the new entity?

Or suppose your organization has decided to enter a new market through product differentiation. What skills and knowledge does your company's workforce need to make this strategic move work? How can you determine whether managers and employees have the required capabilities? What training, development, and recruiting policies would best ensure that your firm has the needed talent to successfully use product differentiation?

As with each type of high-level corporate strategy, each strategic move described in this chapter has different implications for your

HR strategy. You can best help your company select and implement strategic moves by analyzing those moves' human resource implications and putting the right processes and practices in place to ensure that your firm's workforce has the skills and knowledge to make strategic moves successful.

Summing Up

In this chapter, you learned the following:

- Gaining and securing a market beachhead—even in a low-end or low-margin segment—can put your company in a position to eventually expand into more attractive and profitable segments.

- When barriers to market entry are dauntingly high, your organization should avoid a costly direct assault on rivals. Instead, it should try to develop a new and superior process for doing what incumbents are now doing.

- Judo strategy, as conceptualized by David Yoffie and Mary Kwak, is based on three principles: movement, balance, and leverage. Each can help your company compete against larger, stronger, and more established businesses.

- To succeed, product differentiation must be valued by your firm's targeted customers. To provide a defensible position, product differentiation must also be protected by patents or proprietary methods that make its duplication by rivals difficult or impossible.

- Acquisitions and joint ventures offer still other strategic moves for entering or expanding within a market. However, these moves can result in disappointment or failure if your company doesn't carefully identify and work to meet criteria for success.

Leveraging Chapter Insights: Critical Questions

- Which strategic move(s) is your company currently making to
  compete in its industry—gaining a market beachhead? Entering a new market through process innovation or product differentiation? Applying movement, balance, and leverage (principles of judo strategy)? Creating and then dominating a new
  market? Using acquisitions, joint ventures, or mergers to "buy"
  its way into a new market?

- What evidence have you observed or gathered that suggests
  your company is applying the strategic move(s) you've identified in the preceding question? Have you and other executives
  discussed these moves during high-level strategy meetings? Has
  your company indicated its preferred strategic moves through
  internal documents and communications?

- How can you best support your company's strategic moves
  through your HR strategy? That is, what HR programs, policies, processes, and structures will most ensure that your firm
  has the human talent it needs to successfully carry out the
  strategic moves it has selected?

CHAPTER SIX

From Strategy to Implementation

Seeking Alignment

Key Topics Covered in This Chapter

- *The profound differences between strategy creation and strategy implementation*

- *Alignment for implementation*

- *The elements of successful implementation: people, incentives, supportive activities, organizational structure, culture, and leadership*

MANY HR AND OTHER executives enjoy strategizing. SWOT analysis involves plenty of hard work, but once that's done, you can play the part of the armchair general—developing bold initiatives to generate ever more value from your company's workforce, outflank rivals, corral customers, forge better relationships with suppliers, and conquer markets. Strategy, however, is meaningless if you don't pay equal or greater attention to the harder and less glamorous work of implementation. *Implementation* describes the concrete measures that translate strategic intent into actions that produce results. Implementation requires continuous managerial attention at all levels. Unlike strategy creation, which is entrepreneurial and market oriented, implementation is operations oriented. (See "Two Very Different Activities" for more on this.) Implementation excellence is absolutely essential for successful pursuit of any strategy. Applied carefully, it can provide enormous rewards. Consider the case of Herman Miller, Inc.

Michigan-based Herman Miller, Inc., is a leader in the North American office furniture industry and a vendor to major corporations. In the early 1990s, company executives recognized that small businesses represented a fast-growing and underserved market. Unlike deep-pocketed corporate clients, these small enterprises watched every penny and had short planning cycles; they were less interested in Miller's countless feature choices for workstations, desks, chairs, and fabrics than in office furnishings that were relatively inexpensive and that were delivered quickly and on time.[1]

Herman Miller's management responded in 1995 with a new strategy that aimed to provide these smaller customers with a limited range of basic, mass-customized office furniture that was highly affordable, built quickly, and delivered on time. This was a great strategy for addressing a growing market segment, but the company needed more than good intentions to make the strategy successful. Operations within Herman Miller had to change. The organization couldn't simply throw orders from its small-business customers into the same fulfillment machinery and expect to give them what it had promised. But what, precisely, did the firm need to do differently?

Company managers approached the implementation problem by first examining Herman Miller's current key processes—from order taking and order filling to delivering and installing finished products. Based on that analysis, they created a lean new operating unit, which they called SQA (for simple, quick, affordable). They also created a new supply chain for SQA capable of delivering on their promise to customers. All participants in that chain, including outside vendors, were linked through a state-of-the-art information system that ensured both speed and accuracy. Managers and supervisors

Two Very Different Activities

Strategy creation and strategy implementation differ in profound ways. Even the vocabulary used to describe them is very different.

Strategy creation	Strategy implementation
Analyzing and planning	Executing
Thinking	Doing
Initiating	Following through
Starting at the top	Moving from top to bottom
Being entrepreneurial	Being operational
Setting goals	Achieving goals

then got the word out about the new strategy, making sure that everyone—from the sales staff and assembly personnel to delivery and installation employees—understood the importance of being fast, error free, and on time.

These efforts produced exceptional results. Once executives had carried out the new strategic initiatives and fine-tuned them through practice, SQA had collapsed the normal order-to-delivery cycle from the six- to eight-week industry average to just two weeks or less. On-time error-free delivery, which Miller's traditional business had previously achieved only 70 percent of the time, stabilized above 99 percent. Still better, SQA's sales growth soared to 25 percent per year—three times the industry average.

We tell the Herman Miller story to make an important point: strategy in the absence of effective implementation is pointless. Some experts believe that strategy creation is actually less important than implementation. Strategy, these observers maintain, has become a commodity in many industries. That is, any rival can duplicate a company's strategy. In this sense, strategy is not a tool for differentiation. What matters more than strategy is the ability to execute exceptionally well. Stanford's Jeffrey Pfeffer put it this way: "It is more important to manage your business right than to be in the right business."[2] Success, in Pfeffer's view, comes from successfully implementing one's strategy, not just having one. But the ideal, of course, is both to formulate a great strategy *and* to carry it out through outstanding implementation!

Getting from strategy formulation to implementation requires executives to answer numerous questions about their organization's structure, personnel, and resources. As we've seen, any successful strategy must be backed by a coherent set of supporting practices and structures. Most people call this phenomenon *alignment*. In enterprises that have achieved alignment, organizational structures, support systems, processes, human skills, other resources, and incentives all support strategic goals.

Declaring a strategy won't get you far if you fail to create alignment between the strategy and the many large and small things that constitute how your company operates. Companies that fail to achieve

FIGURE 6-1

Alignment for implementation

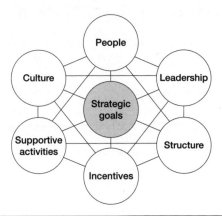

alignment don't get the strategic results they seek. In this chapter, we'll take a closer look at the elements of alignment that you and other implementers of strategy must consider—in particular, the supportive activities, organizational structure, culture, and leadership of the business, as represented in figure 6-1. Notice in that figure how each element is aligned with strategic goals and with each of the other elements, forming a solid platform for implementation and eventual success. In the next chapter, we'll look more specifically at ways to align your HR strategy to your organization's business strategy.

Starting with the Right People

Every manager and every employee in a company—from the executive suite to the loading dock—must participate in implementation if the organization's strategy is to succeed. Senior management has a responsibility to communicate the company's strategic intent to employees, and middle and lower-level managers must reiterate that intent and translate it into the way their subordinates work. Management and the company's HR professionals must also ensure that the company has:

- People with the right skills to make the strategy successful—this is accomplished through hiring and training

- People with attitudes that support the strategy

- The resources that managers and employees need to do their jobs well

Companies don't always get the people side of implementation right. Consultant and author Dwight Gertz has described one company that operated a chain of fresh-baked-cookie shops in shopping malls and other high-traffic areas across the United States. Years of experience had helped management learn which cookies to bake, when, and in what quantities. Executives knew that if store managers simply followed their published operating procedures, sales and profits would follow—they always had.

Unfortunately, the cookie company's recruitment advertising campaign for store manager candidates focused on the theme of "Be your own boss." Not surprisingly, the ads attracted entrepreneurial people who wanted to run things their own way. That would be just fine in some situations, but not this one. The newly hired managers didn't follow the company's success formula, and, not surprisingly, profitability plummeted wherever the entrepreneurial recruits ran things. They made the wrong cookies, or they made too few or too many at different times of the day or week.[3]

In the case Gertz described, the company had a sound strategy and a proven set of operating procedures. But its personnel selection process was out of alignment; the organization was hiring people who were temperamentally indisposed to follow those established procedures. The mind-set of key employees was thus not aligned with the company's formula for making money; instead, that mind-set was neutralizing the formula's power.

Essential ingredients of implementation include the right recruiting system and a rewards system that aligns employees' interests with the success of the strategy. That is nothing more than common sense. To accomplish this, every unit and every employee should have measurable performance goals with clearly stated rewards for goal achievement. And the rewards should be large enough to elicit the desired level of effort.

Where does your company stand on the people part of strategy? Do its rewards programs and human resource practices measurably support the strategy? Do hiring and training aim to get the right people with the right skills into positions where they can make a difference? These are critical questions for HR professionals to consider. The next chapter provides guidance on how to align your HR strategy behind your company's high-level strategy, and how to structure your HR department so you can successfully carry out the HR strategy you've defined.

Defining Supportive Activities

Misalignment of human resource activities is a common, and significant, impediment to effective strategy implementation. But there are others, including activities that few of us would think essential to the success of a particular strategy. Corporate-level strategy, according to Harvard professors David Collis and Cynthia Montgomery, "is a system of interdependent parts. Its success depends not only on the quality of the individual elements but also on how the elements reinforce each other."[4]

Management guru Michael Porter has used the example of Southwest Airlines to illustrate how companies stand a better chance of successfully pursuing their strategy when many seemingly unrelated activities reinforce each other and the overall strategy: "Southwest's . . . competitive advantage comes from the way its activities fit and reinforce one another," Porter wrote.[5] For example, the company's strategy entails competing on the basis of low-cost, frequent service. As figure 6-2 illustrates, many primary activities make that strategy feasible, and these are supported by other activities. Very low ticket prices, for instance, is a primary activity of the strategy; it is supported by high aircraft utilization, the limited use of travel agents, a standardized fleet of aircraft, highly productive ground crews, and

FIGURE 6-2

Southwest Airlines' activity system

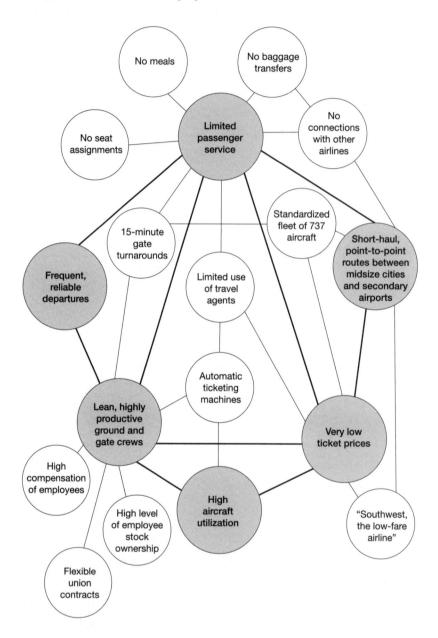

Source: Michael E. Porter, What I s Strategy?" *Harvard Business Review*, November–December 1996, 73.
Reproduced with permission.

so forth. In the absence of any one of these linking activities, Southwest's low-cost strategy would be jeopardized. But together, they make it work. Traditional rivals of Southwest have periodically tried to emulate its strategy by offering low fares and frequent departures, but because they lack supporting activities, all have failed. Per Porter, "Southwest's activities complement one another in ways that create real economic value . . . That is the way strategic fit creates competitive advantage and superior profitability."[6]

Take a minute to review your company's strategy. Ask yourself, "How well is it supported by the organization's other key activities?" For example, if rapid and accurate order fulfillment is a key element of the strategy—as in the Herman Miller case earlier—your company would want to coordinate sales, order processing, manufacturing, and delivery activities, and purge them of errors and wasted time. Do hiring, training, logistics, pricing, and other activities create an interlocking support system for strategy? If they do not, what could be done to link strategy and these supportive activities more effectively?

Crafting the Right Organizational Structure

Successful military leaders have always organized their forces in terms of their battlefield strategies. In the first days of World War II, for example, German army commanders opted for a strategy of blitzkrieg—highly mobile, or "lightning" warfare. This strategy aimed to counter the static trench-warfare strategy that Germany's Belgian and French rivals had carried over from World War I. Speed, surprise, air support, and the concentrated power of fast-moving armored units served as the key elements of the new German strategy. Instead of slogging it out from fixed positions in a long battle of attrition— as both sides had done during World War I—the Germans aimed to pierce or outflank fixed defenses, causing havoc and collapse in the enemy's rear. In some cases, the strategic plan also called for paratroopers to be dropped behind or on enemy flanks to produce a similar result.

This new battlefield strategy demanded a new organization. Instead of the traditional model of deploying a small armored unit in support of the much larger infantry, the Germans reversed these roles. Armor formed the tip of the strategic spear; infantry, artillery, and supply units were organized in support of that tip. Each of those support units was mechanized to keep pace with the fast-moving armor, and all were linked through field communications.

The blitzkrieg strategy contributed substantially to Germany's victories early in World War II. U.S general George Patton was among the first on the Allied side to appreciate its power. Indeed, he reorganized his own forces to meet and defeat mobile German armies in North Africa, Sicily, and France.

As much as businesspeople like to see military analogies in what they are doing, business is not warfare. Nevertheless, the military example of reorganizing people and material in support of a new strategy is instructive and useful. Our earlier story about Herman Miller makes it clear that that company would not have successfully carried out its strategy of fast, dependable delivery of mass-customized office work-stations and furniture without a reorganization of its human, supplier, and manufacturing assets. Like every other enterprise that pursues agility and speed, Miller had to become a lean, nonhierarchical orga-nization where people could make production decisions swiftly and monitor manufacturing processes more effectively.

Take a minute or so now to think about your company's organiza-tion. Are its people, resources, and units aligned with the high-level competitive strategy? How about the HR function? You and other executives have defined goals for the HR function based on the over-arching strategy. Is your unit optimally organized to achieve those goals? If not, what organizational changes might you make? For exam-ple, would it be better to centralize some or all HR activities in your organization? Decentralize HR to create separate human resource cen-ters for each business unit in the company? Outsource some HR activ-ities? Reorganize the HR function into process-specific teams (such as benefits administration, compensation, and so forth)? What organizational structure would best enable the HR function to support the corporate strategy?

Assessing Culture and Leadership

Culture and leadership are the last elements of strategy implementation you need to consider. Both must support the high-level strategy and the day-to-day work required to implement it.

The business literature often refers to company culture. For instance, we have allusions to 3M's culture of innovation and its 15 Percent Rule, which allows R&D personnel to spend 15 percent of their time pursuing whatever ideas appeal to them, as long as those ideas have some commercial potential. We also hear of Wal-Mart's culture of dedication to satisfying customers and driving down costs. And then there's eBay's more playful, collegial, and "can do" culture.

Culture refers to a company's values, traditions, and operating style. Culture is one of those vague qualities that are difficult to measure or describe with precision, but it nevertheless exists and sets a tone for managerial and employee behavior. In a sense, it describes how people view their workplace and how things are done. One company may be highly engineering oriented, pride itself on its tradition of technical innovation and problem solving, and operate with a command-and-control style. Another company's culture, in contrast, may value service quality above all else, with the company operating in a collegial, nonhierarchical manner.

One way to understand a company's culture is to ask, Who are your company's heroes, and what stories do people tell about them? These heroes might be supersalespeople, or master organizers, such as General Motors' Alfred Sloan. St. Paul, Minnesota–based 3M counts Dick Drew and William McKnight among its heroes. Even though these individuals passed from the scene many decades ago, current employees know who they were, recognize their contributions, and tell their stories even today.

Dick Drew, who developed masking and cellophane adhesive tapes in the 1920s and 1930s, was an accomplished inventor—a man who could quickly diagnose a customer's problem and craft a profitable technical solution. His many successful inventions made him a legend in the company. William McKnight spent his entire career with the company, eventually rising from assistant bookkeeper to president, and then chairman (1949–1966). McKnight's great contribution to 3M lore was his business philosophy, whose principles continue to guide the company. He described that philosophy as follows:

> *As our business grows, it becomes increasingly necessary to delegate responsibility and to encourage men and women to exercise their initiative. This requires considerable tolerance. Those men and women, to whom we delegate authority and responsibility, if they are good people, are going to want to do their jobs in their own way.*
>
> *Mistakes will be made. But if a person is essentially right, the mistakes he or she makes are not as serious in the long run as the mistakes management will make if it undertakes to tell those in authority exactly how they must do their jobs.*
>
> *Management that is destructively critical when mistakes are made kills initiative. And it's essential that we have many people with initiative if we are to continue to grow.*[7]

A company's culture may be strong or weak. Strong cultures are difficult to change without great effort, time, and substantial disruption. Thus, companies with strong cultures are wise to adopt strategies consistent with their cultures. Doing otherwise creates implementation problems. For example, it is advisable for 3M, Hewlett-Packard, Nokia, and Siemens to stick to strategies consistent with their cultures of technical innovation; those cultures will naturally support implementation. Companies that find themselves in competitively dead-end positions, however, may have to adopt strategies that are at odds with their existing cultures. The traditional air carriers (United, British Airways, Delta, and so forth) are prime examples of companies that must change their strategies or go under. Yet the strategic options before them will require a difficult set of cultural changes. For some, the "us versus them" tensions between management and labor will have to give way to a more collaborative culture. In these cases, the organizations will have to reinvent their culture and strategy simultaneously—a truly difficult proposition.

Changing company culture to better align it with a new strategy is the responsibility of the CEO and the senior management team. It is a top-down job, and HR professionals can play an important role in the process. How? Help your CEO and the senior management team identify the company's current culture and evaluate cultural alternatives. Provide guidance on how your company can transition from the current to the desired culture. Here are a few ideas for approaching the task:

- **Identify aspects of culture that must change in support of strategy implementation.** Examples may include product quality, customer focus, command-and-control management, and so on. Concentrate on these and leave less-critical aspects of culture alone. You can only do so much.

- **Model the behaviors and values you'd like to see employees adopt.** For example, suppose you've determined that people throughout your company must be willing to take more risks in order to create the entrepreneurial culture your company needs to carry out its strategy. In this case, you'd want to demonstrate that entrepreneurial quality yourself by taking risks in your own role—for instance, by proposing bold new HR initiatives that your company has not considered in the past. If your company's strategy hinges on lowering cost, you can model the right behaviors and values by cutting your own travel and entertainment expenses before you ask others to do the same. Remember, people are watching you.

- **Engage employees in "town meeting" forums to build consensus and commitment to change.** The personal connection between leaders and rank-and-file employees is an essential ingredient in reshaping an organization's culture. Why? It builds trust, which in turn makes it easier for employees to embrace change.

- **Sponsor celebratory events when change milestones are met.** Celebrating the "small wins" that your company's employees have achieved during a change initiative further reinforces cultural change. Apply this practice in your own HR department, and encourage managers throughout your firm to do the same.

- **Set high performance standards.** Help managers throughout your firm establish challenging but realistic expectations of their employees' performance. Faced with ambitious expectations, most people achieve more.

- **Reward people for the results you seek.** When people know that they'll receive praise, recognition, and financial and nonfinancial incentives for achieving clearly defined goals, they're more likely to strive to meet and even exceed those goals.

How well aligned is your company with its chosen strategy? Do you have the right people and reward systems in place? Is the organization—and its many units and functions—structured in a way that supports the strategy? Do other key activities, such as recruit-

---

The Seven S Framework

Over the years, many experts have proposed models for successful strategy implementation. One of the first—and best—of these is "the Seven S Framework," which first appeared in *The Art of Japanese Management*, authored by Richard Pascale and Anthony Athos and published in 1981. The model was adopted by McKinsey & Company, a global strategy consulting organization; many now refer to it as the McKinsey Seven S Framework. The *S*s in this framework are Strategy, Structure, Systems, Style, Staff, Skills, and Superordinate goals. If you'd like to learn more about this framework for strategy implementation, refer to Richard Pascale's *Managing on the Edge*. (See "For Further Reading" at the end of this book for the bibliographic details.)

ment, training, and other processes, support the strategy? Does the organization's culture fit with the business strategy? Assessment tool 6-1 provides a checklist you can use to review the alignment concepts explained in this chapter and to answer these questions.

Assessment Tool 6-1
Alignment Checklist

People

☐ Our people have the necessary skills to make the strategy work

☐ They support the strategy

☐ Their attitudes are aligned with the strategy

☐ They have the resources they need to be successful

Incentives

☐ Our rewards system is aligned with the strategy

☐ Everyone has performance goals aligned with the strategy

Structure

☐ Units are optimally organized to support the strategy

Supportive Activities

☐ The many things we do around here—pricing, the way we handle customers, fulfill orders, etc.—support the strategy

Culture

☐ Our culture and strategy are well matched

For every "no" response, specify the problem and what needs to be done to correct it.

Summing Up

In this chapter, you learned the following:

- Implementation describes the concrete measures that translate strategic intent into actions that produce results. It requires continuous managerial attention at all levels.

- Successful strategy is aligned with a coherent and reinforcing set of supporting practices and structures.

- Alignment is a condition in which organizational structures, support systems, processes, human skills, resources, and incentives support strategic goals.

- To make its strategy work, your company must have people with the right skills, resources, and attitudes.

- Activities such as recruiting, development, pricing, distribution, order fulfillment, and the like must all support the corporate strategy.

- The ways in which the organization and its units and functions are structured can strongly support—or hamper—strategy implementation.

- The organization's culture should be appropriate for the strategy—and vice versa.

Leveraging Chapter Insights: Critical Questions

- What is your company's high-level competitive strategy? Do managers and employees throughout the organization possess the skills, behaviors, knowledge, and attitudes required to play their part in carrying out the strategy? If not, what steps might you take to address the situation?

- Which supportive activities throughout your organization most strongly reinforce implementation of the corporate strategy?

Which seem misaligned? What actions might you take to strengthen these activities' alignment with the high-level strategy?

- How firmly does the overall structure of your organization, as well as the structure of its units and functions, support implementation of the corporate strategy? What structural changes might better serve that implementation? Why?

- In your view, is your organization's overall culture and leadership approach well suited to carrying out the competitive strategy? Why or why not? What cultural and leadership changes might better position your company to carry out its strategy?

CHAPTER SEVEN

Aligning Your HR Strategy

Key Practices

Key Topics Covered in This Chapter

- *Understanding the HR strategy process*

- *Important considerations in selecting an HR strategy*

- *Aligning your HR strategy to corporate strategy*

- *Structuring your HR function to support the corporate strategy*

- *Making a compelling case for your HR strategy and structure*

I N C H A P T E R 6, you learned how important it is for a company's workforce, daily activities and processes, structure, culture, and leadership all to align with the organization's high-level strategy. Only through this alignment can the company successfully implement its strategy. But effective implementation also hinges on the alignment of each *part* of the company with the competitive strategy. In other words, after a company has formulated its high-level strategy, each division, unit, department, and function must define its own plan for supporting that strategy.

For example, if your company has selected a product differentiation strategy in order to compete against new rivals, every part of the organization must think through how it can best help implement that strategy. The marketing department's strategy will probably include developing new types of advertising campaigns that extol the virtues of the company's unique offerings. The sales group's strategy will likely call for reps to visit existing and potential new customers to educate them on the special features and benefits of the organization's products. The R&D department's strategy will almost certainly entail researching the technologies, materials, and processes required to differentiate the company's products. And the IT team's strategy will probably involve identifying ways to better analyze customer preferences and buying patterns.

Like these and other departments and functions in the organization, the HR group will need to develop a strategic plan as well. For example, the HR department's strategy will have to contain ideas for ensuring that the company's workforce has the right skills to support product differentiation, that people are being rewarded for the right behaviors and attitudes, that the HR function is structured in ways that support the corporate strategy, and that HR programs aimed at recruiting, retention, compensation, and training and development all reinforce the company's overarching strategy. Moreover, after divisions, units, and departments have formulated their supporting strategy, their leaders further strengthen alignment by translating unit strategy into individual goals for their employees.

In this chapter, we'll explain how to align your HR strategy behind the corporate strategy—including understanding the alignment process, selecting the right structure for your HR function, and making a compelling business case for the HR strategy and structure you're proposing.

Understanding the HR Strategy Alignment Process

A sound HR strategy, aligned strongly behind the corporate strategy, plays a crucial role in delivering real competitive advantage to your company. But how do you develop an aligned HR strategy? Some experts propose the following overall process—which includes the SWOT analysis described in earlier chapters:[1]

1. **Diagnose HR's strengths and weaknesses.** Ask, "Given the high-level strategy our company has defined, what are the most critical areas where HR can enable implementation of that strategy?" For example, does your HR group excel at attracting talent away from rival companies? Are you unusually good at leading major change initiatives? Have you cultivated particularly strong relationships with executives and managers throughout your organization? Also identify the most critical areas where HR will be a constraint on strategy implementation.

2. **Assess external and internal developments' implications for HR's ability to support the corporate strategy.** Consider outside changes that may influence the HR function's ability to help implement your company's high-level strategy. For

instance, assess changes in HR technologies, regulatory developments affecting working practices, the intensity of industry competition for talented workers, changes in recruiting and training methods, and so forth. Also evaluate internal trends and developments that can affect HR's ability to carry out its part of the corporate strategy. These might include cultural problems such as resistance to change, difficulties with transferring knowledge and best practices across the organization, changes in retention rates owing to employees' heightened demand for specific career opportunities, higher turnover as your company's workforce ages, and so forth.

3. **Paint a picture of the kind of organization your company needs to be in order to carry out its strategy.** Ask, "What organizational structures, employee skills, behaviors, and attitudes does our company require in order to implement the competitive strategy we've defined?" For example, do you need decentralized decision making? An entrepreneurial culture in which people are willing to take risks? An emphasis on continuous performance improvement? A tolerance for frequent large-scale change? Top-notch skill in leveraging new technologies or analyzing customer needs?

4. **Assess the gap between your ideal future organization and your current organization.** Compare the required structures, skills, behaviors, and attitudes you identified in step 3 to your organization's current position. Identify gaps between what you need and what you have.

5. **Define the human resource changes needed to close the gaps.** What HR programs, projects, and policies would help create the kind of organization your company needs to be in order to successfully implement its strategy? Would these include new performance management systems? Outsourcing of certain activities? Different training programs? New recruiting methods? Brainstorm everything that comes to mind.

Developing Your HR Strategy: Crucial Considerations

By using the overall process just described, you formulate a possible HR strategy. But defining a strategy doesn't necessarily mean that the selected strategy will succeed. To be successful, your HR strategy must meet two criteria: (1) it can be implemented in your organization; and (2) it strongly supports the corporate strategy.

To determine whether your HR strategy meets the first criterion—that is, it's able to be implemented—you need to weigh several considerations. For example, think about the resources available to your HR department—including funding, time, personnel, space, and technology: Are these resources adequate for carrying out the HR strategy you're proposing? Also consider the level of talent in the department: Does your HR staff possess the knowledge, skills, and attitudes needed to implement the HR strategy you've formulated?

Another consideration involves the company's values. Specifically, does the HR strategy you're proposing fit with the organization's picture of how it should operate, how people should be treated, and other manifestations of values? For instance, if your HR strategy calls for outsourcing, offshoring, or downsizing, consider your company's stand on these practices. In an organization that has avoided offshoring, or that has declared an unwillingness to downsize except as an absolute last resort, an HR strategy that hinges on these practices may not be well received.

Of course, it's also important to take into account financial and legal considerations when formulating an HR strategy. For example, suppose the HR strategy you've sketched out contains a program that somewhat supports the corporate strategy but is extremely expensive—such as a new HR information system designed to improve the efficiency of recruiting and hiring processes. If the program isn't legally required, you might conclude that it's best to drop it from your strategy.

Other considerations include the impact of your strategy on other business units' strategies. One statement you can make with

unwavering certainty about a company's HR function is that its
strategy affects every other unit or department in the organization—
because every part of the organization consists of people. By contrast, some departments' or functions' strategies don't necessarily
exert a major impact on every other part of the organization. To
illustrate, the logistics department's decision to centralize processing
of returned products in order to support a corporate strategy em-
phasizing cost cutting and efficiency may have little or no implica-
tion for the marketing department.

So, owing to HR's intricate connections with every other part
of the organization, it's important to take other units' strategies into
account while developing your HR strategy. For example, if several
departments' strategies hinge on hiring huge numbers of people
with specific skills in order to support the corporate strategy, this
requirement will need to figure in your own strategy.

To evaluate the second criterion for a successful HR strategy—it
strongly supports the corporate strategy—ask yourself these questions:[2]

- **"Does my proposed HR strategy directly affect the company's strategic objectives in a positive way?"** Examine each
  component of your HR strategy, and ensure that a cause-and-
  effect link exists between that component and one or more
  components of the corporate strategy. For example, suppose
  your company has defined a strategy that hinges on improving
  customer satisfaction, among other things. And you've formulated an HR strategy that contains a component entailing
  enhancing employee retention. You know from research and
  your years in the HR industry that as employees gain experience on the job, they develop more knowledge and skills for
  serving customers better—which in turn leads to greater customer satisfaction. Thus you can clearly demonstrate that this
  part of your HR strategy strongly supports a key component of
  the corporate strategy.

- **"Do our HR department's actions support the proposed HR
  strategy?"** You may have developed an entirely appropriate

HR strategy, in which every component clearly supports some component of the corporate strategy. But suppose your HR department's everyday actions—the ways in which HR practitioners typically are spending their time and allocating resources—differ from those required to carry out your HR strategy. In this case, your strategy stands little chance of supporting the corporate strategy. Take the example of enhancing employee retention, in the preceding bullet point. If improving retention is a key component in your HR strategy, but your department typically invests its time and money in programs and activities that have little to do with retention, your HR strategy will not align behind the corporate strategy.

- **"Have I assigned a weight to each component of my HR strategy?"** In any corporate or departmental strategy, not all strategic objectives carry the same weight, or importance. This is also true of the components of your HR strategy. To clarify the relative importance of each component of your strategy, assign a weight to each. This process can help you determine how to allocate resources to carrying out each strategy component. For example, if you've assigned "improving HR customer satisfaction" a weight of 50 percent and "reducing error rates" 5 percent, this suggests that you should spend half of your budget and time on activities related to improving satisfaction, and only 5 percent of your budget and time fixing errors. If your resource allocations can't be made in ways that reflect the weight of each component in your strategy, then your strategy will not support the corporate strategy.

Asking these questions can help you assess the strength of your HR strategy's alignment with corporate strategic objectives. Assessment tool 7-1 provides a checklist with additional criteria that can help you discern whether your HR strategy is aligned. And "HR in Action: Aligning Intuit's HR Strategy" shows how one HR department aligned its strategy.

Assessment Tool 7-1
Signs of Alignment

For each statement below, check whether you agree or disagree. Then interpret your score using the instructions at the end of the assessment tool.

1. Some of the objectives in my HR department's strategy use the same language as the objectives in the corporate strategy.

   Agree   Disagree

2. I can show a direct cause-and-effect connection between each element of my HR department's strategy and one or more objectives in the corporate strategy.

   Agree   Disagree

3. A non-HR company officer or an outside expert has assessed my HR department's strategy and deemed it aligned with the corporate strategy

   Agree   Disagree

4. Other senior managers are willing to directly fund one or more of the programs proposed in my HR department's strategy.

   Agree   Disagree

5. HR budget expenditures reflect the different weights I've assigned to the different components of my HR department's strategy.

   Agree   Disagree

6. The proposed allocations of HR staff members' time reflect the different weights I've assigned to my HR department strategy's components.

   Agree   Disagree

7. My HR department's strategy will enable me to measure outcomes (such as "staff turnover," "leadership bench strength," or "revenue per employee") that are important to the corporate strategy.

Agree   Disagree

8. Other senior managers in the company have ranked HR as in the top 25 percent of all functions that contribute to corporate goals.

Agree   Disagree

9. HR specifically rewards the same activities that take place in support of each corporate strategic objective.

Agree   Disagree

10. HR accomplishments are listed in my company's annual report.

Agree   Disagree

Interpreting your score

The higher your number of "Agree" responses, the more firmly your HR strategy is aligned with the corporate strategy.

SOURCE: John Sullivan, *Rethinking Strategic HR: HR's Role in Building a Performance Culture* (Chicago: CCH, 2004), 334–335.

HR in Action: Aligning Intuit's HR Strategy

Software company Intuit, based in Mountain View, California, had defined a corporate strategy in the early 1990s that hinged on deepening its seven thousand employees' commitment to and happiness with the organization. Intuit's human resource department began formulating an HR strategy to support the company's competitive strategy. For Intuit's HR group, the biggest challenge lay in finding a way to help managers measure their employees' engagement with the company, identify problem areas, and develop action plans for producing higher employee engagement. Decreasing engagement, the HR team theorized, worsened turnover—which only increased costs for the company and deprived it of the talented employees it needed to succeed in the highly competitive software industry.

As a key component in its strategy, the HR group developed a "voice of the employee" surveying process based on the company's "employee value proposition"—which is a contract Intuit has with its employees. That proposition includes commitments from the company to its employees such as investing in them to help them grow and letting them know how they're performing. The ultimate goal of the survey? Using the resulting data to show managers patterns of practices that produce stronger employee engagement. All this required correlating certain items in the survey with turnover, and demonstrating to managers that focusing on those items had been statistically shown to reduce turnover.

Intuit's HR strategy also included use of technology. For example, employees had access to all survey data through a computer-based system in the company. This system contained a Web site that posted the hundreds of action plans developed by managers to address issues raised in the survey process. Managers who hadn't logged on or updated their action plans in a while received automatic reminders to do so. The site was searchable by manager name, providing strong incentive for managers to be accountable for their plans. The system also helped managers get ideas by viewing their colleagues' action plans. Another result of this "public forum" use of technology was an increase in employees' trust in their managers and in the company.

The HR strategy also emphasized face-to-face collaboration between managers and their employees to identify what sparked negative responses to survey statements such as "My business unit makes good decisions" and to brainstorm possible solutions to the problem. These discussions, HR leaders maintained, need to focus on issues that fall within a manager's control.

Another key component of Intuit's HR strategy was a modification of its compensation system. Whereas the company used to use a "peanut butter" system—spreading pay across all employees—it began moving to a pay-for-performance approach. Leaders were assessed based on what they had done to improve employee engagement. That assessment, in turn, contributed to an overall performance rating that affected their pay and bonus.

Finally, the HR strategy was backed by a policy of letting managers go who did not take the survey process and follow-up actions seriously, or who failed to turn around poor survey results relatively quickly.

Because Intuit's HR leaders had developed a strategy that aligned clearly behind the corporate strategy, they had the active support of the company's CEO. Indeed, rather than viewing the survey process as an HR-specific function, the CEO saw it as "how you run your business."

SOURCE: Charlotte Garvey, "Connecting the Organizational Pulse to the Bottom Line," *HR Magazine*, June 2004.

Structuring Your HR Function Strategically

There are numerous ways to structure, or organize, your company's human resource function in order to support the organization's overall competitive strategy and enable implementation of the HR strategy you've selected. Indeed, along with HR programs, policies, and projects, your HR structure constitutes a key element in your HR strategy. The many possible HR structural forms available differ in several ways—including degree of centralization, use of technology, strategic impact, emphasis on certain activities over others, and implementation difficulty. Moreover, each structure has its advantages and disadvantages. In selecting a structure for your HR function, keep in mind that there's no one "best" structure. Rather, the most effective HR professionals choose a structure that most fits their company's needs. Indeed, some companies use a blend of several structures to arrive at an approach that optimally suits their type of business and strategic priorities.

Experts have identified the following ten HR structures as particularly familiar to most companies:[3]

1. **Personnel.** HR serves as an employee advocate, specializing in transactions such as payroll and benefits. The department is centralized and organized by functional units. HR makes little use of technology other than to handle centralized administrative activities and has minimal outreach, allowing managers extensive unfettered discretion. This structure produces transactional excellence but has minimal strategic impact on profitability and employee productivity.

2. **Generalist.** HR decentralizes so as to provide different services that fit the unique needs of each business unit. HR generalists located in each major business unit deliver most services and report directly to the unit's general manager, while centralized HR serves as support staff for the generalists. Local managers know and trust the generalists, who handle most transactions locally rather than through extensive use of technology. This structure has medium strategic impact, because solutions to strategic problems are transferred slowly across business units, and generalists operate independently of one another.

3. **Business partner.** HR's role is organized into four areas: service delivery, employee commitment, change management, and strategic actions. The strategic elements of HR are centralized, and a moderate number of generalists handle nonstrategic activities. HR has an extensive senior management staff and relies significantly on external consultants. The emphasis is on strategic relationship building among executives throughout the organization, including HR. Use of technology is medium, and strategic impact is medium.

4. **Call center.** Basic HR questions are answered through a centralized HR unit that's available continually during working hours. Call centers report directly to HR operations and oper-

ate independently of HR generalists and other HR functional departments. They have little direct impact on how the rest of HR is organized. Use of technology emphasizes telephone and knowledge-based systems, and the structure has minimal strategic impact.

5. **Outsourcing.** HR managers identify HR functions that provide the company with no competitive advantage. These functions are handled by vendors with proven superior capabilities. HR managers focus on the specific areas within HR that exert a strategic impact by solving the company's complex people problems. The HR organization is streamlined, though vendor management may become a major new responsibility. There is minimal use of technology, and strategic impact can be moderate to high.

6. **Centers of excellence.** The company establishes groups of internal consulting experts to solve the most difficult HR problems directly, then HR generalists use the knowledge gained from the experts to share solutions across units. Centers operate independently of other HR functional units and report to a senior HR manager or the vice president of HR. Use of technology is minimal, and strategic impact can be high if the centers maintain the same quality standards as external consulting firms.

7. **Self-service.** In this advanced variation of the call-center structure, HR answers and transactions are shifted to the company's intranet. Managers and employees have access to easy-to-use HR Web sites through which they can handle their own basic transactions and find answers to basic HR questions. Access to the site is global and around the clock. Use of technology is high, and strategic impact is minimal.

8. **Fact-based decision making.** HR strives for continual improvement in people management through extensive use of metrics. HR provides data on the metrics directly to line managers, who use the information to make people decisions.

The HR department may also engage in forecasting to anticipate problems, and establish R&D teams to develop new people management tools. Metrics and analytics managers report directly to the senior decision maker in every HR functional unit. Use of technology such as analytics software, reporting applications, and business intelligence applications is pervasive throughout the organization. Strategic impact is high because "guesswork" is removed from HR decisions, which are made closer to the "customer."

9. **e-HR.** Technology is the mainstay of every HR function and system. HR eliminates paper and operates cheaply, quickly, and globally. HR also uses technology to establish e-learning programs, engage in workforce planning, conduct analytics, assess job candidates online, track job applicants' status, and generate management reports. Most day-to-day HR decisions—including compensation, candidate assessment, retention, and employee relations—are made by line managers. An HRIT group manages the e-HR effort, with an eye toward eventually computerizing every process and HR function. Strategic impact is high because managers make more informed and accurate people decisions.

10. **Performance culture.** Every people-related system focuses on measuring, recognizing, and rewarding productivity and results. The notion of "performance" permeates the entire organizational culture and everyone's way of thinking. HR doesn't view itself as "owning" people programs and employee productivity; rather, managers and employees themselves own these things. The HR department resembles a consulting organization, providing advice and metrics rather than direct service. Use of technology is high (to provide managers with daily performance information), and strategic impact is high if HR can influence the entire workforce to accept accountability for productivity.

As you can see, each of the preceding structures has unique characteristics, including degree of strategic impact. How do you select the right HR structure for your company? Don't assume that the best structure is the one with the highest strategic impact. For example, in a "commodity business" (such as a company that makes only one type of metal fastener), investing heavily in the creation of a performance culture may be a mistake. Why? This HR structure is particularly complex, expensive, and difficult to implement, and continual improvement often has little relevance in commodity businesses. The most effective HR structures take into account not only the company's strategic priorities but also its type of business and the conditions in which it is operating. Table 7-1 provides guidelines for deciding which HR structure might be best for your company.

TABLE 7-1

Selecting an HR structure

To choose the most appropriate structure for your HR function, take into account your company's strategic priorities and type of business.

If your company's strategic priorities call for . . .	And your company is . . .	Then consider this HR structure
Reducing costs, complying with regulatory requirements, and perfecting basic transactions	A small, medium, or large company where a single person runs HR in a union environment; most "rules" are defined by the union contract	Personnel
Providing excellent hands-on, localized HR services delivered by generalists	A medium to large firm that is geographically dispersed	Generalist
Focusing more on strategy and less on transactions, and involving HR practitioners more heavily in formulating strategy	A medium or large organization that's suffering from an inability to compete adequately in its industry	Business partner
Freeing up HR generalists' time so they can play a more strategic role	A large corporation	Call center
Focusing more on core competencies and less on activities that service providers could do better	An especially small or large organization that has adequate available outsourcing support	Outsourcing
Providing internal "consulting quality" help to solve advanced HR problems	A large, global corporation that uses many external HR consultants	Centers of excellence

continued

TABLE 7-1 *continued*

Selecting an HR structure

If your company's strategic priorities call for . . .	And your company is . . .	Then consider this HR structure
Encouraging managers and employees to become more self-sufficient	A global business or an organization with a strong IT staff	Self-service
Making savvier use of metrics and analytic tools to continually improve the way work is done	A medium or large technology-driven organization with enterprise-wide software applications	Fact-based decision making
Reducing paperwork, accelerating HR processes, and shifting HR decisions to managers	A large, global organization	e-HR
Transforming the organization's culture so everyone is focused on performance and results	Operating in a highly competitive environment and wants to be "number one" in employee productivity	Performance culture

Source: John Sullivan, *Rethinking Strategic HR: HR's Role in Building a Performance Culture* (Chicago: CCH, 2004), 45–63.

Making the Case for Your HR Strategy

You've formulated a potential HR strategy that aligns with the corporate strategy, including an HR structure that meets your company's strategic priorities and business conditions. But that doesn't mean your ideas will receive widespread approval in your organization. As with any proposal, you need to make a compelling business case for the HR strategy and structure you've selected. You must demonstrate to other executives, as well as to the line managers whose cooperation you need to implement your ideas, that your plan aligns with your company's strategy. You also need to show that your plan will give the firm a significant competitive edge and that it will generate considerable economic value.

In other words, you need to call on your powers of influence and persuasion to "sell" your strategy ideas to the rest of the executive team. Experts suggest that as you think about how best to present your proposed HR strategy, you ensure that your presentation answers the following questions:[4]

- **Does your HR strategy meet the company's goals?** Lay out your company's key strategic objectives, showing precisely how each element in your HR strategy supports achievement of those objectives. Describe the estimated impact of your HR strategy in measurable terms. If possible, show how the HR strategy you're proposing will be difficult for rival companies to copy. Explain how the strategy is superior to alternative plans. And convey a sense of urgency: your company *needs* to put its corporate strategy into action now to remain competitive—and the HR strategy you've selected will enable the firm to implement its strategic plan as quickly and effectively as possible.

- **Does it fit with the organizational culture?** If your HR strategy involves decisions and plans that don't fit with the organization's culture, it has little hope of succeeding. If you're unsure of the fit, hire a consultant to conduct a quick cultural-fit assessment. Convince other executives that your strategy fits the culture, by using key buzzwords (such as *continual improvement*, *ownership and accountability*, and *competitive edge*) that reflect executives' major strategic concerns. If possible, cite historical precedents in which your company embraced and carried out a major strategic initiative.

- **Does it align with existing processes and systems?** Demonstrate that the components of your proposed HR strategy align (or at least don't conflict) with your company's existing major processes and systems. Without that alignment, you'll find it more difficult to sell your ideas or, if you do sell them, to carry them out.

- **Will it give your company a competitive advantage?** Provide a side-by-side comparison of how your HR strategy is superior to rival companies'. Point out the ways in which it is difficult for competitors to discern and adopt. List the best HR practices applied at leading rival companies, and show how you've benchmarked the components of your proposed strategy against those practices. Share your views of where competing organizations are headed strategically. If implementing your

HR strategy will take significant time, show that you've calculated rival companies' progress toward their strategic goals by
the time your plan is put into action. Describe what you've
done to counter that progress. Explain how you expect rival
companies to respond to your firm's strategic changes and how
your plan will counter those responses.

- **Will it succeed?** List the critical success factors (inside and
outside your company) for your HR strategy, as well as common implementation problems such strategies face. Show that
your company has the critical success factors covered and that
you have a solution for typical problems.

- **Will it generate measurable economic value?** Using the
language of dollars and numbers, estimate your HR strategy's
economic impact on the company. How will your strategy's
programs, policies, and projects enhance revenue, income, profit
margins, customer value, and shareholder value? When will the
company start seeing these improvements? How will you leverage existing resources (rather than asking for significant up-front
money) to jump-start creation of the economic value you're
envisioning? What return on investment (ROI) do you expect
your HR strategy to generate? (For example, if you expect a
particular HR program to return at least $1.15 for every $1.00
invested, you can boast an anticipated 15 percent ROI.)

- **Does your HR team have the credibility and talent required
to carry out the HR strategy?** Your fellow executives will
have more confidence in your HR strategy if they view you and
your team as trustworthy and competent, if they know that you
can attract any additional talent needed to implement the strategy, and if you clearly lay out the steps needed to put your strategic plan into action. Their confidence will grow further if you
show that you've undertaken a pilot project to test the feasibility
of your strategy, if you regularly provide milestones for assessing
the progress of the strategy implementation, and if you can show
how you'll respond if things go awry during implementation.

Clearly, winning buy-in for your HR strategy is no easy feat. But with careful preparation and attention to the many details you'll need to cover in your presentation, you can vastly sweeten your odds of succeeding. If you need more information on how to gain support for your strategy ideas, see *The Essentials of Power, Influence, and Persuasion* volume in this series.

Summing Up

In this chapter, you learned the following:

- The HR strategy alignment process comprises five steps: diagnosing HR's strengths and weaknesses, assessing external and internal developments' implications for HR's ability to support the company's strategy, envisioning the kind of organization your company must become in order to carry out its strategy, assessing gaps between this ideal future organization and the current organization, and defining the HR changes needed to close any gaps.

- Considerations to keep in mind while formulating an HR strategy include whether it's feasible, how well it expresses your company's core values, how expensive it is, how it will impact other units' strategies, and how strongly it supports your company's high-level strategy.

- How your HR department is structured, or organized, is a key part of your HR strategy. You read about ten possible HR structures: personnel, generalist, business partner, call center, outsourcing, centers of excellence, self-service, fact-based decision making, e-HR, and performance culture. Each structure has pluses and minuses and differs in terms of degree of decentralization, use of technology, strategic impact, and other dimensions. To select a structure, consider your company's strategic priorities, type of business, and conditions in which it's operating.

- To win other executives' and managers' support for your proposed HR strategy, you need to demonstrate that the strategy meets your company's goals, fits with the organizational culture, aligns with existing processes and systems, will give your company a distinct competitive advantage, stands a good chance of succeeding, will generate measurable economic value, and is backed by a sufficiently trustworthy, credible, and talented HR leader and team.

Leveraging Chapter Insights: Critical Questions

- Think about the competitive strategy you and other executives have defined for your company. In what ways can your HR department help carry out that strategy? In what ways might it constrain implementation of the corporate strategy? What external and internal business developments may influence your HR group's ability to help implement the high-level strategy? What HR changes are needed to close any gaps between the kind of organization your company needs to become to carry out its strategy, and the kind of organization it is currently?

- Given your responses to the preceding questions, what HR programs, policies, and projects would most help you formulate an HR strategy that aligns with the corporate strategy?

- Given your company's strategic priorities, as well as the type of business it's in and the kind of conditions under which it's operating, what might be the most appropriate structure for your HR department? Consider the ten possible structures described in this chapter. Does one of them in particular seem most appropriate? If so, why? Or would a blend of several be more effective?

- What information will you gather in order to make a compelling business case for the HR strategy you've developed?

How will you show that your strategy meets the company's goals, fits with the organizational culture, aligns with existing processes and systems, will give your company a competitive advantage, will succeed, and will generate economic value? How will you demonstrate that you and your team have the personal qualities and professional talent to carry out the HR strategy?

CHAPTER EIGHT

Action Plans

The Architecture of Implementation

Key Topics Covered in This Chapter

- *Agreeing on goals for your HR strategy*

- *Adopting performance measures*

- *Determining the who, what, and when of getting the work done*

- *Determining the level and type of resources needed to do the job*

- *Identifying all important interlocks between units and outside entities*

- *Making a financial estimate of your plan's impact*

ONCE YOU'VE DEFINED your HR department's strategy and won support for it from the rest of the executive team, how do you successfully carry it out? Effective implementation hinges on turning your strategic plans into action plans that get executed by your HR unit. To boost your chances of reaching the goals spelled out in your HR strategy, those action plans must lay out practical steps, measure progress over time, ensure that people have the resources they need to carry out the plans, and enable implementers to keep the plans on track.

Action plans are where strategic planning and implementation overlap. They are also where you and other executives can make vital and visible contributions to your organization's success. This chapter segments the action planning process into a number of key steps. Once we've explained each of those steps, we'll present an example of one HR leader's formal action plan. You can use that plan as a prototype for your own HR action planning.[1]

From Strategic Plan to Action Plans

An *action plan* is a document reflecting what must be done in order to achieve the objectives laid out in your HR department's strategy. Leaders of other units in your company also develop action plans to carry out their unit strategies. Your action plan begins with the specific contributions your unit can make to the company's strategy and the unit goals expressed in your HR strategy. It then identifies all the steps required to achieve them, as well as the measures by which you assess progress toward the goals. This is represented graphically in figure 8-1.

Here, each of a company's operating units has determined its unique contributions to the company's strategic goals. These contributions, in turn, become unit goals, which each unit aims to achieve through a set of measurable action steps. Consider this example.

Pedalpower Bicycle Company (PBC) has developed a new strategy for expanding its sales in the fragmented North American bicycle market. It will target the profitable upper tier of street bikes. PBC bikes will be designed to appeal to quality-conscious adult cyclists who regularly pedal to work or use their bikes for errands around town, or simply for recreation. Consequently, PBC bikes will be rugged and come equipped with wide, puncture-proof tires, chain guards (to protect trousers from oily chains), and detachable fenders

FIGURE 8-1

Unit goals, metrics, and action plans

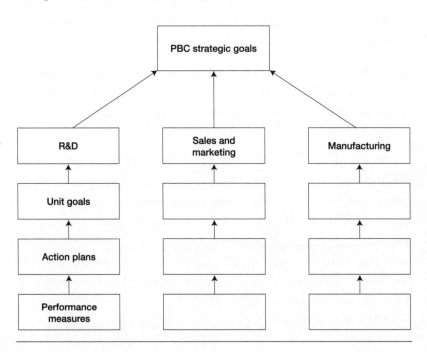

for rainy-day riding. Racers, trail bikers, and kids are not in the target market. The strategy calls for unit sales of four hundred thousand by the end of the third year.

To further differentiate itself, the new PBC products will feature a modular design, making it possible for consumers and dealers to customize their orders and have them delivered quickly. This customization strategy has been successfully implemented in Japan and South Korea by an Asian manufacturer, but has not been applied to PBC's target market in North America.

Though every unit of PBC will have to contribute to the strategy through specific strategic plans, three units in particular will be most affected: product development, sales and marketing, and manufacturing. To support the company's new strategy, the product development unit set four goals for itself:

1. Work with marketing to determine customer requirements and pricing constraints by January 2, 2006.

2. Based on goal 1 results, design three prototypes for market testing by April 1, 2006.

3. Based on goal 2 results, create manufacturing specifications for three customizable models by August 1, 2006.

4. Concurrently work with manufacturing on design for manufacturability. Deliverable: a list of no more than sixty components capable of producing several thousand uniquely configured bikes. Deadline: October 1, 2006.

Notice in this example how PBC's product development unit translated the company's high-level strategic goal into specific, measurable unit-level goals. The product development manager and her team will then develop detailed action plans supporting each goal. The sales and marketing, manufacturing, and other operating units—including HR, IT, finance, and so forth—will do something very similar. The collective goals of all these units will then be rolled up into a complete implementation plan.

Next we examine each step in the action planning process.

Set Unit Goals

A company's strategy is the natural starting point for both corporate- and unit-level goals. The strategy articulates how the organization as a whole will direct its efforts over a multiyear period. Individual units take companywide strategic goals and deconstruct them into unit goals with clear targets and performance measures. For example, a direct-mail sporting goods company might have a strategic goal of gaining a 15 percent market share within three years. The company's individual units would then define their own goals supporting the high-level objective. For instance, the HR department might set out to provide training programs that help the sales force sell to new customer segments. Meanwhile, the customer service group might decide to raise its customer satisfaction index from 73 to 90 over the next two years, and to raise it to 95 percent by the end of the third year. And the marketing department might come up with a unit goal of increasing customer loyalty by 20 percent during the same three-year period, while the national sales force would focus on increasing average account revenue by 15 percent as a unit goal. The action plans of several of these different units might have a common goal of developing a new customer database by the end of year 1.

In effect, the company's high-level strategic goals cascade down to the units, which devise goals for their parts of the corporate strategy, as we saw in figure 8-1. Unit managers respond to this cascading process by negotiating performance goals with each of their teams or direct reports, as described in figure 8-2.

In most companies, senior executives examine unit goals to ensure that they:

- Support and are compatible with the company's strategy

- Add up to a complete, collective plan for achieving the company's strategic goals

While reviewing proposed unit goals, executives keep an eye out for goals that conflict with those of the company or with those of other units. They also ensure that all the strategic initiatives required

FIGURE 8-2

Linking corporate, unit, and team/individual goals

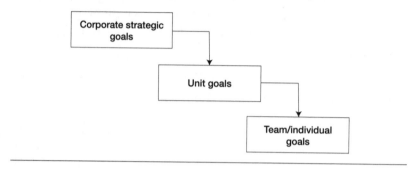

to achieve the company's high-level goals show up somewhere within the collective unit plans.

Agree on Performance Measures

Once you settle on an HR strategy and develop a plan to reach the goals spelled out in that strategy, you must determine how you'll measure the HR group's performance in terms of those goals. Your performance metrics should be relevant and clear—for example, "Reduce workforce turnover by 10 percent annually for the next three years." Performance metrics should also reflect changes you can actually measure. For example, one company's marketing department set a performance metric involving increasing market penetration in Latin American countries. From a practical standpoint, using this metric would be difficult, if not impossible—because Latin America is a large region with numerous local markets.

Many systems are available for measuring performance. Managers have traditionally looked to accounting measures as performance indicators. Key among these are revenues from sales, sales per employee, gross profits, profit margin, return on invested capital, and return on assets. These are more useful at the enterprise level than at the unit level. Here are examples of performance areas that might be measured by three different corporate units:

HUMAN RESOURCES UNIT	MARKETING UNIT	MANUFACTURING UNIT
• Training	• Sales	• Unit volume produced
• Recruiting	• Market share	• Cost
• Employee turnover	• New product sales	• Efficiency
• Benefits costs	• Pricing	• Quality
• Compensation/wages	• Distribution	• Process improvement
		• Process innovation

Once you've determined your HR unit's key performance areas, you decide how you'll measure success in each area. Using those measures, you can then define your unit objectives. For example, for your HR unit, two key performance areas and their corresponding measures and objectives might be:

KEY PER- FORMANCE AREA	MEASURES	OBJECTIVES
Recruiting	Time to fill technical positions	• By end of year 1, number of days to fill each technical position will be no more than 42.
		• By end of year 2, number of days to fill each technical position will be no more than 38.
	Percentage of management jobs filled from within	• By end of year 1, percentage of management jobs filled from within will be 50.
		• By end of year 2, percentage of management jobs filled from within will be 60.
Training	Number of hours of training for new employees (less than 1 year)	• By end of year 1, number of hours will be 85.
		• By end of year 2, number of hours will be 115.
	Number of hours of training for experienced employees	• By end of year 1, number of hours will be 45.
		• By end of year 2, number of hours will be 65.

Whichever performance measurement system your company or unit uses, you need objectives that are "SMART"—that is, specific, measurable, achievable, realistic, and time bound. Here are some examples of unit objectives that meet those criteria, along with others that do not:

GOOD OBJECTIVES	NOT–SO–GOOD OBJECTIVES
Add twenty new systems engineers in the next year who are capable of handling the new programming language.	Add new systems engineers who are capable of handling the new programming language. [These measures do not meet the criteria of specific, measurable, or time bound.]
Raise sales 10 percent annually over the next three years.	Improve sales over the next year. [Not specific or measurable.]

Formulate Action Steps

Once you've identified SMART objectives for the key performance areas in your HR strategy, the question is, How will you achieve those goals? The answer is through *action steps*. Action steps are the who, what, and when behind carrying out a strategic initiative and achieving assigned goals. The sum of these steps should complete the job. Every step should have an "owner" who publicly agrees to take responsibility for it. Steps that lack clear owners are often done haphazardly or neglected.

Action Steps and Substeps

In approaching a strategic objective, it's vital to identify action steps and substeps. Ask, "What are all the steps that must be taken for us to accomplish this goal?" Then, for each step you've identified, ask, "Can this step be broken down into substeps?" By asking that same question over and over for each step and its component substeps, you will eventually reach a point where steps can no longer be subdivided. At that point, you will have identified every action step required to carry out the strategic objective. Project managers use this approach all the time to en-sure that they've correctly assessed the scope of the job and all its associated tasks. They use the term *work breakdown structure* to refer to this process. They go further by estimating the amount of time each step will require. Here's an example that shows some of the substeps that might be involved in hiring new workers for a key position:

MAJOR STEP (OR TASK)	LEVEL 1 SUBSTEPS	LEVEL 2 SUBSTEPS	LEVEL 2 SUBSTEP DURATION (DAYS)
Hire twenty systems engineers in the next year who can handle the new pro-gramming language	Determine recruiting strategy	Research effective-ness of Internet recruiting	5
		Develop and place recruiting ad	1
	Establish work space for newly hired en-gineers	Reconfigure cu-bicle layout on third floor	4
		Purchase and in-stall office equip-ment and furniture for new hires	3

Note: for a blank work breakdown structure worksheet, see figure A-2 in the appendix.

Determine Needed Resources

Your action plan is not complete it if fails to recognize the resources HR needs to implement its share of the corporate strategy. Re-sources typically include many of the following:

- People

- Money (per budget)

- Technologies

- Office space

- Support from other departments

- Strategic partners

- Time

- Training

Managers often make the mistake of underestimating their resource needs. If they overlook this step or take shortcuts, they run the risk of having too few resources to execute their plans successfully. To avoid this scenario, ask yourself these questions when assessing your resource needs:

- How will this new action plan affect the HR team's ongoing day-to-day work?

- Can our existing resources cover the steps laid out in the action plan in addition to business-as-usual activities?

- If not, what additional resources will our unit need?

- What new skills will our people need to execute the HR action plan?

- What training will be required, and at what cost?

- What new systems or technology will we need to support the plan? At what cost?

As you think about the resources your unit needs, remember to look beyond what the group needs today and consider what it might need in the coming years. By forecasting skills and competencies needed in the future and by hiring for "tomorrow," you can help your HR unit keep pace with industry changes and build a competitive advantage. For example, suppose your company's long-term strategy calls for leveraging an up-and-coming technology—and designing new products using that technology. You may anticipate a need for employees skilled in the technology a year down the road. In this case, you might include the training of some employees in that technology *now* in your action plan. That way, you can help your company lay the foundation for changes that will come later.

Planning ahead, thinking strategically, and leveraging current resources is a key management skill in a world of constrained resources. In defining required resources, strive to set things up so that you have whom and what you need—when you need them.

Identify Interlocks

Few organizational units work effectively in isolation. They need to collaborate with others at least to some degree—both inside and outside the company—to accomplish their strategic goals. We refer to these points of cross-functional collaboration as *interlocks*. Interlocks don't appear on organizational charts, but they nevertheless play an important role in how strategy-related work gets done. Interlocks can take the form of a task force, an interdepartmental team, or cooperative relationships among individuals within a department who work together. A growing percentage of work in business organizations is now completed through interlocks. (See *The Essentials of Power, Influence, and Persuasion* volume in this series for more information on the power of informal collaboration in organizations.)

Interlocks result in two types of exchanges: giving and receiving. Sometimes, a unit will need to receive work, information, or support from other units in order to carry out its action plans. At other times, a unit will need to give work, information, or support to other units so that they can implement their own action plans. Typically, several groups need to collaborate to carry out a strategic initiative, and the interlocks can be substantial. Suppose, for example, that your company's strategy calls for growing its market share by 30 percent over the next five years. This corporate goal will likely exert an impact on many (if not all) units in the company. In developing action plans, units throughout the organization will find that they need to collaborate to implement their plans. Here are some potential interlocks:

THE HEAD OF . . .	MIGHT NEED PEOPLE FROM . . .	TO HELP WITH . . .
HR	Sales	Developing a plan for recruiting new sales reps
Sales	Human resources	Designing a series of courses on effective cross-selling
Marketing	Information technology	Building a customer database that distinguishes market segments
Product development	Finance	Clarifying new business models

As collaboration across units and departments increases, companies often form cross-functional teams comprising representatives from each of the units that have interlocking interests and obligations. Using the earlier example of the company that wants to grow market share, this organization may decide that its strategic goal necessitates creating a cross-functional team. In this case, the team might be led by someone from marketing and include others from HR, product development, sales, and information technology.

When cross-functional teams are created, they typically develop a charter that outlines members' roles, responsibilities, key milestones, deliverables, and decision-making processes. With clear expectations and shared assumptions, the teams can operate as smoothly as possible.

Some managers find interlocks challenging for the simple reason that they lack formal authority over the people involved. A cross-functional team, for example, may be led by the representative of one function who has no power to discipline or reward team members—some of whom may enjoy higher rank in the organization. The head of this team must lead without benefit of formal power or authority. (*The Essentials of Power, Influence, and Persuasion* offers helpful guidelines for leading when you're not officially in charge.) And as for resources, interlock team members must look to one another and, early in the initiative planning stage, ensure that their combined resources are up to the job.

To ensure accountability in any interlock relationship you participate in, document all your interlock needs, expectations, and obligations. If you can't reach agreement on any of these with other participants in the interlock relationship, identify this as an area of risk in your action plan.

Failure to agree on interlock arrangements can spark intense conflict between groups in organizations—especially when resources are tight. For example, Sue, a marketing manager, may approach Larry, the head of information systems, and explain that she needs help.

> *"We need a database to keep track of all customers and to record all transactions in what we call the 'active seniors' segment," Sue tells Larry. "Our goal is to expand that segment by twenty-five percent over the next two years. Could one of your people become a regular member of the task force we've set up to address that goal? We plan to meet once every two weeks over the coming year."*
>
> *Larry responds, "I'd like to help, Sue, but frankly, I can't spare anyone. We have our own goals, too, you know."*

When such conflicts arise, discuss and try to resolve them immediately. That way, you stand a better chance of keeping your HR action plan on course.

Estimate the Financial Impact

The final piece of your HR action plan is an estimate of the costs associated with the plan. For example, if your plan calls for setting up an e-HR system, you'll need to develop a clear estimate of the cost of operating the system. You'll also want to estimate the savings you anticipate the new system will achieve for your company, owing to efficiencies gained. (See *The Essentials of Finance and Budgeting* in this series for more information on developing this part of your action plan.)

Now that you've read about the various elements of a strategic action plan, see "Tips for Crafting Your Action Plan" for additional guidelines.

Tips for Crafting Your Action Plan

- **Keep it simple.** An overly complex plan will confuse and frustrate anyone who looks at it. So if your flowchart of activities looks like the wiring diagram for a complex piece of machinery, revise it with an eye toward simplicity and coherence.

- **Involve the people who will execute the plan.** You'll boost your HR action plan's chances of succeeding if you don't impose it on the people whom you'll ask to help you carry out the plan. If implementers are involved in developing the action plan, they'll feel more committed to its success. Remember, too, that a plan devised solely by senior-level strategists is less likely to reflect the realities of the business and the organization's true capabilities than a plan built on the ideas of the people on the front line—the people who will need to do the work outlined in the plan.

- **Structure your action plan in achievable chunks.** Overly ambitious plans are usually doomed to failure. People look at them and say, "We'll never get this done—not in our lifetimes." They'll feel defeated from the beginning and won't likely extend themselves to reach the goals in the plan. The lesson here? Build an action plan that is both manageable and achievable.

- **Specify roles and responsibilities.** Like every endeavor, an action plan should detail clear roles and responsibilities. Every planned outcome should be the acknowledged responsibility of one or more individuals. Those "owners" should publicly state that they accept the responsibility. Doing so puts them on record as taking responsibility for results.

- **Make it flexible.** Business strategies seldom follow planned trajectories or timetables. Competitors counterattack. Customers don't behave as anticipated. Mistakes happen. Thus, a good implementation plan is a living document open to revision. Organizations and units that lock themselves into rigid schedules, goals, and events ultimately find themselves detached from the shifting world in which they must do business.

A Sample HR Action Plan

Now that we've discussed all key parts of the unit action plan, let's wrap them up into a sample. What follows is the action plan for the human resources function in APC, an electric utility company.[2] (The plan has been simplified for illustration purposes.)

But first, let's get the big picture: APC had just defined a new strategy hinging on drastically improving overall performance in order to remain competitive in the age of utility deregulation. That meant finding ways to reduce costs as well as increase workforce productivity throughout the organization. The company had already divested low-performing divisions to jump-start its strategy. LeNita Shaw, director of HR, analyzed costs and productivity throughout the company's business units to identify further opportunities to make improvements.

Her analysis suggested several possibilities. Specifically, in some technical units—such as fleet management (the unit responsible for purchasing and maintaining vehicles and equipment)—established labor agreements had spawned certain problems. For example, employees were promoted to higher positions based on seniority, not ability. And longtime employees whose jobs were abolished for some reason had the right to take a lower-grade position but be compensated at their previous pay grade. Result? Lower productivity at higher costs. Moreover, with APC's recent divestitures, many employees had been given the option of staying with APC rather than moving to the companies that had acquired APC's former divisions. Those who chose to stay were placed in different jobs. Many of these employees accepted the jobs as a stopgap measure until a better position was posted—creating a revolving door in certain positions. The high turnover only increased APC's costs and lowered productivity, because employees didn't remain in positions long enough to master the required technical skills. This posed a real problem, since vehicle and equipment technologies were changing rapidly.

After reviewing the situation, Shaw developed an HR strategy focused on lowering costs and boosting productivity in these troubled business units. She made a compelling case for her strategy to the rest of the executive team and the heads of the relevant business units, and they encouraged her to propose an action plan for implementing the strategy. Here's a look at her plan, with examples provided for each component:

- **Goals.** (1) Develop a battery of technician and mechanic selection tests that resemble a battery developed earlier, which had the blessing of the technicians' and mechanics' union. (2) Improve technicians' and mechanics' skill levels through training.

- **Performance metrics.** (1) For selection tests: newly developed tests pass internal and external validation process, in one pass, by end of second quarter this year. The tests must also be approved by union leaders. (2) For skills improvement: technicians and mechanics receive training on changing vehicle and equipment technologies by year end and pass end-of-course assessment tests with scores of 80 or above out of 100.

- **Action Steps.**
  Developing selection tests

WHAT	WHO	WHEN
Decide how to update older tests to meet current technical standards.	Technical experts in affected business units	October 2006
Submit proposed revised tests to testing consultant for review.	Head of technical training	December 2007

Training technicians and mechanics

WHAT	WHO	WHEN
Document latest technology changes in utility vehicles and equipment. Develop courses.	Technical experts in affected business units	November 2006
	Technical training specialists	January through March 2007

- **Resources.** Hire one outside testing consultant to review new selection tests. Borrow two trainers from one of the business units not affected by the HR strategy to assist trainers from affected units.

- **Interlocks.**

HR WORKS WITH . . .	TO . . .	WHEN
Legal	Ensure that revised selection tests meet all hiring regulations and don't inadvertently discriminate against applicants	Start November 2006
Union leadership	Check that new selection procedures are acceptable	November 2006
Education and development services department	Get their advice about performance assessment and career development for technicians and mechanics	November 2006

- **Financial impact estimate.**

  Costs

  Test development and review: $75,000
  New training courses: $50,000 × 30 employees = $1,500,000
  Total costs: $1,575,000

  Benefits

	YEAR 1	YEAR 2	YEAR 3
Number of technicians/mechanics passing training courses	10	10	10
Savings from technicians'/mechanics' greater on-the-job accuracy, speed, and efficiency	$600,000	$600,000	$600,000

  Savings from training: $1,800,000

	YEAR 1	YEAR 2	YEAR 3
Turnover in affected units	70%	50%	30%
Savings from reduced turnover	$550,000	$950,000	$1,350,000

Savings from reduced turnover: $2,300,000

Return on investment:

$4,100,000 (savings) − $1,575,000 (costs) = $2,525,000 (return)

As you can see, an action plan is a rational, building-block approach to getting a big job done. It begins with the top-tier question, What are we trying to accomplish? It then systematically gathers the resources and creates all the mechanisms required to do the job.

Unfortunately, even the best-conceived action plan is vulnerable to events, conflicts, and people problems that can make it run off the tracks. Your job is to ensure that your HR action plan stays on track and stays aligned with your unit strategy and the corporate strategy. That is the subject of our next chapter.

Summing Up

This chapter explained the following:

- Your action plan begins with strategic goals and identifies all the steps required to achieve them.

- Action planning starts at the top, with your company's strategic goals, and cascades down through the organization by defining the measurable action steps that each unit and subunit will contribute to those top-level goals.

- Once you settle on HR's strategic goals and a plan to reach them, your unit must find ways to measure its performance on those goals. Performance metrics should be SMART: specific, measurable, achievable, realistic, and time bound.

- The best way to achieve the goals of your action plan is through action steps. Action steps are the who, what, and when of carrying out a strategic initiative. The sum of these steps should complete the job.

- Every action step must have an "owner" who publicly agrees to take responsibility for it. Steps that lack clear owners are often done haphazardly or neglected.

- All action step owners must ensure that they will have the resources (time, money, people, training, etc.) needed to get the job done.

- Most strategic initiatives require interlocks, or points of cross-functional collaboration.

- The most effective action plans estimate the costs associated with carrying out the plan, as well as possible savings and other benefits.

Leveraging Chapter Insights: Critical Questions

- What strategic goals does your HR unit need to achieve in order to support your company's corporate strategy?

- What metrics will you use to assess your unit's progress toward those strategic goals?

- What action steps need to be taken—by whom and by which dates—so that your HR strategy can be implemented successfully?

- What resources will your unit need to carry out its strategic plan?

- What interlocks will your unit be involved in while implementing the HR strategy? To which units will you owe work, information, or support? From which units will you need work, information, or support?

- What is the potential financial impact of your HR strategy on the company—in terms of likely costs and benefits?

CHAPTER NINE

How to Stay on Course

Sensing and Responding to Deviations from Plan

Key Topics Covered in This Chapter

- *A practical model for successful implementation*
- *Using progress reviews to monitor implementation*
- *The value of informal checks by executives and managers*
- *Common causes of implementation failure*
- *Creating contingency plans to address potential setbacks*

S ET IT AND FORGET IT? That might be possible with using a fine timepiece, but not with implementing your HR strategy. Actions plans provide instructions for achieving specific goals, but people don't always follow instructions. Or they misinterpret those instructions. Or their instructions fail to address all workplace and market realities. Or something in the environment—over which they have no control—changes. No action plan can foresee the many obstacles and changing conditions that you will face over the weeks and months it takes to implement your HR strategic plan. Thus, midcourse adjustments and interventions are inevitable and necessary. This chapter offers suggestions for keeping implementation of your HR strategy on course.[1]

A Model for Staying on Course

Not every strategic plan succeeds. Several months after a new strategic initiative is launched, both management and employees may sense that things aren't working out as anticipated. Goals are being missed. Financial results aren't even close to what the planners had anticipated. The first instinct is to blame the new strategy and the people who cooked it up: "Whatever made them think that this strategy was a good idea?" True, the plan may be ill conceived. But it's equally likely that implementation of the plan has gone off track. As Larry Bossidy and Ram Charan write in their popular book *Exe-*

cution: "The strategy by itself is not often the cause. Strategies most often fail because they aren't executed well."[2]

If you've been in the business world for a while, you can probably remember strategic initiatives that never delivered what they promised. What caused these plans to fall short of expectations? Did the problem lie with the strategy or with the way your company or department implemented it?

Assuming that you've done a good job of developing action plans around each goal in your HR strategy, you can reduce the chances of failure by closely tracking plan implementation and promptly addressing unanticipated problems. If you identify small problems and pounce on them before they can grow into big problems, there's a good chance you can get your HR strategy back on track. Figure 9-1

FIGURE 9-1

Finding and fixing implementation problems

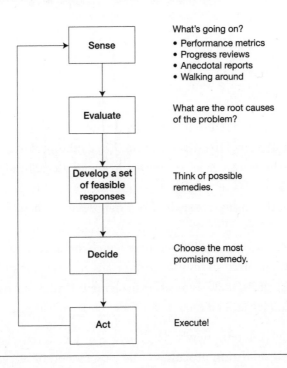

is a straightforward model for accomplishing this. In the model, you and other executives continuously search for deviations from your action plans or for plans that are falling short of expectations. Your search tools are:

- The performance metrics you've built into your action plan

- Periodic progress reviews

- Anecdotal reports from people on the scene

- Direct observation by "walking around"

By constantly testing for the plan's performance, you produce data that helps you evaluate the situation. What is going wrong? What are the root causes of implementation problems? Asking these questions helps you generate potential remedies. Brainstorming with other executives can often produce additional ideas for fixing problems and removing barriers to success. The next steps are to select and execute the remedy most likely to get implementation of your plan back on track.

Progress Review

Periodic progress review is a powerful tool for monitoring implementation of your HR strategic plan. Using the performance metrics you've built into each action step, you can gauge how well people are doing relative to plan. Consider this example, based on the example of the utility company from the previous chapter.

LeNita Shaw, director of HR at utility company APC, has launched the plan for her HR strategy, which included goals centering on developing selection tests for technicians and mechanics in under-performing units such as fleet management and improving these workers' skill levels. The metrics for these two goals were as follows:

1. For selection tests: newly developed tests pass internal and external validation process, in one pass, by end of second quarter this year. The tests are also approved by union leaders.

2. For skills improvement: technicians and mechanics receive training on changing vehicle and equipment technologies by year end and pass end-of-course assessment tests with scores of 80 or above out of 100.

Unfortunately, by the end of the second quarter, the new selection tests aren't close to being completed. Falling short of that goal would put Shaw's plan seriously behind schedule. Shaw needs the union leaders to review the proposed new tests, and they have just a short window of time available to do so. If Shaw misses that window, she'll be hard pressed to get the help she needs from the union leaders in reviewing the tests. When Shaw investigates, she discovers that the technical experts in the affected business units who had agreed to provide input on the tests have taken longer than anticipated.

So, if finding time to provide input on the tests is the problem, why is that? "We've been too short handed to do the work," says the head of vehicle technology in the fleet management unit. "We had enough resources when we agreed to your action plan, but then Brenda left, and we've haven't been able to replace her yet."

The problems depicted in this example are all plausible. The question is, Why has so much time slipped by without these problems' being identified and corrected? Weekly or monthly progress reviews are the best mechanisms for catching problems like the one that now jeopardizes Shaw's HR strategy implementation. Had she instituted this type of review, she would have spotted the technical group's personnel shortcomings early, before the larger, schedule-busting problem developed. This would have given her an opportunity to address the root problems rather than trying to recover after the fact.

What sort of oversight does your HR group provide for important strategic activities—activities that could delay the completion of key goals? If your oversight is weak, what changes might you make to strengthen it?

Performance Measures

As described in the previous chapter, every important strategic goal—at the company and the unit level—should be linked to one or more performance measures: number of new hires, number of employees trained, manufacturing costs per unit, sales per sales representative, cycle time for completing a business process, and so forth. And, as stated earlier, each of these should have a time component: for example, "Employees will complete training within two months after their start date." Executives and managers should use these metrics and dates to identify where progress is and isn't being made. Metrics that aren't moving in the right direction—or are moving too slowly—should send a signal that you need to intervene, to find the sources of the problem, and to fix it. And remember, it's always easier to fix problems when you catch them early. For more information on assessing progress on a strategic plan, see the section "Evaluating an HR Initiative's Strategic Impact" in chapter 11.

Quarterly Reviews

Formal quarterly reviews are another important tool for assessing progress and ensuring that your action plan is being implemented. Consider asking the managers and team leaders who report to you to submit one- to two-page reports for each of the action plans they are implementing. These reports should address the following points:

1. What has been accomplished on the plan

2. What hasn't been accomplished

3. Key issues or problems that need resolution

4. Decisions or resources the manager or team leader needs from you

5. Performance on key objectives, when relevant

It's valuable for you to submit a similar report to your CEO or other supervisor, to help ensure that everyone remains "in the loop" on how your plan is progressing.

The act of producing a quarterly report in itself can spur an executive, a manager, or a team leader to keep a close eye on the progress of implementation. Note: the appendix contains a handy progress-review worksheet (see figure A-3). Consider using it as you develop progress reports for your strategy implementation, or consider giving a copy of it to the managers and team leaders reporting to you.

Informal Checks

Progress reviews are a formal and systematic way of identifying implementation problems. But informal checks made by curious and observant managers are every bit as valuable. Some senior executives make the mistake of compartmentalizing strategy initiatives into two distinct activities: planning and doing. "We executives do all the strategic thinking and planning. Our people do the implementing." This attitude is a prescription for failure. Executives and managers need to stay close to the implementation action and look for problems with their own eyes in addition to gathering information from implementers who report to them. Instead of waiting for progress reports to arrive at their desks, they must routinely *see* and *be seen* on the front lines.

Of course, progress reports from your subordinates are useful, but they have a way of putting a positive spin on whatever is going on. The people who write them are often loath to admit problems—especially when there is some hope of resolving them. Reports are no substitute for the evidence you can gather by simply watching people work and listening to what they have to say. Straightforward questioning of people in your department and in the various operating units affected by your HR strategy can reveal important information you might not find in progress reports. "How are things going?" "Are you getting the resources you need?" "What is blocking progress?" "How could I help you?"

For the senior manager or executive, asking questions costs very little, but it can uncover important hidden problems. Being seen is equally useful. Showing up, participating in executive meetings, lending a hand with some of the more challenging tasks, and demonstrating other forms of personal involvement provide tangible evidence that what's going on in the company is important. By showing up, you help send the message that the HR strategy matters and has the weight of upper management behind it. When other leaders and employees see this behavior, they will likely feel more committed to carrying out their part of the strategy as well.

Common Causes of Implementation Failure

Even the most carefully thought-out action plans can get derailed. Consider these common causes.

Plans Are Expanded

During the execution of action plans, a project may increase in scope. For example, an HR group might decide to add courses to a training program or send a course curriculum through several extra rounds of development. Spending time on additional work cuts into the resources intended to carry out the original plan.

Antidote: ensure that all requests for plan expansion come to you or to someone you've charged with managing implementation of your HR strategy. Determine how these requests will impact your action plan and what additional time and resources will be needed to satisfy the requests *and* keep the plan on track. You or the person you've designated will have the authority to either deny the expansion request or approve the resources needed. Outsourcing certain parts of the action plan may be a feasible solution if you've ruled that plan expansion is essential.

Plans Are Trimmed

A project may be cut back during implementation. This might be done to reduce costs or speed up implementation. While such measures might save money and time, they may also cause an action plan to fall short of achieving its original objectives.

Antidote: again, a plan change of this nature should be adjudicated at the top. If the plan is being trimmed to save time, examine the reasoning that went into the original deadline. If you had decided to complete a particular activity by the end of the calendar year, consider how firm that deadline needs to be. Is there anything special about the end of the year? Would your HR strategy be imperiled if the implementation period were lengthened by a few months? Ask yourself whether a trimmed-down plan finished on time is of greater value than the original plan finished somewhat later.

Resources Are Inadequate

With some plans, people end up having insufficient time to work on special strategic initiatives because their regular duties consume too much time. This situation may stem from inaccurate resource estimates, an increase in project scope, or competing priorities. Whatever the cause, this truth remains: if everyone takes on too much work, resources will be strained.

Antidote: be flexible and maintain a reserve. When experienced military commanders commit their troops to battle, they do so with the assumption that the clash will produce unforeseen dangers and opportunities. They hold a force in reserve to respond to these developments. A strategy implementation project is similar. It's impossible to foresee with absolute certainty what resources a strategic initiative will require and what problems will develop. Consequently, build flexibility into your plans, and hold some additional funds, equipment, or people in reserve. In a word: be prepared for resource shortfalls.

Interlocks Fail

A group that your unit depends on for a strategy-related deliverable or collaboration may alter its plans and, therefore, fail to fulfill its interlock obligations to you. In many cases, this occurs because that group's manager has failed to free up necessary resources or has other priorities. In other cases, the executive or manager who developed a strategic plan neglected to consider interlocks during the action planning stage.

Collaboration between units is always an issue in any organization, unless these units routinely work together. Causes of collaboration problems include the following:

- Poor communication ("We don't know what they want from us")

- Misalignment of goals or priorities

- Antagonism between unit managers

- Different working styles (e.g., one unit is entrepreneurial; the other, bureaucratic)

- Lack of incentives for collaboration

If you sense the existence of any of these problems, take a closer look at the interlocks section of your HR action plan and brainstorm ways of strengthening any weak areas.

Antidote: communication. As you develop your HR action plan, state in unambiguous terms, "This strategy implementation is a key goal for the company. I expect us to work together to make it succeed." Also, keep in mind that the more you involve other unit leaders in developing your action plan and providing input, the more likely they'll be to honor any interlock agreements you make with them.

People Resist Change

A new HR strategy produces more than a change in a company's competitive stance; it can also upset the status quo inside your organization, triggering resistance to change. "The reformer has enemies in all those who profit by the old order," that old strategist Machiavelli warned his readers. And what held true in sixteenth-century Italy remains true today. Some people clearly enjoy advantages that they view as threatened by change. They may perceive change as endangering their livelihoods, their perks, their workplace social arrangements, or their status in the organization. Others know that their specialized skills will be rendered less valuable after particular changes are carried out. For example, when a supplier of automotive hydraulic steering systems switched to electronic steering technology in the late 1990s, long-term employees with expertise in hoses, valves, and fluids suddenly had less value in the organization. The know-how they had developed over long careers was displaced by the electrical engineering skills the company was actively recruiting.

Anytime people perceive themselves as losers in a strategic change initiative, expect resistance. Resistance may be passive: people refuse to commit to goals. Or it may be active: people directly oppose or try to subvert the goals.

Antidote: identify potential resisters and redirect their angst. Here's how to start:

- Determine who has something to lose if your HR strategy is successfully implemented. Communicate the why of the strategy to them. Explain the urgent need to move away from established routines or arrangements.

- Emphasize the benefits of the new HR strategy to potential resisters. Those benefits might be greater future job security, higher pay, and so forth. There's no guarantee that these benefits of change will exceed the losses for these individuals. However, explaining the benefits will help shift their focus from negatives to positives.

- Help resisters find new roles that enable them to make genuine contributions *and* mitigate their losses.

- Many people resist change because it represents a loss of control over their daily lives. Return some of that control by making resisters active partners in your strategy implementation program.

If you've encountered stiff resistance from a few of your own HR team members and the preceding interventions fail, move resisters out of your unit. You cannot afford to let a few disgruntled individuals subvert the entire group's progress. But don't make them "walk the plank." Do what you can to relocate them to positions where their particular skills can be better used. That's what the innovator of electronic steering systems did. That company still had plenty of business supplying hydraulic systems to car and truck manufacturers, so it employed its hydraulic specialists in those units even as it hired electronic engineers for its expanding new business. And just as you relocate resisters out of your own unit, explain to other unit leaders the importance of doing the same.

See *The Essentials of Managing Change and Transition* volume in this series for helpful guidelines on addressing change resistance.

Contingency Plans

Every action plan contains the risk that something unforeseen or unforeseeable will come along and delay or derail implementation of the plan. Your response? Develop contingency plans for these potential problems. A *contingency plan* is a course of action you prepare in *advance* of a potential problem. It answers this question: "If *X* happens, how could we respond in a way that would neutralize or minimize the damage?" Consider these examples of contingency plans:

- FirstBank, a large financial-services company, had decided to adopt new information technology. The HR department had developed a unit-level strategy that contained the goal of hiring twenty-five new information systems professionals within six months who could help set up and run the new IT platform. Before implementing the HR action plan, the director of HR developed a contingency plan. "If we're only able to find fifteen qualified IT hires within the stated time frame, we will consider hiring IT consultants and outsourcing some of our IT work that must be completed, until we can hire the ten remaining full-time IT employees specified in the plan."

- The Acme Company set up a two-year project to modernize its manufacturing facilities. Senior management regarded the two-year deadline as extremely important. Recognizing the real risk that the deadline might not be met, the sponsor agreed to set up a reserve fund that could be used to hire outside help if the project fell behind schedule. This contingency plan included a monthly progress review and a provision that falling three or more weeks behind schedule would trigger release of the reserve funds.

- TechoWhiz, Inc., was banking on its software project team to develop a new version of its integrated office application suite, one that would include all the bells and whistles, and seamless linkages to the Internet. Not wanting to miss the announced release date and its expensive marketing rollout, the team developed a contingency plan for dealing with any unfinished elements of the program. That contingency plan was clear: any new elements not ready for the official release date would be packaged as a downloadable add-on to be made available at a later date to all registered users of the new version. Staffing for the development of this add-on was planned in advance, with budgeting conditional on the amount of needed work.

The real benefit of a contingency plan is that it prepares you to deal quickly with an adverse situation. When disaster strikes, you

Make Someone Responsible for Each Serious Risk

Just as you assign every task in an action plan an "owner," it's wise to make someone responsible for each serious risk in your action plan. That person should monitor the assigned risk, sound the alarm if the risk appears to be moving from potential problem to real problem, and be prepared to take charge of the consequences.

don't have to spend weeks trying to figure out what you should do or how you will find the funds to deal with a new situation.

Has your unit identified the risks in your HR action plan? Have you developed contingency plans for dealing with them?

Keeping your HR action plan on track might not be as interesting or enjoyable as formulating your HR strategy. And it may not seem as glamorous. But staying on course is a vital job. In the end, a well-executed mediocre strategy generates more value than a brilliant strategy that falls apart during implementation.

Summing Up

In this chapter, you discovered that:

- Strategy failures often stem from poor implementation.

- You can sense deviations from your HR action plan through several mechanisms: performance metrics, periodic progress reviews, anecdotal reports, and direct observation.

- Weekly or monthly progress reviews are the best mechanisms for catching implementation problems before they grow into major impediments to success.

- If you are overseeing implementation of your HR action plan, don't create a climate in which people are afraid to report problems in a timely way.

- Don't wait for progress reports on your HR plan. Augment reports by getting out on the front lines of implementation, observing and asking questions.

- Common causes of HR implementation failures include plan expansions, plans that are trimmed, inadequate resources, inter-lock failures, and resistance by people who see themselves as losers under the new strategy.

- Every HR action plan contains risks—some unforeseeable. Create a contingency plan for every serious risk.

- Make someone responsible for managing every serious risk in your action plan.

Leveraging Chapter Insights: Critical Questions

- Examine the action plan for the HR strategy you've developed. How will you review progress once implementation of the plan begins? Whom will you talk with? How often will you check in with them? What will you ask them?

- What kinds of progress reports will you require from implementers charged with carrying out parts of your HR action plan? What information will you ask for in the reports? Who will submit them? How often? What reports will you submit to your own supervisor?

- Which goals in your action plan are the most essential to stay on track? For example, which goal, if it gets derailed, will prevent the remaining goals in your plan from being achieved?

- What do you see as the major risks inherent in your action plan? What contingency plans might you develop to address those risks? Who will take ownership of each risk?

- If you've begun implementation of your HR action plan, how are things progressing? If some items are behind schedule, what might be the cause? Consider typical causes such as expanding or trimming the plan, failing to get interlock agreements met, and encountering change resistance.

CHAPTER TEN

The People Side of Implementation

Getting the Right People on Board

Key Topics Covered in This Chapter

- *How to enlist the support and involvement of key people in a change initiative*

- *Supporting your HR action plan with consistent behaviors*

- *Enabling structures (i.e., training, pilot programs, and a reward system)*

- *Celebrating milestones*

- *The importance of relentless communication*

THE PREVIOUS TWO CHAPTERS could give the impression that implementing your HR strategy is a mechanical process: just develop a blueprint of action steps, tell the people around you to execute those steps, and check periodically for compliance and progress. The reality is that people are the most important part of any strategy implementation. Many HR executives find that harnessing managers' and employees' energy and commitment to strategic change can be their greatest challenge. When you call on others to carry out your action plan, you need to make them feel that they've had something to say about the plan. They must know that the plan's success is vital. They must be motivated to do the right things well. And they must have meaningful incentives for all their hard work.

The record shows that implementation of strategic plans rarely proceeds smoothly. In some cases, external factors upset schedules or divert managers' attention. Technical glitches hamstring progress. But the most common obstacle to implementation is people problems. People make mistakes. Key players quit or are transferred. Different groups forget to communicate with each other. Untrained individuals get assigned to jobs they can't handle. Managers alienate the employees charged with critical action steps.

This chapter addresses the people side of implementation and shows you how to steer clear of people-related problems.

Enlist the Support and Involvement of Key People

Your HR action plan will stand a far better chance of being carried out successfully if it has the backing and involvement of key people—and not just the CEO and his or her court. It goes without saying that top-level involvement is essential. But you must also enlist the support of managers and employees whom others respect: individuals with proven technical skills, people with access to vital resources, and the informal leaders to whom people naturally turn for direction and advice when they encounter obstacles. How can you pinpoint these people? Authors Michael Tushman and Charles O'Reilly offer this suggestion:

> *To determine who these key individuals are and what their responses to the change might be, ask: Who has the power to make or break the change? Who controls critical resources or expertise? Then think through how the change will likely affect each of these individuals and how each is likely to react toward the change. Who will gain or lose something . . . Are there blocs of individuals likely to mobilize against or in support of the change effort?*[1]

Enlisting support entails building an effective team of change makers who can work in unison toward the stated goals in your HR strategy. But how can you be sure you've picked the right people for this team? See assessment tool 10-1 for a set of questions that will help you discern whether your team has the right stuff. Also see "Tips on Who Should *Not* Be on the Team."

Assessment Tool 10-1
Does Your Implementation Team Have the Right Stuff?

For each question, answer yes or no.

1. **Are enough of your company's key players (people in relevant positions of power) members of the team?**

   Yes   No

2. **Do members of the team have the relevant expertise to do the job and make intelligent decisions?**

   Yes   No

continued

3. Does the team include the needed range of perspectives and disciplines to do the job and make intelligent decisions?

Yes   No

4. Does the team include people with sufficient credibility so that other employees and management will treat their decisions seriously?

Yes   No

5. Does the team include true leaders?

Yes   No

6. Are the team members capable of forgoing their personal interests in favor of the larger strategic goal?

Yes   No

Your total score:

Interpreting your score

If you answered yes to most of these questions, the team guiding your implementation effort is strong and in a good position to succeed. If you said no to any questions, consider revisiting your team choices.

SOURCE: John P. Kotter, *Leading Change* (Boston: Harvard Business School Press, 1996).

Tips on Who Should Not *Be on the Team*

In his book *Leading Change,* John Kotter recommends that you keep three types of people off your implementation team:

1. **People with big egos.** Big egos, per Kotter, fill the room, leaving little or no space for anybody else to participate or

contribute. People with big egos don't always understand their own limitations and how those limitations can be complemented by the strength of others.

2. **Snakes.** Kotter describes a *snake* as the kind of person who secretly poisons relationships between team members. "A snake is an expert at telling Sally something about Fred and Fred something about Sally that undermines Sally and Fred's relationship."

3. **Reluctant players.** These are people who lack either the time or enthusiasm to provide energy to the team. Be wary of including these people on your team. Keeping them off may be difficult, however, since some reluctant players may have the expertise and/or organizational power you need.

Implementing a new HR strategy is difficult enough without having these people on your team.

SOURCE: John F. Kotter, *Leading Change* (Boston: Harvard Business School Press, 1996), 59–61.

Support the Plan with Consistent Behaviors and Messages

Once you've articulated the need for your HR strategy convincingly and established broad support for your plan, maintain that support through a set of consistent behaviors and messages. Inconsistency in either will send a damaging signal—that you're not serious about implementing your new HR strategy or that you're unwilling to do your part.

Consider this example: not many years ago, one of the American Big Three automakers underwent a painful strategic restructuring. Everyone was asked to sacrifice by giving up benefits today in order to achieve greater competitiveness, job security, and prosperity tomorrow. Thousands of middle managers were laid off, and the company's union was asked to forgo pay and benefit increases. Because the company had made a convincing case for change, people had gotten the message and tightened their belts; even the unions pitched in. Within months, however, senior management awarded itself and other key people with substantial bonuses and pay increases. Once that inconsistent behavior became public, the bonds of trust between management and the rank and file—and union leaders—unraveled. Collaboration turned to open hostility that simmered for nearly ten years.

At about the same time, a company in another industry was likewise supporting a belt-tightening and restructuring program. But this one did so with highly visible and consistent deeds. Its CEO set the pace by selling the corporation's three jets and taking commercial flights on his travels—in coach class, to boot. And no more limos to meet him at the airport. "I don't mind taking a cab," he told the business press. "They can get me to where I'm going just as fast." The company's other traveling executives followed their boss's lead. People noticed.

Which of these companies do you suppose was more successful in building support for its change program?

SQA, Herman Miller's successful low-cost office furniture unit, also used a consistent set of messages to support its strategy of on-time, accurate fulfillment of orders. Everyone understood that this was the unit's key measure of success. So SQA managers came up with several ways to reinforce that message. For example, every morning they posted the previous day's percentage of on-time orders at every entrance to the plant. It was impossible to enter or leave without knowing how the unit had performed the day before. Managers also added the latest on-time order statistic to every internal e-mail message. "Yesterday's percentage of on-time accurately filled orders was 99.2 percent." The vice president of operations even adopted the practice of randomly asking employees whether they knew the previous day's performance score. A correct answer was rewarded with either a crisp $100 bill or a day off with full pay.

What messages or behaviors would be consistent with the implementation of *your* HR strategy?

Develop Enabling Structures

Enabling structures are the activities and programs that underpin successful implementation of a strategic plan. As such, they're critical parts of the overall plan. Such enabling structures include pilot programs, training, and reward systems.

Pilot programs give people opportunities to grapple with the challenges in a strategic plan on a relatively small, manageable scale. Pilots are test beds in which you and your implementation team can experiment with and debug initiatives before rolling them out more broadly. An example of a pilot program for your HR strategy might include asking a particular unit in your company to test-drive the new performance management methodology that your strategy calls for. A pilot can be a valuable proving ground, since it's almost always easier and less risky to change a single department or unit than an entire company.

Training programs can hold equal value. Motorola and General Electric developed formal training programs that served as key enablers for the quality strategies adopted by these companies. Xerox did the same when it set up its companywide benchmarking program in the mid-1980s. Every Xerox employee received a copy of "the little yellow book," as they called the company's how-to manual on benchmarking methods, and skilled trainers were placed in almost every operating unit of the company. You can set up training programs for your HR strategy as well. For example, if your strategy calls for adopting a new e-HR system, you could establish a program that trains employees on how to use the system.

Reward systems also play an enabling role. People generally adopt behaviors that produce rewards and abandon those that don't generate rewards. Thus, if your HR action plan asks people to either work harder, work smarter, or work in new ways, your reward system must align with those desired behaviors. Crafting the right incentive program is a complex task that hinges on the unique characteristics of your situation and the policies your company has established. But keep in mind that rewards don't always need to take the form of bonuses and other financial incentives. In designing a reward system, also consider nonfinancial incentives that people value—such as opportunities to take on a plum assignment, a special team dinner to celebrate achievements, and free company products.

Celebrate Milestones

The road to implementing any strategy can prove long and frustrating. People tend to grow tired or lose interest if those who formulated the strategy don't take steps to keep everyone's spirits and energy lifted. You can keep people fired up about your HR strategy if you identify milestones—even small ones—and celebrate them as they are achieved. (See "Tips for Celebrating Short-Term Wins.") Celebrating a series of short-term wins can:

- Neutralize skepticism about your strategy and implementation efforts.

- Provide evidence that people's sacrifices and hard work are paying off.

- Help retain support.

- Keep up the momentum.

- Boost morale.

Tips for Celebrating Short-Term Wins

You can help your implementation team celebrate short-term wins in many ways—not all of them requiring significant amounts of money. Here are just a few ideas for celebrating and keeping your strategy implementation team pumped up:

- Treat implementers to a catered lunch—and bring in an outside speaker who can talk about his or her company's success in achieving something similar.

- Visit individuals in their offices and thank them personally, describing in specific terms what you appreciated about their contribution to the implementation.

- Deliver handwritten notes of thanks and appreciation to successful implementers.

- Mention implementers' achievements to managers and executives of influence who can open new opportunities for these dedicated, creative individuals.

- Create a "hall of fame" wall with photos of implementation team members and short descriptions of what they accomplished.

- Create a publicly posted timeline showing the strategic plan's milestones that have been reached, and depicting the individuals who made each achievement possible.

- Hand out gift certificates to local restaurants, theaters, or other cultural attractions.

- Arrange for implementers to get free or discounted company products or services of their choice.

- Conduct an implementation team meeting during which each member states what he or she most appreciates about the teammate sitting to his or her left.

- Arrange for the team to have a celebratory lunch with the company president or general manager.

- Stage a potluck supper for the team at your home; hand out prizes, balloons, or fun gifts in appreciation of the team's achievements.

- Publish an article about your team's accomplishments in the company newsletter, naming each individual and noting his or her contributions to the implementation effort.

There is a fine line between celebrating a successful milestone and making a premature declaration of victory. Crossing that line could dissipate the sense of urgency you need to keep people motivated and moving on toward future hurdles. John Kotter, who lists "declaring victory too soon" among the reasons that many strategy implementations fail, says that both change initiators and change resisters have reasons for making this mistake. "In their enthusiasm over a clear sign of progress," he writes, "the initiators go overboard. They are then joined by resistors, who are quick to point out any opportunity to stop change . . . [T]he resistors point to the victory as a sign that the war has been won and the troops should be sent home."[2] Catastrophe follows if the weary troops accept this argument and go back to their usual activities.

So instead of declaring victory as soon as parts of your HR strategy have been successfully put into action, use the credibility and momentum gained from these short-term wins to muster an attack on the next milestone in your plan.

Communicate Relentlessly

Communication is the most important tool in your HR strategy implementation arsenal. Leverage your communication skills to make it clear:

1. What your HR strategy is

2. Why the strategy is important

3. How effective implementation of your HR strategy will benefit the company and employees

4. What role each person will play in implementing the strategy

These four points should form the core of any pep talk you deliver about your strategy to managers and employees. And these same four points should also inform every communication to your direct reports and their subordinates when you discuss you HR strategy.

Communication is an effective tool for motivating managers and employees to embrace change, for overcoming resistance to a new strategy, for preparing people for the pluses and minuses of change, and for giving them a personal stake in helping to carry out the strategy you've defined. Effective communication can set the tone for the difficult work ahead. But don't rely on a single announcement to keep your strategy implementation on track. Be sure to use ongoing communication. Consider these tips for communicating during implementation of your HR strategy:[3]

1. **Specify the nature of the new strategy and the results you're aiming for.** Slogans, themes, and phrases don't define what your strategy is expected to achieve. Instead, communicate specific information about how the new strategy will affect workforce productivity, customer satisfaction, product or service quality, market share, sales, and other important measures of organizational success.

2. **Explain why.** Too many executives and managers leave employees in the dark about the business reasons behind a new or revised strategy. You may have spent lots of time studying the problem your HR strategy intends to address and digging out the relevant facts, but that doesn't mean others are privy to that same information. To help them understand the need for your strategy, share with other executives and managers (as well as your own direct reports) the various strategic options available and why your plan is better than the others.

3. **Explain the scope of the strategy change, even if it contains bad news.** Some people will be more affected than others by implementation of your HR strategy. And that leads to lots of fear-generating speculation. Fear and uncertainty can paralyze a team, unit, and entire company. You can short-circuit fear and uncertainty with the facts. But don't sugarcoat them. If your HR strategy calls for some layoffs or other difficult changes, be up front about it. If some people will need training to acquire new skills, say so. Also explain the things that will *not*

change. Balancing change with continuity and familiarity can help calm fears of the unknown.

4. **Develop a graphic representation of the implementation action plan that people can understand and hold in their minds.** This graphic representation might consist of a flow-chart of the steps that must be taken to carry out your HR strategy, or a graphic image of what the changed HR department or company will look like. Regardless of the details, keep the depiction clear, simple, and memorable.

5. **Predict the negative aspects of implementation.** With any strategic change, there are bound to be negatives—including hard work, changes in assignments, and frustrating setbacks. If you prepare people for these, you can help them take these difficulties in stride once your plan's implementation is well under way.

6. **Explain the criteria for success and how it will be measured.** Define success for your strategic plan clearly, and devise metrics for assessing progress toward that vision of success. Metrics are key parts of your action plan. If you fail to establish clear measures for what you aim to accomplish through your HR strategy, how will anyone know whether they are moving forward or at least headed in the right direction? Measure progress as you move forward—and then communicate that progress to the people who are implementing your plan.

7. **Explain how people will be rewarded for success.** As stated elsewhere, people need incentives for doing the added work that carrying out a new strategy requires and for handling the inevitable disruptions. Be very clear about how individuals will be rewarded for progress toward the goals defined in your strategy.

8. **Repeat, repeat, and repeat the purpose of change and actions planned.** If your initial announcement of your HR strategy doesn't generate questions, do not assume that people have accepted the need for change. Instead, they may simply be surprised, puzzled, or shocked by what you've proposed. So

follow up your initial announcement meeting with another meeting. Then back this up with communications that address individual aspects of your strategic plan.

9. **Use a diverse set of communication styles.** Some people are most receptive to the printed word or to flowcharts. Others respond best to stand-up presentations. Since every audience contains people with different learning styles, provide a mix of media—a dedicated newsletter, events, e-mails, and stand-up presentations—to keep people informed, involved, and keyed up about your HR strategy. These communications should be honest about successes and failures. If people lose trust in what they are hearing, they will tune you out.

10. **Make communication a two-way proposition.** Remember that strategy implementation is a shared enterprise. So spend at least as much time listening as telling. You'll help keep others involved and motivated. Leaders need feedback, and the hard-working implementers need opportunities to share their learning and their concerns with leaders who listen.

11. **Be consistent.** You are the boss when it comes to your HR strategy, and people will have their eyes on you. They will listen to your words, but will also look for inconsistencies between your words and the messages you communicate through your body language and behavior. Do you speak about your strategy with genuine enthusiasm? Does your tone and manner signal confidence in the implementation project, or do you appear to be merely going through the motions? Try to see yourself as others see you—and address any gaps between your spoken and unspoken messages.

Understand HR's Unique Role in the People Side

As a human resources executive, you play a central role in defining an HR strategy. At its core, your strategy explains how your organization's workforce must be differentiated in order to carry out the high-level strategy. That is, what skills will be needed in which positions? What behaviors and attitudes must your firm's workforce demonstrate? But without the right people occupying the right positions and carrying out the right activities at the right level of talent throughout your organization, your strategy (as well as the high-level strategy) stands little chance of succeeding. Part of your job, then, is to help other executives, senior managers, and line managers implement strategy through effective strategic leadership of their teams and employees. Effective strategic leaders communicate strategy clearly to their people; articulate the performance, behaviors, and attitudes they require of their teams; and take steps to address any shortfalls on these dimensions.

How might you help other leaders throughout your organization improve strategy implementation? Experts recommend these practices:[4]

- **Design performance management methodologies.** A company's performance management methodology enables managers to understand what's expected of them to carry out the corporate strategy and to cascade those expectations to their subordinates. The best performance management method also contains metrics for assessing whether the firm has enough sufficiently talented players in the right positions and whether employees understand the business's strategy and their part in executing it. Performance management also includes processes for recognizing and rewarding top performers in key positions ("A" players) and either improving or removing mediocre performers ("C" players). Finally, good performance management means conducting effective performance appraisals on time—and clarifying expectations at the beginning of clearly defined performance periods.

  By providing this kind of performance management model to other executives and managers throughout your firm, you sweeten the odds that these leaders will successfully carry out their part of the corporate strategy.

- **Design "A," "B," and "C" tracking systems.** Develop a way for executives and managers to identify "A," "B," and "C" players on their teams. This requires defining—as clearly as possible—top-notch performance (in terms of concrete outcomes and desired behaviors and attitudes) for each position under an executive's or a manager's control. Though such metrics might by necessity be imprecise, merely defining them encourages accountability among leaders for making smart workforce decisions. After all, if a manager doesn't know who his underperformers are, he can't coach them to improve their performance or remove them from his team so as to ensure successful execution of strategy.

- **Help leaders get feedback.** Design surveys through which each executive's and manager's boss and direct reports evaluate his or her leadership behavior. Respondents rate the leader's effectiveness on numerous criteria, including (1) creating a strategic mind-set (communicating business strategy and plans for executing it, informing employees about strategic progress); (2) employee development (coaching performance improvement, teaching job-related skills, mentoring high-potential players); (3) leading change (setting stretch targets, building teamwork, embodying a compelling vision, sharing information); and (4) performance management (clarifying expectations, providing frequent and honest feedback, allocating rewards appropriately, taking corrective action when necessary). Results from such surveys can help leaders identify and strengthen weak areas in their abilities—thereby improving their capacity to carry out strategy.

- **Provide extra help to line managers.** Many lower-level managers, especially supervisors, have been promoted into management because of their great skill as individual contributors. Thus they often find it particularly difficult to make the painful workforce choices that must be made to ensure successful execution of strategy. Why? Such decisions often affect people whom they view as friends—former peers with whom they may have worked on teams.

    Your job is thus to help these leaders make the hard workforce choices necessary to implement company strategy. You can do so by providing crystal-clear, position-specific guidelines for defining "A," "B," and "C" performers. Also explain to line managers that making decisions about mediocre performers is a critical part of their job. Ease their concerns by reassuring them that such employees will be treated with dignity and respect, and will receive help from the company in transitioning to other opportunities. Do everything you can to ensure that employees who are let go can exit the organization as smoothly and painlessly as possible. Finally, it's even more important that line managers' strategy leadership skills are evaluated through surveys of their direct reports.

When you help other leaders in your company lead their work-forces in ways that support the strategic direction the organization has defined, your enterprise has a far better chance of garnering the desired results from its strategy. The sidebar "HR in Action: Enabling a Strategic Divestiture" describes how several HR practitioners helped their companies deal effectively with people issues during a time of intense strategic change.

HR in Action: Enabling a Strategic Divestiture

Among large companies especially, divestiture (the selling of parts of an organization) is playing an increasingly large role in high-level strategy. Why? Many companies' competitive strate-gies call for focusing more tightly on core capabilities and let-ting underperforming units go to acquirers that have more of the resources needed to turn a divested unit around.

In companies considering divesting one or more units, the HR team plays a critical role in ensuring the success of the strat-egy during every phase of the effort. For example, before attracting buyers for a soon-to-be-divested unit, HR prepares a detailed examination of base salaries, as well as other costs (such as benefits), to determine the unit's financial liability. It also identifies key talent throughout the company, so that the firm's "brainpower" doesn't get sold off. When Mitsubishi Corporation decided to divest an underperforming U.S. chemical company, for example, company president and top HR executive Dave Siporin identified forty key players (managers and technical experts) and developed a proposal for retaining them.

Sometimes assessing current performers in the unit results in the decision not to divest after all—or to postpone the decision. Tom Capizzi, vice president of worldwide HR at guidance equipment maker Thales Navigation, identified certain managers who could lead a turnaround of a potentially divested unit if given several months to prove themselves. Because of Capizzi's analysis, the company decided to pull the divestiture deal from the table and wait six months.

HR leaders can also help enhance the purchase price of a divested unit by assessing and improving the unit's human capital. In one divestiture situation, Thales Navigation's HR team brought in interim management to run the unit, in order to increase the perceived value of the unit in the eyes of potential acquirers.

Finally, an HR team must take steps to ensure a smooth transition of the divested company to its new owner—and preserve morale and productivity in the remaining businesses as the divestiture process unfolds. This means developing and implementing a communication campaign to prevent sabotage, calm possible union unrest, and grapple with other negative events that may harm the unit's performance or perceived value before the divestiture deal is closed. It also means offering incentives that encourage key people to remain in high-leverage positions during and after the transition. In the Mitsubishi divestiture, for example, the HR group created three groups of employees—all with different termination dates. The first group was let go when the divestiture deal was announced; the second received incentives to stay on until the deal closed; and several individuals were offered positions with the acquiring company.

SOURCE: Robert J. Grossman, "Must See (People Assets) Inside!" *HR Magazine*, September 2004.

In the end, the people side of implementation of your HR strategy should be your most important concern. Without the commitment and hard work of many others in your organization, the action plan you've spent so much time and thought on may well go to waste.

Summing Up

In this chapter, you learned these key practices for getting the right people on board while implementing your HR strategy:

- Get the right people involved in implementation. That should include individuals with proven technical skills, people with access to vital resources, and the informal leaders to whom people naturally turn for direction and advice when they encounter obstacles.

- Keep troublemakers and people with big egos, too little time, or no enthusiasm off your implementation team.

- Be consistent in your behavior and messages. Don't ask people to make sacrifices on behalf of your new strategy if you, as the leader of the strategy, are not willing to make those same sacrifices yourself.

- Use enabling structures—pilot programs, training, and reward systems—to support successful implementation of your HR strategy.

- Celebrate as you and your implementation team achieve important milestones on your strategic action plan. You'll boost your chances of maintaining momentum, support, and morale.

- Resist any urge to declare victory at the first signs of successful implementation.

- Keep up a steady stream of communications about the implementation of your strategy. Remind people about what the strategy's purpose is, why it's important, how it will benefit the

company and everyone in it, and what roles people are
expected to play to ensure that the strategy succeeds.

- Be open to communication (concerns, suggestions, ideas) from
others on the front lines who are carrying out their parts of
your HR strategy.

Leveraging Chapter Insights: Critical Questions

- Think about the HR strategy you've defined. In your company,
who are the key people who will help carry out that strategy?
How might you best enlist their support and involvement in
implementing your strategy?

- What messages about your HR strategy are you sending to the
people who are implementing the strategy? Consider your oral
and written statements, as well as your behaviors. Are you
sending consistent messages? Are you demonstrating as much
commitment to the strategy as you're expecting from your
implementers?

- What enabling structures are you using to help ensure successful implementation of your HR strategy? Consider pilot programs, training, and reward systems. How effective are these
structures? What changes might you make to improve their
effectiveness?

- How do you help your implementation team celebrate milestones? Are these celebrations sufficient to keep the team motivated and performing? If not, what changes could you make?

- Of the eleven tips offered earlier for communicating about
your HR strategy, which do you apply regularly? Which do you
need to use more consistently? What steps might you take to
apply some of these practices more effectively?

- In what ways do you help other executives and managers execute the corporate strategy through effective leadership of their

people? Do you provide tools for leaders to assess their strategy implementation abilities? For identifying their "A," "B," and "C" performers? For rewarding top-notch players and either coaching or removing mediocre employees? How might you provide even stronger support for other leaders seeking to carry out their part of the corporate strategy in their units?

CHAPTER ELEVEN

Implementing Human Capital Initiatives

The Rubber Meets the Road

Key Topics Covered in This Chapter

- *Implementing workforce planning initiatives*
- *Carrying out new recruiting strategies*
- *Executing retention initiatives*
- *Ensuring successful compensation design*
- *Launching effective training and development programs*
- *Knowing when your HR initiative has paid off*

I N P R E V I O U S C H A P T E R S, you've learned about the importance of developing an action plan for your HR strategy, determining how you'll keep the plan on track, and getting the right people on board—and motivating them—to successfully carry out your plan. In this chapter, we focus on ways to implement HR initiatives and programs in the key functional areas of workforce planning, recruiting, retention, compensation, and training and development. Such initiatives represent where the "rubber" of your HR strategy meets the "road": carry out these initiatives skillfully, and you'll vastly boost your chances of generating the value promised by your strategy. But part of generating value is demonstrating in concrete, measurable terms what a strategic initiative has accomplished. Thus we end this chapter with a discussion of how to evaluate an HR initiative's strategic impact.

Let's start our examination of implementing HR initiatives by looking at a particularly vital functional area in the human resources discipline: workforce planning.

Workforce Planning

The most effective HR strategies include workforce planning initiatives. *Workforce planning* is the process by which you determine the types of skills, the numbers of employees with those skills, and the locations in the company those employees should serve so that your organization can carry out its competitive strategy. A successful workforce plan ensures that your company has the right number of people, with the right capabilities, in the right places, at the right time. You avoid talent surpluses and shortages, which in turn helps stave off the need for layoffs or panic hiring.

Thoughtful workforce planning can also generate concrete financial results—by enabling an organization to boost productivity over the long run, cut labor costs, and reduce time to market. One company's workforce plan resulted in such superior customer service that the organization's customers became exceptionally loyal. Increased customer loyalty in turn accelerated sales while decreasing customer-acquisition costs, and it enabled the company to charge premium prices.[1]

There is no standard process for creating a workforce plan. For example, in some companies, workforce planning is centralized in the HR function. In others, the process is decentralized: unit leaders develop a workforce plan for their part of the business and then submit them to HR for review. In these cases, unit leaders supply specific documents with their workforce plan—including their unit strategy and information about each employee's performance and promotion potential, career advancement plans, skill levels, and cross-function potential.[2]

Just as there's no one "right" process for developing a company-level workforce plan, there's no standard format for such a plan. However, many workforce plans contain the following components:[3]

- **Forecasting.** What are your estimates of the sizes of the available labor pool, the demand for labor according to your company's strategy, labor cost, your company's anticipated growth once its strategy is implemented, and the magnitude of the organization's output (in terms of production or creation of services) that the strategy is intended to achieve?

- **Succession planning.** Which leaders will be retiring or moving on to another position, and who will fill those positions? How quickly will successors need to be ready to fill vacated leadership positions?

- **Recruiting.** Given your company's strategy, what are your estimates of the organization's head-count needs, positions that will need to be filled or created, locations in the company where specific individuals with certain skills will have to be placed, the required timing of those placements, and labor sources.

- **Retention.** What are your company's turnover rates in various units? Do any of those rates pose a danger, given your company's strategy? If so, who is at risk for leaving? And how will you reduce turnover?

- **Redeployment.** Can your company put its workforce in the best possible position to carry out its strategy by moving some individuals into positions with higher strategic impact?

- **Contingency workforce.** What percentage of your company's workforce should be contingent, and which jobs are most appropriate to be filled by contingent workers?

- **Potential retirements.** Who in your company is eligible for retirement? When are they likely to retire? Do they need to be replaced? If so, who will fill their vacated positions? Might some retirees be able and interested in alternative work arrangements, such as a part-time schedule or a consulting role?

- **Performance management.** Who are the top-notch, average, and suboptimal performers throughout your company? How will people who cannot get their skills up to par be managed out of the organization?

- **Career development.** What career paths interest employees in your company? How quickly do they want to move up their career ladder? What specific steps in various career paths can your company offer its workforce? What forms of support (career counseling, professional-development programs) will your firm need to offer to satisfy employees' career interests while also developing a workforce that can support the high-level strategy?

- **Backfills.** Would your company benefit from a backfills plan? Through backfills, certain positions have someone waiting in the wings to fill in if needed—for example, if the incumbent unexpectedly leaves the company. If you do need a backfills plan, which positions will you designate for backup? And who will serve as the understudy for each of those positions?

- **Job rotations.** Can your company benefit by rotating certain individuals through various roles so that these employees acquire specific skills and knowledge? If so, who will be eligible for such rotations, and which positions will be involved? How will you post information for available positions?

- **Skills inventory.** What skills does your company's current workforce possess? What skills will it need in the future in order to make the corporate strategy succeed? Where are the gaps?

- **Metrics.** How will you determine the effectiveness of your workforce plan? Will you define metrics such as "Percentage of vacant positions filled within designated time frame," "Number of employees redeployed after first full year of program," "Ratio of contingent to traditional workers by quarter end"?

As you can see from the preceding list, workforce planning can encompass many other key areas in the HR function—particularly recruiting, retention, and development. Moreover, workforce planning clearly requires the ability to gather and analyze enormous quantities of information. Forecasting can prove especially challenging. If you don't have the time or resources to prepare your own forecasts, consider paying an outside consultant or information specialist to provide you with raw data and possibly their interpretations and analyses of the data if you need them.[4] And if other responsibilities prevent you from preparing a comprehensive workforce plan, a few key tactics can collectively serve as a "plan B." These include having a strong redeployment process that lets you move people from areas of lower strategic importance to business units or roles with higher priorities, setting aside a larger-than-normal contingency workforce, and requiring managers of key positions to designate someone in advance to take that position if it becomes vacant.[5]

For a closer look at a component of one company's workforce plan, see "HR in Action: Succession Planning at BP Amoco." The following guidelines can also help you develop a workforce plan for your own enterprise:

- **Link workforce planning to corporate strategy.**[6] In developing your workforce plan, always keep in mind the longer-term direction the company is striving to achieve through its corporate strategy. That way, you'll be more likely to ensure that members of the workforce have the skills, behaviors, and attitudes required to steer the company in the desired direction.

- **Balance short- and long-term needs.**[7] In addition to identifying the required workforce for your company's future and determining steps to create that workforce, you must assess your company's current workforce needs and make the changes necessary to meet them. Thus you continually conduct two gap analyses: one between your company's present workforce capability and present need, the other between its present capability and future needs.

- **Clarify the high-level strategic objectives your workforce plan will satisfy.** For example, will the workforce changes your

HR in Action: Succession Planning at BP Amoco

Succession planning is a vital component of many workforce plans. If companies lack bench strength, they'll be caught off guard when top performers vacate strategically important positions. Succession planning is often used to build up bench strength in a company's executive and managerial ranks, but it can also help with developing an organization's talent pool generally. Here's the succession plan that BP Amoco developed for its top positions.

BP Amoco takes succession planning very seriously and has created a disciplined system for guiding high-potential individuals into the top jobs in the organization. The supporting structure for this system is a set of development committees within each business. These committees link to HR committees within each business, which in turn link to the group-level HR function. Incumbent leaders and the HR leader for each committee draft succession plans according to their knowledge of direct reports and others. The committees then finalize the plans according to their personal knowledge of "high potentials."

Promising individuals are grouped according to their stage of development, rate of progression, and perceived ability to reach the top few jobs in the company. They're given development opportunities keyed to how many years in the future they'll likely qualify for a top job. For example, people who are fifteen to twenty years away from a top job acquire some cross-functional experience where they get a strategic overview of the business and deepen their understanding of their division's unique issues. Those who are ten to fifteen years away from a top job acquire international experience and gain cross-business exposure, as well as have people management and bottom-line responsibilities. Individuals five to ten years away from a top job attend international business school and leadership programs. For people only five years away from a top job, development becomes individually focused—and these individuals are expected to take a lead role in developing others.

By establishing a disciplined approach to succession planning, backed by a solid infrastructure and development process, BP Amoco laid the groundwork for ensuring that it has a reliable supply of leadership talent—even decades into the future.

SOURCE: Linda Holbeche, *Aligning Human Resources and Business Strategy* (Burlington, MA: Elsevier Butterworth-Heinemann, 2001), 281–284.

plan entails help your company carry out its strategy of reducing costs, entering new markets, improving product innovation,
transforming the organization's culture, or some other strategic
imperative?

- **Balance organizational and employee needs.**[8] In developing
  a workforce plan, remember that few companies today can
  merely put people in roles based solely on the organization's
  needs—as if the individuals involved were pieces on a chess
  board. These days, high-potential workers are more discrimi-
  nating about their career opportunities and less willing to let
  their employer move them around at will, with no regard for
  their interests or aspirations. In the sections of your workforce
  plan involving succession planning, recruitment, retention,
  definitions of new roles, redeployment, and so forth, consider
  whether your plan accommodates valued workers' career plans
  as well as meets your company's needs. If the two aren't aligned,
  you'll have a harder time implementing your workforce plan.

Recruiting and Selection

As a key element in most workforce plans, strategic recruiting initiatives play an important role in a company's ability to carry out its
competitive strategy. Especially in tight labor markets, the recruiting
strategies you use can determine whether your organization has the
talented employees it needs, when it needs them. But even when the
labor market is on the employers' side, competition among companies for employees can still prove stiff—especially over individuals who
possess highly specialized technical skills. Moreover, job candidates—
especially those from Generation X (under thirty years of age)—are
demanding more from potential employers than just a paycheck.
Many employees today want opportunities to sharpen their skills, enhance their marketability in the job market, balance family and community life with work life, and get involved in exciting projects led by
sharp, accomplished people.

To attract the best employees to your company, you may have to convince them that working in your organization will present them with all of these opportunities and more. Whether you recruit through newspaper ads, campus visits, employee referrals, search firms, the Internet, or some combination of these and other sources, always tie your recruiting initiatives to your company's strategy. That means first defining the implications of the strategy—such as how your company's needs will change, how much it will grow, what costs it is expecting, how much flexibility it will require to serve customers (for example, twenty-four-hour service), and how much change and innovation it will need to accommodate.[9] And it means assessing your current workforce and identifying gaps in skills and knowledge that can be filled only through recruiting new employees from outside.

To ensure that your recruiting and selection initiatives serve the company's competitive strategy, consider applying these guidelines:

- **Balance external recruiting with internal development.**[10] Don't view recruitment's purpose as only filling gaps in your workforce. Instead, use recruiting initiatives to bring into your organization the kinds of skills and experience that can't easily be built from within. Strike the right balance: overreliance on external recruiting can cause internal job candidates to leave in search of better promotion opportunities elsewhere. Overreliance on internal development can cause stagnation among the company's workforce. By clarifying the purpose behind a particular recruiting initiative, you boost your chances of generating the desired value. For instance, if you want to bring a fresh perspective into your workforce, recruiting external "change agents" who will challenge the status quo once they're hired may be the best strategy to suit this purpose.

- **Win technical experts.**[11] Individuals with highly specialized technical expertise often inspire the most intense competition among employers. To win these experts, first decide whether your company's needs justify the kinds of expense it takes to get top high-tech players. If so, you may need to offer hefty signing bonuses in addition to top-grade salaries; hire a search firm to entice desirable individuals away from competitors; and include flexible work arrangements, creative perks (such as computer giveaways, weekly car washes, and in-office massages).

- **Target desirable candidates.**[12] Ask key managers throughout your firm who the most desirable individuals are that are currently employed by other companies. By pre-identifying them, you can focus your time and resources on persuading a narrower group of high-potential players to come to work for your firm. Whenever new people start work at your company, ask them to recommend promising friends and colleagues from their former employer. Reward them for successful recruitment of top talent. In targeting any potential candidate, look especially for individuals whose departure from a rival company would severely hurt that competitor.

- **Hire before you need to.** Recruit people into key positions in your firm *before* the need for their talent becomes urgent. That way, you'll avoid the delays inherent in getting new hires up to speed—delays that can impede your company's ability to serve customers, get new offerings to market, and carry out other crucial activities.

- **Use recruiting to attract learners.** You want to recruit people who are open to continually learning and improving their skills. To that end, hold professional seminars and open houses at your company to get these potential candidates in the door—and get them excited about your organization. During these events, introduce them to high achievers who are currently working on intriguing, leading-edge projects in your company. Bring in outside experts who can deliver compelling presentations on your company's industry, products, or other aspect of the business.

The key point to remember in crafting recruiting strategies is that how you implement those strategies affects the quality of your workforce not only today but also tomorrow. Every job posting you publish in a newspaper or on the Internet, every conversation and meeting managers conduct with a candidate—all of these actions send a message to the labor pool about your company. Your company's recruiting practices communicate volumes about its culture, values, ethics, and standing in the industry. And everyone who receives those messages will pass along their impressions to their colleagues and friends—who will weigh the information while making their own career decisions. For many companies, well-crafted recruiting initiatives can strongly support a strategy that entails becoming an "employer of choice."

For a case study of one company that designed effective recruiting initiatives, see "HR in Action: Savvy Recruiting at Cisco."

HR in Action: Savvy Recruiting at Cisco

As the new millennium opened, Cisco Systems, which makes networks for the Internet, was hiring an average of more than one thousand new employees every three months—in Silicon Valley, one of the tightest job markets in the United States. Moreover, the company's employees were extolling Cisco's virtues as a great place to work—demonstrating a depth of loyalty unusual in an industry marked by high turnover rates. How has Cisco scored these admirable achievements? Its recruitment strategies have played a large role.

For one thing, Cisco uses creative means to find promising new hires. For instance, it holds focus groups with ideal recruitment targets—discerning where they spend their time and how they conduct their job hunting. Then the recruitment team sets out to find high-potential recruits—by infiltrating microbrewery festivals, arts fairs, and other places talented workers frequent.

The recruitment team also makes savvy use of technology. For example, the team relies heavily on the Internet to find high-potential job candidates—having learned that the most desirable candidates aren't looking through want ads. After post-ing Cisco's Web site in company ads, the team discovered that most of the hits on the site came during the workday. It deter-mined to make job hunting on company time easy, developing software that enabled people to rapidly profile themselves on Cisco's Web site—and replace the profile with a screen disguise if the boss walks by.

In addition, Cisco strategically uses employee referrals in its recruiting strategies. Soon after anyone who's surfing the com-pany's Web site clicks on the link "make friends @ Cisco," a Cisco employee contacts the person to describe life at the com-pany and refer him or her to a hiring manager. Every time a referral is hired, the Cisco employee gets a bonus of $500 to $1,000. Merely making a referral wins an employee prizes. The payoff? Referral rates at Cisco are double the industry norm.

Finally, Cisco's recruitment team works hard to get the message out about the company's appealing culture and core values. To attract talented new employees, the team touts Cisco's complement of employee-friendly services, such as on-site stores, dry-cleaning services, fitness centers, ATMs, oil changes for employees' cars, and mobile dental clinics for which people can make appointments through e-mail. The recruitment team also makes clear that the company values its employees highly: senior managers get cubicles in the center of the office space, while employees get the windows. And all offices are the same dimensions: 12 feet by 12 feet.

SOURCE: Charles A. O'Reilly III and Jeffrey Pfeffer, *Hidden Value: How Great Companies Achieve Extraordi-nary Results with Ordinary People* (Boston: Harvard Business School Press, 2000), 70–77.

Retention

Like recruitment, retention initiatives aimed at keeping valued em-ployees constitute a key element in any successful HR strategy. To carry out its corporate strategy, a company needs a stable, high-per-forming workforce. By developing ways to retain your company's best workers, you generate the following important benefits for the organization:[13]

- The longer effective workers stay in the company, the more time you have to make them feel valued and respected as individuals who can make a unique contribution to a clear, shared purpose. Your reward? The level of commitment required for employees to carry out their part of the high-level strategy.

- When people have worked together for a long period, they achieve operational efficiencies, generate more innovative ideas, and enhance their productivity.

- Retaining employees increases the workforce's stability—enabling people to form and cultivate positive, trust-based relationships with teammates, customers, suppliers, and supervisors.

But developing the right retention initiatives involves more than just trying to keep every employee for as long as possible. You need to adapt your initiatives to your industry, to job-role realities, and to labor-market trends. For example, in some industries—such as the nuclear power industry—specialized skills and deep familiarity with the business are essential. Thus it's vital to hold on to talented employees as much as possible. As far as labor-market trends are concerned, you would want to invest more in retention during a tight market (especially labor shortages for specialized skills) and possibly less when labor supplies are plentiful.

No company wants 100 percent retention: there will always be underperformers that an organization must weed out, and firms benefit from fresh ideas offered by newcomers. And of course, 0 percent retention is equally inappropriate, because constant turnover spawns damaging instability. Thus key questions to ask yourself in developing retention initiatives include these: What retention rates do we need to carry out our corporate strategy? What rates are appropriate for our industry, and for labor-market realities? What are the costs of letting turnover increase, and can we tolerate those costs?

Other changes in the business landscape are making developing the right retention strategies increasingly daunting for HR professionals. For example, more open markets, globalization, and skilled employees' greater awareness of their marketability and options have brought the notion of the lifetime employment contract into question. Today, it's simply unrealistic for any manager to expect to hang on to every valued worker indefinitely. In addition, brutal corporate restructurings that have resulted in massive layoffs have engendered mistrust in and skepticism about the "employment relationship" among many workers. While compensation is very important, today's savvy employees want more than a paycheck before they give their loyalty to a company: they want assurances that the company will help them sharpen their skills and their employability, as well as give them opportunities to do challenging, meaningful work that makes a difference. In a bitter irony for many organizations, the very talents that are most desirable in the workforce—the ability to get things done, innovate, serve customers, and so forth—are exactly the skills that most help people find jobs with rival companies.[14]

Any successful retention strategy must start with an understanding of why valued employees leave a company *and* why they stay. According to some experts, the main reason skilled workers leave is lack of challenge in their work. Other reasons include lack of appreciation and recognition, increased workloads, lack of work/life balance, slow pace of change, and intensifying office politics. Conversely, good people tend to stay if they have opportunities for personal achievement and challenge, variety in their work, autonomy, positive interpersonal relationships within teams, increasing influence on the company's strategic direction, and opportunities for significant personal development.[15]

With these realities in mind, consider the following ideas for designing the most effective retention initiatives—most of which you'll want to show hiring managers how to implement:[16]

- **Avoid overselling your organization while recruiting.** If, in order to attract a desirable new hire, you or a hiring manager tout career development opportunities that simply don't exist at your organization, you can't expect the new hire to remain long at your company.

- **Consider retention bonuses.** During mergers and other times of major organizational change, a "stay bonus" can help you keep key players in place—protecting the organization's stability and ensuring that your workforce has the skills needed to weather the change.

- **Help people clarify their development needs.** Career counseling and professional-development workshops can enable employees to clarify their long-term goals—in turn making it easier for you to design appropriate development opportunities.

- **Design variety and challenge into job roles.** The more opportunity people have to learn new skills, meet new people, and gain exposure to exciting ideas, the more likely they'll stay with your company. Job rotations, attendance at conferences, stretch assignments, and other opportunities can all help provide variety.

- **Support professional education.** Many companies have found that by supporting professional education—footing some or all of the tuition bill for an undergraduate or graduate degree or a technical certificate program—they encourage learning-minded employees to stay.

- **Create a sense of ownership in the company.** Stock options and other financial rewards, if appropriate for your company, can help cultivate a sense of personal ownership in the company among workers. When people see a direct link between their work and the company's financial performance—and the accompanying individual rewards—their commitment to the organization tends to intensify.

- **Foster affinity and fun.** Cultivate a lighthearted but professional atmosphere, especially during times of stress. You'll encourage a sense of teamwork and affinity among workers—the feeling that "we can get through this, and have fun doing it."

- **Coach managers.** For some people, their relationship with their boss is the primary reason they decide to stay with a company—or defect. Work with managers throughout your company to ensure that they're practicing all the important principles of good management: supporting their teams, developing their people, linking personal goals to company goals, recognizing and rewarding talent, inviting creative input from employees, and so forth.

In addition to the preceding suggestions, consider using these techniques:[17]

- **Practice prevention.** Rather than waiting for a turnover crisis, proactively determine which valued players are most at risk for leaving, and calculate their departure's impact on the organization. Target retention initiatives to at-risk groups. You can identify at-risk individuals by searching the Web for resumes posted by your company's employees, asking workers to identify who's looking for new jobs, and hiring an executive-search professional to tell you who the prime candidates are for poaching by other firms. Also, ask key employees why they stay—then reinforce the positives while eliminating anything that frustrates them. Hold "stay interviews" every six months for at-risk employees.

- **Block poaching by rival companies.** Use competitive intelligence to anticipate rival companies' moves. For example, if you learn that a competing firm is planning to move into a new line of business, you can bet that it'll be sniffing around other companies for needed talent. Put processes in place to make it difficult for rival organizations to lure away your firm's top talent—for example, by "rerecruiting" high performers with exciting new opportunities at your company.

- **Tailor recognition to employee needs.** Encourage managers to develop customized "appreciation" plans for each employee, depending on what people value most. Appreciation plans might involve plum assignments, opportunities to deliver presentations to important audiences, articles about an employee's achievements in the company newsletter, a chance to have lunch with the CEO, a handwritten note of thanks delivered personally, and so forth.

- **Learn from recruitment rejections and defectors.** Whenever a potential new hire turns down a job offer from your company, ask what led to the decision. The person's responses can generate a wealth of valuable comparative data on matters such as pay rates, development opportunities, cultural advantages, and other characteristics of rival companies. Likewise, six months after a key employee defects, conduct an exit interview to discern the reasons. Waiting a bit to hold the interview boosts your chances of getting a more candid response.

- **Get rid of deadwood.** Many people leave a company because they feel forced to work with mediocre performers who "drag down" their team and the organization overall and don't do their share of the hard work. By letting chronic underperformers go or redeploying them to parts of the company where they can make more of a contribution, you enhance the remaining team members' productivity, morale, and job satisfaction.

Clearly, retention raises numerous complex questions while also presenting a wealth of opportunities to design creative initiatives. See "HR in Action: Retaining Valued Workers at TopFlight Airways" for a case study of how one company used cultural transformation to boost retention *and* profitability.

HR in Action: Retaining Valued Workers at TopFlight Airways

How does TopFlight Airways (a pseudonym for a U.S. airline) do it? In one study of TopFlight Airways' reservation call centers, researchers learned that the company's call centers boast a turnover rate of just 3 percent—in an industry plagued by much higher rates. Call-center reps are staying at TopFlight Airways— even though they earn less than their counterparts at other airlines *and* have longer commutes.

What's going on? The company's retention initiatives have played a large role in this startling achievement. For example, Top-Flight Airways strives hard to make the company a fun place to work. Hallway posters claiming, "It wouldn't kill you to laugh,"

continued

and "Don't be afraid to laugh at yourself," send the message. The organization also cultivates a sense of ownership in its workforce by offering a profit-sharing plan. Employees literally own roughly 10 percent of the firm's stock. In addition, the company fosters affinity among its employees—going so far as to promote its employee couples on its Web site. People often cite the benefits package offered to workers—including free flights and flexible scheduling—as one reason they stay despite the below-average wages.

By designing smart retention strategies, TopFlight Airways has set a positive spiral in motion: when valued employees stay, they create a productive, stable company and a positive work culture that attracts additional job applicants. More and more employees relate their appreciation for the company to friends and family, creating a positive reputation in the community. This reputation attracts additional applicants, saving the company money on wages and recruiting. And thanks to low turnover, orientation and training costs have decreased—further enhancing profitability.

SOURCE: Jack J. Phillips, series ed., and Patricia Pulliam Phillips, ed., *Retaining Your Best Employees: Nine Case Studies from the Real World of Training* (Alexandria, VA: ASTD and SHRM, 2002), 135–150.

Compensation

The compensation initiatives you design exert a profound, widespread impact on behavior throughout your company—and strongly determine how successfully managers and employees deliver the performance needed to support the high-level strategy. For example, evidence suggests that as you increase the percentage of an employee's pay that is "at risk"—that changes depending on his or her productivity—performance increases.[18] Moreover, compensation sends a signal to the workforce about what the company values most. To illustrate, if you and other members of the executive team claim that you value teamwork, but your company rewards people for individual achievement, you're sending mixed messages about which behaviors and attitudes you want your workforce to demonstrate.

Compensation influences many other important HR initiatives as well. For example, the salary and bonus you name in a job offer to a desirable candidate will play a large role in whether the person decides to accept a job with your company—thus affecting your recruitment efforts. Likewise, pay raises influence your retention initiatives—as current employees consider their salary prospects while deciding whether to stay with your company or head for a competitor that's dangling an attractive offer in front of them.

Finally, designing effective compensation initiatives can become especially challenging during major change—for example, when two companies are merging or one is acquiring the other. In this case, the HR group must either join disparate payment plans into one program that fits the new entity or discard the original programs and create a new one. And of course, new and old employees in a merged organization will worry about what's going to happen with their pay, so HR must also develop and deliver an effective communications plan to inform and reassure them.[19]

In sum, your approach to compensation determines many different outcomes—including how well your company attracts, retains, and motivates its people to give their best; how effectively the workforce implements the organization's strategy; and how successfully other HR initiatives are carried out. To design appropriate compensation initiatives, consider these guidelines:[20]

- **Be flexible.** Don't assume that the compensation strategies your company has used in the past will work today or tomorrow. In today's dynamic economy—with extensive global and technological change and corresponding fluidity in corporate strategies— the "We've always done it that way" approach doesn't work. The most effective HR teams review their compensation strategies regularly—for example, every year—to ensure that they're appropriate for emerging business realities. Signs indicating the need for changes in your compensation policies include increasing employee turnover and inability to hire top job candidates.

- **Articulate your purpose.** Develop a compensation philosophy: a concise, clear statement that communicates what your company's compensation programs mean to achieve, what your company values most, and what pay elements (such as wage increases or bonuses) will be consistent across the company. Examples include "We pay competitive base salaries and we reward performance" and "We want to attract, motivate, and retain employees—our most critical resource." Communicate your compensation philosophy to the entire workforce so employees know that pay scales aren't arbitrary and that everyone is trying to adhere to a shared philosophy.

- **Consider size.** In small companies, it may be appropriate for the founder of the senior team to make personal decisions about individual pay, given their firsthand familiarity with their workforce. But in larger organizations, top executives have less familiarity with managers and employees—thus these companies must develop a fair, equitable program that can be administered efficiently. Such programs shield HR professionals from individual managers' pressuring them to customize compensation within their departments.

- **Inform yourself.** Stay up to date on industry compensation standards. Every time your company hires a new employee or has a job offer turned down by a desired candidate, find out what compensation these individuals were offered by other potential employers. Also ask recruiters and executive-search professionals what the market rates are.

- **Tie compensation to corporate strategy and culture.** Ask whether your compensation initiative serves the high-level competitive strategy your company has defined. For example, if the organization is entering new markets requiring highly specialized skills, does your initiative accommodate paying a premium for rare talent that rival companies are also trying to capture? If successful execution of the corporate strategy hinges on developing homegrown talent, does compensation support this goal? Likewise, ask whether your compensation initiatives will help foster the kind of culture—team-based? individual achievement? egalitarian?—your company needs in order to execute its strategy.

- **Get senior managers' input.** In designing a compensation initiative, collaborate closely with high-level management to ensure executives' buy-in and ensure that your initiative meshes with the company's strategic objectives. As an HR professional, you possess the most knowledge about labor markets, compensation survey tools, job design, and compensation-related legal issues. But without senior management's buy-in and input, you'll have difficulty winning approval for your ideas.

- **Look beyond pay.** Consider intangible as well as tangible (financial) compensation—such as perks, benefits, and quality of the work environment. Many not-for-profit organizations, which often can't offer high pay, stress the quality of life and robust benefits employees can gain by working for the enterprise—including generous retirement and vacation programs and a positive, collaborative work environment. If your company isn't in a position to offer high pay, define and communicate other forms of compensation that current and potential employees may value just as much—if not more than a hefty paycheck.

- **Coach managers on compensation.** Ensure that managers know how to handle compensation-related discussions with their employees. For instance, if your company has ranked jobs and their associated salaries differently according to the uniqueness of the talent involved, coach managers to explain to employees how this decision supports the company's need to obtain and grow the specific skills required to implement its strategy. The question "Why are some people paid more?" is always awkward—but the more managers can show a link between compensation strategies and corporate strategy, the greater the chance that all employees will understand and accept your firm's pay structure.

To learn how one HR professional developed effective compensation initiatives, see "HR in Action: New Compensation Schemes at Insteel Wire Products."

HR in Action: New Compensation Schemes at Insteel Wire Products

Rhonda Hiatt, HR manager at North Carolina–based Insteel Wire Products, Inc., had long wanted to emphasize pay for performance in her company's compensation initiatives. The long, hot summer of 1999 gave her an opportunity to win executive support for her ideas. That year, turnover in the company's manufacturing plants had soared (along with temperatures), while morale had eroded. Employees were complaining not only about the heat on the shop floor but also about the lack of pay increases—though salary surveys showed that the firm was already paying competitive rates.

Hiatt knew something had to change if Insteel hoped to reverse the exodus and restore morale. Hiatt proposed some ideas to the company's director of operations, who expressed interest. The two began collaborating with general managers from the plants, revising Hiatt's ideas as a result of their input.

Ultimately, Hiatt's plan called for fundamental changes not only in pay but also in work structure and training. For example, previously welders had operated a machine for an entire shift while being helped by two assistants. Under Hiatt's plan, all three employees had equal status in the pay hierarchy and took turns operating the machine. As a result, all three employees began earning similar pay. In addition, Hiatt's group revised Insteel's existing training manual and distributed it to all employees— informing them that they could earn more pay by mastering specific skill sets within designated time frames. Employees were given between one and three months to move up to a new skill level, which enabled them to earn more money, more quickly. They could earn even more by maintaining specified efficiency levels on their equipment or by taking courses that enabled them to train other employees. The optional levels rewarded those who wanted to move up but didn't penalize those who opted not to advance. Employees could even use achievement of these new skill levels as springboards into management.

These new initiatives paid off quickly—and dramatically. From 1999 to 2000, turnover at one of the company's plants plummeted from 34.3 percent to 20 percent. Morale also improved. According to Hiatt, the summer of 2000 was the first time she didn't hear employees clamoring for pay raises. Indeed, Hiatt's plan proved so successful that Insteel implemented it at several other facilities.

SOURCE: Patrick Mirza, "Mission Possible: Compensation Strategy Cooled Long, Hot Summers," *HR Magazine*, December 2000.

Training and Development

Training and development initiatives constitute additional core components of most HR strategies. Why? For one thing, the quality of the learning opportunities offered by a company is one major criterion people use when deciding whether to accept a job offer or stay with an employer. Today, high performers look for employers that can help them learn continually and thereby improve their skills and marketability. Moreover, in a fast-changing business world, it's vital that every manager and employee in a company continually learn so as to help the organization keep pace with and benefit from change. Yet a fast pace also makes it harder for people to find time to learn. (Witness the increasing number of employees claiming they're too busy to attend an on-site course or too exhausted by their mounting responsibilities to work through a degree program at night.) The fact that today's companies need workers to master a wide range of skills—in areas such as customer relations, leadership, and basic business literacy—only increases the importance of training and development.

For all these reasons, the training and development initiatives you develop must enable workers to acquire new knowledge and master new skills as rapidly and effectively as possible—and at a pace that keeps them stimulated and energized but not overwhelmed. Such initiatives must also take into account the reality of people's work lives—acknowledging their limited time outside of work and respecting their available energy.

In addition, training and development initiatives must be carefully geared to different levels in your organization. Clearly, executive- and leadership-development programs will look very different from training curricula designed to get employees up to speed on the latest technology adopted by the company. And different employees will have different skills-development needs—ranging from communication, people management, and strategic thinking to interpersonal skills, financial literacy, and business planning. Finally, different people learn best through different means—including taking courses, reading books, watching others, being coached or mentored, and using trial and error to master new skills. The most effective training and development initiatives take individual learning styles into account.

Given the many criteria your training and development initiatives must meet in order to generate the desired value, it's no surprise that designing such initiatives can pose a daunting challenge. Here's a selection of guidelines that can help you create effective initiatives:[21]

- **Tie training and development initiatives to corporate strategy.** For example, if your company's competitive strategy calls for raising quality standards, you shouldn't devote the greatest portion of your training budget to change-management training initiatives.

- **Consider company culture and values.** Does your company want to emphasize self-sufficiency in employees' learning, or do you view development as a partnership between your organization and its workforce?

- **Balance company, unit, and individual needs.** Though high-level company needs take priority in your design of training and development initiatives, such initiatives must also take unit- and individual-level needs into account. Company-level initiatives often focus on matters such as leadership, quality improvement, culture change, new-hire orientation, and so forth. Unit-level learning often emphasizes job-related training. And individual-level learning often seeks to help people master new skills that will enable them to progress toward their desired professional future.

- **Invite managerial input.** As always, it's valuable to invite input from other executives and managers in designing your training and development programs. These individuals can shed light on which specific skills and knowledge the company needs its workforce to acquire, which parts of the organization need what type of development, and how learning opportunities can best be provided (for example, through on-site workshops, one-on-one tutoring, and self-paced study).

- **Leverage online learning.** Emerging technologies in online learning have presented HR professionals with valuable new opportunities to design effective training and development initiatives. For example, self-paced learning modules can provide just-in-time training to new managers seeking guidance on various aspects of their role—such as hiring and firing, giving a performance review, coaching, and building a business plan. Many companies are using online training resources in a blended learning environment—whereby classroom or workshop facilitators help them complete an online module and develop plans for applying their learning on the job.

For a case study of how one company created valuable training and development initiatives that dovetailed with an effort to retain star performers, see "HR in Action: Developing High Flyers at Chesterton Finance."

Every HR initiative—no matter which key area it covers—entails a complex array of tasks. To implement such initiatives successfully, you need to organize the tasks involved, as well as track progress once implementation begins. See the appendix for two worksheets—work breakdown structure (figure A-2) and project progress report (figure A-3)—that can help.

HR in Action: Developing High Flyers at Chesterton Finance

Chesterton Finance had to make some tough decisions. Owing to poor business performance, the financial-services firm had put a freeze on promotions and required executives and managers to justify every penny spent. The company's HR team, in partnership with several business heads, argued that the company was at risk of losing some of its best employees unless it could offer them development opportunities. The key challenge lay in deciding where to focus the limited resources available for such an initiative.

The HR team decided to use a selection of leadership competencies it had defined to serve as the content of a series of development workshops for high flyers at risk of defecting. The desired outcomes of the initiative were leadership-development plans created by each participant and his or her manager.

To ensure that the resulting plans were relevant, managers helped participants identify their learning objectives before the workshops started. The HR team briefed the managers ahead of time to make sure they understood their role in the initiative. The team also provided managers with tools (such as 360-degree feedback surveys) to help them prioritize objectives with their employees. In defining learning objectives, each participant had to prepare responses to questions such as, "If I were to learn how to deal more effectively with X leadership challenge, how would the company, my team, and I benefit?" and "How will I know that I'm making progress toward X objective?"

After the workshops, participants met with their managers and developed an action plan for building on their learning. The HR team then followed up with the participants over the next eighteen months—at three- and six-month intervals. The thought and care that went into this initiative paid big dividends. First, the workshops made participants feel valued by the company and thereby boosted morale during a difficult time in the organization. Second, participants' enhanced leadership skills translated into bottom-line results. For example, one learner explained that, thanks to the workshops, he was leading his team more effectively. Though market conditions were as tough as ever, his team had outperformed all other comparable teams within a year of the workshops—producing millions of dollars' worth of extra sales revenue.

SOURCE: Adapted from Linda Holbeche, *Aligning Human Resources and Business Strategy* (Burlington, MA: Elsevier Butterworth-Heinemann, 2001), 192–193.

Evaluating an HR Initiative's Strategic Impact

Regardless of the array of initiatives you develop for your HR strategy, the rest of the executive team will likely call on you to explain—in concrete, measurable terms—how strongly those initiatives will support the corporate strategy. To assess an HR initiative's potential for exerting a strategic impact, you can use informal methods as well as more formal approaches based on metrics. Let's explore the informal methods first.

Some experts maintain that an HR initiative with strong strategic potential has distinctive characteristics. Specifically, such initiatives:[22]

- Have been developed to meet the company's future needs.

- Have goals defined in business terms—such as "Raise revenues 5 percent," "Accelerate time to market 10 percent," or "Reduce customer complaints 3 percent."

- Are "owned" by the head of HR—meaning that he or she has assumed total accountability for producing the results promised by the initiative, even though HR doesn't have total control over the resources affecting the initiative's success.

- Intend to deliver results that will be felt outside of HR—such as in several business units, and by customers and other stakeholders.

- Have the attention of the CEO and other top executives.

- Are mentioned in the company's annual report or the CEO's annual report of his or her accomplishments.

- Prompt regular meetings between HR and non-HR executives.

- Prompt senior managers outside of HR to want regular progress reports.

- Would noticeably affect total corporate revenue or profit if discontinued.

- Have been benchmarked by competing companies.

- Promise to give the organization a distinct competitive advantage.

Though not every strategic HR initiative will meet all of these criteria, those that meet at least 75 percent of them will likely exert sufficient strategic impact. As you might imagine, strategic HR initiatives look different from nonstrategic initiatives. Table 11-1 shows several examples.

In addition to informal methods of assessing an HR initiative's strategic potential, metrics can provide valuable insight. Metrics (also known as measures) enable you to communicate the business results your initiative is intended to achieve, as well as determine whether you've achieved the desired results. Effective metrics meet several specific criteria:[23]

- They state what your initiative seeks to achieve—for example, "Reduce turnover by year end."

- They specify the time in which the desired results will be achieved.

- They compare the intended result with a benchmark number (such as last year's turnover, or a competing company's turnover).

- They use clear language that everyone understands.

TABLE 11-1

Strategic versus nonstrategic HR initiatives

Initiative type	Strategic approach	Nonstrategic approach
Recruiting	Identifying the best sources of candidates to improve new hires' on-the-job performance	Reducing hiring costs by using cheaper but lower-quality sources—resulting in below-average on-the-job performance
Interviewing	Comparing candidates' interview "scores" to their on-the-job performance and retention rate after hiring, to see how well interviews predict performance	Attending interviews, asking good questions, and providing the standard types of information about your company to candidates during interviewing
Training	Adding new training programs that generate measurable improvements in on-the-job performance after employees participate	Offering a standard array of training classes each year because they are popular and well attended
Retention	Alerting managers ahead of time that specific employees are likely to quit, and explaining how to use tools to retain them	Tracking turnover rates in each manager's group and reporting your findings to managers
Compensation	Educating managers on how to use compensation tools that directly affect their employees' productivity	Suggesting that managers give across-the-board raises even if no evidence ties raises to productivity or retention

Source: John Sullivan, *Rethinking Strategic HR: HR's Role in Building a Performance Culture* (Chicago: CCH, 2004), 313.

- They state a target expressed in some measurable form—such as "100 percent of deadlines met in the first quarter of next year," "A 30 percent reduction in time to market by end of fiscal year," "Doubling of total revenue within three years," or "20 percent improvement in employee satisfaction and morale by year end as measured by survey responses."

Well-developed metrics offer numerous benefits. For one thing, they reduce the likelihood of confusion about what an initiative is after. They also help you focus on high-priority actions—as suggested by the maxim "What gets measured, gets managed." In addition, metrics make it relatively easy to gather feedback on how your initiative is performing once you've launched it. You can use that feedback to make midcourse corrections to keep your initiative on track. Finally, using metrics demonstrates that you're comfortable with the language of numbers and data—often a key criterion for earning credibility as a knowledgeable businessperson.[24]

In selecting metrics for your HR initiatives, you have a bewildering array of possibilities to choose from. Table 11-2 shows some examples of metrics you might select for various types of initiatives. The key goal in defining metrics is to ensure that they meet the criteria described earlier—and that you can explicate the connection between your metrics and your company's strategic goals. For example, "By reducing turnover, we increase employees' knowledge and familiarity with customers—which in turn enables employees to better serve customers. Happy customers buy more from us and tell

TABLE 11-2

Examples of HR initiatives metrics

Initiative type	Examples of metrics
Workforce planning	• Number of vacancies in specifically ranked positions • Percentage of positions that have a designated backfill • Line manager satisfaction with employees' level of skills
Recruiting	• Time to hire • Number of vacant positions filled by external candidates • Percentage of new hires referred by current employees
Retention	• Turnover rate per department, business unit, and division • Employee satisfaction as measured by survey responses • Number of stay interviews conducted
Compensation	• Total bonuses earned by individual contributors • Percent pay increase within executive ranks • Ratio of guaranteed and at-risk compensation
Training and development	• Percentage of workshop participants who pass the end-of-course text • Percentage of employees who have created development plans reflecting their manager's input • Number of leadership course attendees who report at least a 3 percent increase in team productivity post-course

Source: John Sullivan, *Rethinking Strategic HR: HR's Role in Building a Performance Culture* (Chicago, CCH, 2004), 208–210.

others about our company—thus they're more profitable to serve, and they reduce the cost of acquiring new customers." If you can't trace the cause-and-effect links between a particular HR metric and a high-level strategic objective, that's a reliable sign that you may have chosen the wrong metric—or that your initiative may not have a strong enough potential strategic impact.

One metrics-based methodology for assessing HR initiatives' strategic potential comes from a framework known as the Balanced Scorecard. (See chapter 12 for more information on this methodology.) HR experts Brian Becker, Mark Huselid, and Dave Ulrich have adapted the Balanced Scorecard framework to the human resources profession—showing how to define HR goals, metrics, and initiatives specifically to align with high-level corporate strategy.

Summing Up

In this chapter, you learned that:

- HR initiatives represent where the "rubber" of your HR strategy meets the "road"—they're the programs, policies, and projects you launch to put your HR strategy into action.

- HR initiatives focus on various areas. In this chapter, we covered workforce planning, recruiting, retention, compensation, and training and development.

- A workforce planning initiative is an overarching HR effort that can include recruiting and retention, along with other elements such as succession planning, leadership development, and contingency workforce strategies.

- No matter what focus an HR initiative has, it's vital that the initiative clearly support high-level strategic goals.

- There are several ways to gauge an HR initiative's potential impact on the corporate strategy. Some HR professionals use informal assessment methods—such as determining whether an initiative is future focused, is defined in business terms, and has the attention of top executives.

- HR professionals can also use metrics to evaluate an initiative's possible impact on corporate strategy. A well-crafted metric fulfills specific criteria (such as stating the results an initiative intends to achieve and stating a target—a desired specific level of achievement). The HR scorecard, based on the Balanced Scorecard performance management methodology, is one metrics-based approach.

Leveraging Chapter Insights: Critical Questions

- List one or two strategic initiatives you've defined for workforce planning, recruiting, retention, compensation, and training and development.

- For each initiative, how clearly do the intended outcomes support the corporate strategy? What changes might you make to strengthen the alignment between your initiatives and the high-level strategy?

- Examine the metrics you've chosen to assess progress on each initiative. How well do your metrics fulfill the criteria for effectiveness described in this chapter? What changes might make your metrics more effective?

- For what additional HR areas—besides those covered in this chapter—have you developed strategic initiatives? Evaluate these initiatives' strategic potential using the same criteria discussed in this chapter.

CHAPTER TWELVE

Strategy as Work in Progress

Keep Looking Ahead

Key Topics Covered in This Chapter

- *Why HR executives must evaluate strategy effectiveness*

- *Using financial ratios, the Balanced Scorecard, and market analysis to measure strategy effectiveness*

- *Warning signs of strategy peril*

- *Leading strategic change*

I F YOU CREATE a winning HR strategy and implement it well, you might cruise along for years without problems. But no strategy—whether corporate- or unit-level—remains effective forever. Something in the external environment eventually changes, rendering the strategy ineffective or unprofitable. It is difficult to think of an industry in which this has not happened. As Clayton Christensen reminded readers of the *Harvard Business Review* several years ago:

> It is sobering to review yesterday's list of great corporate strategies: Ford's mass production of standard automobiles; General Motors' adoption of vertical integration and design of cars tailored to the preferences of customers in each tier of the market; Xerox's strategy of selling copies rather than copiers; and Sears's sales of reliable, reasonably priced merchandise through stores located in growing suburbs. Guided by brilliant strategies, these companies rose to prominence. Yet when conditions in their competitive environments changed, each found it extraordinarily difficult to change strategic direction.[1]

Unfortunately, all too many executive teams are unable (or unwilling) to recognize when their strategies have become less potent—if not obsolete. Owing to myopia or hubris, they fail to understand how the external environment is changing and do not come to grips with that change by altering their strategy. Strategy re-creation, then, is an ongoing requirement of good management. To quote Michael Porter, it is "a process of perceiving new positions that woo customers from established positions or draw new customers into the market."[2]

This chapter explains how you and the rest of your executive team can assess the effectiveness of your company's current strategy and recognize warning signs that the strategy is losing its power. The temporary nature of successful strategy should caution every leader to continually scan the external environment for new threats and emerging opportunities, and to reassess their company's and unit's strengths and weaknesses, as described earlier in this book. What you learn through that scanning should inform your thinking about whether it's time to alter or replace your current strategy.

As we've made clear throughout this volume, you can help your executive team conduct a SWOT analysis and revise the corporate strategy—as well as conduct similar processes to continually revise your HR strategy.

How Well Is Your Strategy Working?

The strategy model presented in the introduction to this book (figure I-1) indicated feedback loops from the performance measurement piece of the model back to the very beginning of the strategy creation process. Measurement tells leaders how well their strategy and its implementation are working. Substandard measures should spur them to look once again at the external environment for emerging threats and opportunities and to their internal environment for existing capabilities and weak areas. This section profiles three ways to assess how well a corporate or HR strategy is performing: financial analysis, the Balanced Scorecard, and market analysis.

Financial Analysis

The proof of a strategy's power or weakness is ultimately reflected in a company's financial statements: particularly its balance sheet and income statement. The balance sheet describes the assets owned by the business and ways in which those assets are financed—with the funds of creditors (liabilities) and the equity of owners. The income statement (sometimes referred to as the profit-and-loss statement) indicates the cumulative results of operations over a specified period. (See *The Essentials of Finance and Budgeting* volume in this series for more information on these and other financial statements.) By comparing these results from one year to the next, you can gauge the effectiveness of both your company's strategy and its implementation through operations—though separating the two is often difficult.

Consider the case of Parker & Smith, a furniture manufacturer whose multiperiod income statement is represented in table 12-1. In this statement, the company's retail sales demonstrate steady growth even as Parker & Smith has held its operating expenses in check. Something is going well here. The company's corporate sales, however, are flagging from one year to the next. If corporate sales are an important piece of this business's strategy, then something is going wrong—either with the strategy or its execution. This piece of quantitative information should prompt Parker & Smith's executives to look closely at the problem.

TABLE 12-1

Parker & Smith multiperiod income statement

	2005	2004	2003	2002
Retail sales	$2,200,000	$2,000,000	$1,720,000	$1,500,000
Corporate sales	$1,000,000	$1,000,000	$1,100,000	$1,200,000
Total sales revenue	$3,200,000	$3,000,000	$2,820,000	$2,700,000
Less cost of goods sold	$1,600,000	$1,550,000	$1,400,000	$1,300,000
Gross profit	$1,600,000	$1,450,000	$1,420,000	$1,400,000
Less operating expenses	$800,000	$810,000	$812,000	$805,000
Depreciation expense	$42,500	$44,500	$45,500	$42,500
Earnings before interest and taxes (EBIT)	$757,500	$595,500	$562,500	$552,500
Less interest expense	$110,000	$110,000	$150,000	$150,000
Earnings before income tax	$647,500	$485,500	$412,500	$402,500
Less income tax	$300,000	$194,200	$165,000	$161,000
Net income	$347,500	$291,300	$247,500	$241,500

Source: HMM Finance.

Managers can also gain insights into the effectiveness of the company's strategy by examining the ratios of key figures drawn from the enterprise's balance sheet and income statement. Ratios help an analyst or a decision maker piece together a story about an organization's original position, its current condition, and its possible future. In most cases, the story told by these ratios is incomplete, but it's a start. Consider these ratios.

Profitability Ratios

Profitability ratios associate the amount of income earned with the resources used to generate that income. Barring ineptness in operational implementation, the firm's strategy should produce as much profit as possible from a given amount of resources. The profitability ratios to remember are return on assets (ROA), return on equity (ROE), return on investment (ROI), and operating margin (or earnings before interest and taxes, EBIT).

Return on assets relates net income to the company's total asset base and is figured as follows:

ROA = net income / total assets

For example, Parker & Smith's ROA for 2005 would be $347,500 (net income, from the company's income statement) divided by $3,635,000 (total assets, from the company's balance sheet)—which is .09, or 9 percent. The higher the percent, the greater the indication that the corporate strategy is effective. ROA relates net income to the investment of all the financial resources under management's command. It is a useful measure of effective resource utilization without regard to how those resources were obtained or financed—which shouldn't be considered in an examination of a strategy's effectiveness.

Return on equity relates net income to the financial resources invested by shareholders. It is a measure of how efficiently company leaders have leveraged shareholders' stake in the business—providing further clues to the strategy's effectiveness. ROE is calculated as follows:

ROE = net income / shareholders' equity

For example, Parker & Smith's ROE for 2005 would be $347,500 (net income, from the income statement) divided by $1,885,000 (shareholders' equity, from the balance sheet), which is .18, or 18 percent. Again, the higher the percent, the more likely the company's strategy is paying off.

The term *return on investment* is often used in business discussions that involve profitability. For example, expressions like "We aim for an ROI of 12 percent" are common. Unfortunately, there is no standard definition of ROI, since "investment" may be construed from many perspectives. Investment might represent the assets committed to a particular activity, the shareholders' equity involved, or invested assets minus any liabilities generated by a company's taking on a major strategic initiative. ROI might also refer to the internal rate of return, a very specific calculation of return. So, when someone uses the term *return on investment, always* request a clarification. Ask, "How are you calculating 'investment'?"

Many executives use the earnings-before-interest-and-taxes margin (EBIT margin), more generally known as the *operating margin,* to gauge the profitability of a company's operating activities. The operating margin ignores the interest expenses and taxes over which current management may have no control, thus giving a clearer indicator of leaders' performance. To calculate the operating margin, use this formula:

Operating margin = EBIT / net sales

For example, Parker & Smith's operating margin for 2005 would be $757,500 (EBIT, from the income statement) divided by $3,000,000 (net sales, also from the income statement), which is .25, or 25 percent. As with the other ratios, a larger percent suggests the possibility that the company's strategy is performing well.

None of these ratios is a sure or only indicator of a strategy's strength or weakness, because each reflects both the strategy *and* its execution. And as we've seen, a strategy can be perfectly sound—but if it's not executed skillfully, it won't generate value for the company. Nevertheless, ratios that are weaker than those of peer companies, or ratios that are growing weaker from one year to the next, should set off alarm bells in the executive suite and encourage senior management to investigate the causes. Is it the strategy that has flaws, or is the strategy being poorly executed?

The Balanced Scorecard

Financial ratios tell the tale of business performance, and generations of businesspeople have tried to manage using them. But financial ratios aren't buttons we can push to make things happen—instead, they represent the outcomes of dozens of other activities. Thus they are lagging, or backward looking: they show the results of past efforts. Worse, traditional measures can send the wrong signals. For instance, profit measures that look very good this year may be the result of dramatic cuts in new-product development and reductions in employee training. On the surface, current high profitability can make today's state of affairs look rosy, but cuts in project development and training may jeopardize tomorrow's profits. Nor do lagging measures directly assess organizational assets such as customer satisfaction and organizational learning, which improve profitability in the long run.

Frustrated by the inadequacies of traditional performance measurement systems, some managers have shifted their focus to the operational activities that produce financial results. These managers follow the motto "Make operational improvements, and the performance numbers will follow." But which improvements are the most important? Which are the true drivers of long-term, bottom-line performance? To answer these questions, Harvard Business School professor Robert Kaplan and his associate David Norton conducted research on a number of companies with leading-edge measures of performance. From this research, they developed what they called the *Balanced Scorecard*, a performance measurement system that gives top managers a more comprehensive view of their business. The Kaplan/ Norton scorecard methodology includes financial measures that indicate the results of past actions. And it complements those financial measures with three sets of operational measures that relate directly to customer satisfaction, internal processes, and the organization's ability to learn and improve—assets that drive future financial performance. In this sense, the scorecard assesses both the company's strategy and its operational implementation.

FIGURE 12-1

The Balanced Scorecard links performance measures

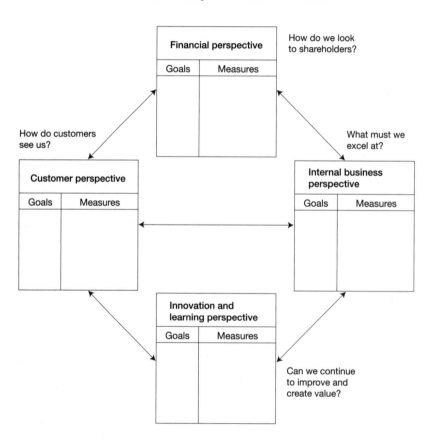

Source: Robert S. Kaplan and David P. Norton, "The Balanced Scorecard," *Harvard Business Review*, January–February 1992, 72.

Kaplan and Norton have compared the Balanced Scorecard to the dials and indicators in an airplane cockpit:

For the complex task of navigating and flying an airplane, pilots need detailed information about many aspects of the flight. They need information on fuel, air speed, altitude, bearing, destination, and other indicators that summarize the current and predicted environment. Reliance on one instrument can be fatal. Similarly, the complexity of managing an organization today requires that managers be able to view performance in several areas simultaneously.[3]

Kaplan and Norton's framework uses four scorecard "perspectives" to link performance measures and galvanize managerial action. Collectively, these perspectives give top management timely answers to four key questions:

- How do customers see us? (The customer perspective)

- What must we do to excel? (The internal perspective)

- Can we continue to improve and create value? (The innovation and learning perspective)

- How do we look to our shareholders? (The financial perspective)

Figure 12-1 indicates the linkages between the four perspectives. The advantage of the Balanced Scorecard over traditional measures is that three of the four perspectives (customer, internal, innovation/learning) provide more than just results—they act as levers that managers can manipulate to improve future results. For example, if the company isn't meeting the target customer-satisfaction scores it has defined in the customer perspective of its scorecard, management has a fairly clear idea where to intervene. Used together, the Balanced Scorecard and traditional ratio analysis can help managers understand the effectiveness of their strategy *and* identify areas where implementation needs work. Moreover, the scorecard can help each unit and function in a company define, implement, and monitor a strategy that directly supports the high-level strategy. In many companies that use this methodology, each unit (and sometimes each team and individual) develops its own scorecard containing goals and targets related to corporate-level strategic objectives. See "The HR Scorecard" to learn more about how the Balanced Scorecard methodology relates to the human resource function.

The HR Scorecard

Like the Balanced Scorecard, an HR scorecard contains four perspectives, each of which has corresponding strategic objectives, measures, and targets:

- **Financial.** This perspective might contain objectives such as "Maximize shareholder value" (as measured by metrics such as "Total shareholder return" or "Revenue per employee") and "Maximize human capital performance" (as measured by metrics such as "Total HR cost per employee" and "HR return on investment").

- **Customer.** This perspective may comprise objectives such as "Provide responsive quality service to employees" (as measured by metrics including "Employee-satisfaction survey results" and "Benefit center–satisfaction percentage").

- **Internal processes.** This perspective might contain objectives such as "Ensure a strategy-focused workforce" (as measured by metrics such as "% productivity-improvement goals established" and "% compensation schemes aligned to strategy").

- **Learning and growth.** This perspective may comprise objectives such as "Build strategic competencies" (as measured by metrics including "Leadership-development participation" and "Critical skill attainment").

There are two key points to keep in mind about the HR scorecard. First, it provides a balanced picture of how well your HR department's strategy (as expressed by the objectives, initiatives, and metrics you've established) supports the corporate strategy. *Balanced* in this sense means that your HR scorecard shows how you will make changes in your workforce's capabilities (learning and growth), your operations (internal processes), and your service to your customers in order to generate the strategy-related financial changes your company desires. Thus the scorecard encourages you to think about how you'll "pull" each of these four important "levers" to effect strategic change.

Second, the scorecard is balanced in the sense that it encourages you to define both lagging and leading indicators. Consider the metric "Number of participants in leadership-development program." This is a leading indicator because participation in leadership-development programs will exert a significant impact on your company's future bench strength. The best HR strategies contain a mix of lagging and leading indicators.

SOURCE: Brian E. Becker, Mark A. Huselid, and Dave Ulrich, *The HR Scorecard: Linking People, Strategy, and Performance* (Boston: Harvard Business School Press, 2001), 74.

Market Analysis

Not too many years ago, executives at a major publisher of college textbooks seemed pleased with the company's results. Revenue from sales was going up year after year, faster than expenses. There seemed to be plenty of bonus money to go around—to shareholders, company managers, and the sales force. Only two disturbing facts intruded on this happy picture. First, the company's unit sales had remained flat for three years in a row. Revenue growth had stemmed from price increases, a tactic that surely could not work forever. Second, revenues depended heavily on the continued vitality of five books. Although the publisher actively promoted 180 current titles, five of them accounted for a whopping 38 percent of the company's total revenue. And each of these products had been in the market for over fifteen years. Not one of the many other books this publisher had introduced during that fifteen-year period had come close to establishing a strong position in the market.

On the surface, this publisher's strategy appeared to be working. But market analysis revealed that the company was simply treading water—going nowhere and being kept afloat by a handful of aging products. Although the sales force was earning annual bonuses for regularly hitting its expanding revenue quotas, it was making no gains in the marketplace. And though the publisher's editors were developing and releasing new books every year, the company was living off past successes.

Clearly, this company needed to look at its strategy and operations and identify what was going wrong.

Market analysis is a big subject, but you can capture many of its benefits if you focus your attention on just a few activities:

- **Customer acquisition.** Is your company succeeding at acquiring new customers at an acceptable cost?

- **Customer profitability.** Are your organization's current customers profitable to serve? Some companies focus solely on the number of new customers or new accounts they corral—even though many of those customers are a drag on profits. (For example, these customers buy only low-price items and demand lots of expensive service.)

- **Customer retention.** Is your enterprise retaining its most valuable customers at a reasonable cost?

- **New products/services.** Are the firm's new offerings, whether products or services, successful and profitable?

- **Market share.** Is your company gaining or losing share in markets that matter?

Negative answers to any questions on this short list should encourage you and other executives to reexamine your company's current competitive strategy.

Warning Signs

Strategic problems seldom appear overnight. But often some early warning signs reveal that something is going awry. This section describes two of those signs and suggests ways you and other executives can respond.

The Appearance of New Competitors

Every successful and profitable strategy creates an unwelcome problem: it attracts competitors like bees to flowers. Unless hurdles are placed in new players' paths, the market will eventually become crowded, and competition and overcapacity will erode profits for everyone. Some new entrants to a market may bring something different and superior to consumers—for example, their product or service is more convenient to purchase.

Consider the example of the video rental stores that still populate many towns and urban neighborhoods. When movies were first made available on VHS cassettes (and Sony's "Beta" format), entrepreneurs set up rental shops to serve local markets. And many did very well. This was a fairly easy business to enter, requiring little in the way of technical know-how or capital. When the initial vendors' profitability became evident, other aspiring entrepreneurs flocked to the market, driving down prices and cutting back sales for almost all players. Eventually, in the United States, the market for videos was taken over by big national chains such as Blockbuster and Hollywood Video. These operators had advantages of scale that small, local competitors couldn't match. Result? Many of the original entrepreneurs went out of business.

The profitability of the big video rental chains, in turn, has attracted innovative competitors. These rivals use pay-per-view, downloadable movies, and postal-based rentals to claim shares of this market.

If your business is successful, that's because it provides something unique that customers value—or it sells or delivers its product or service in a manner they value (faster or more convenient). These qualities differentiate your company and give it a competitive advantage. But if new entrants begin emulating your company's strategy, the competitive advantage of that differentiation disappears.

Now ask yourself, "How easily can other companies copy the unique qualities of our company or its products?" If they can do so easily, be prepared to share the market with them and many others.

Market invasion by imitators is commonplace, and few market leaders can bar the door completely. Consider the case of Apple Computer and its popular iPod digital music player. Apple introduced the iPod in November 2001. It was not the first such device to be offered, but its design qualities and ability to store up to one thousand songs quickly made it a big success—the biggest for Apple since its Macintosh line of computers. The company sought to protect itself from direct imitators by developing a patented design and by farming out pieces of the iPod's manufacture to a mix of suppliers operating under nondisclosure agreements. As of this writing, Apple still has a major chunk of the market and is maintaining it through new releases of improved models. However, this tactic has not stopped other vendors, including formidable ones such as Hewlett-Packard, Dell, Sony, and Samsung, from muscling into the market and carving out sizable pieces for themselves.

How can your company defend its market share from invasion by would-be rivals? Many executives use these tactics:

1. **Deliberately erect barriers to entry.** For example, a fast-food restaurant owner in a small town might buy up the pieces of real estate most attractive to a potential rival.

2. **Don't maximize profits.** If you are the market leader, seek market-share dominance over profit maximization. This may sound like heresy, but it often makes sense. By establishing a pricing structure that produces only modest profits, you'll attract fewer competitors to your market.

3. **Exploit the *experience curve* to establish yourself as the low-cost leader.** This is particularly important in technology industries. If you can learn sooner and faster than competitors, you'll maintain a cost advantage. And that advantage may prove large enough to discourage competitors from horning in on the business.

If none of these antidotes is feasible, your organization must alter its strategy in a way that differentiates your offering to customers and gives the company a competitive advantage.

The Appearance of a New Technology

The fates of many businesses hinge on the technologies they use to create and distribute their products and manage their operations. Just as those technologies account for an organization's success, the eclipse of those technologies results in its failure. For example, during the nineteenth century, harvesting ice from lakes and ponds was a huge and profitable business, particularly in New England. Ice harvested in the Boston area was packed by the Tucker Ice Company and its emulators into specially insulated vessels and shipped to Gulf Coast cities, England, and as far away as India and China. It was a wonderfully profitable business—until mechanical refrigeration technology was developed and disseminated around the world. Because of that innovation, the fortunes of the big ice companies gradually melted away.

The rise of digital photography provides a more current example. Ever since the late 1830s, imaging depended on technology involving the exposure of light to a film or a glass plate coated with photosensitive chemicals. That technology improved over the years. Kodak built an empire on chemical-based photography and dramatically advanced the field—producing film, processing chemicals, and photographic paper for both the amateur and professional markets. The company also marketed cameras for consumers.

The first substantial threat to chemical-based photography emerged in the early 1980s when Sony, an electronics company, introduced a camera using digital technology. The rapid rise of digital photography—which makes the use of film, chemicals, and most papers obsolete—directly threatened Kodak and its manufacturing infrastructure. Worse, Kodak lacked superior competencies in digital imaging, at least initially. The universe of competitors also shifted dramatically. Kodak's main rival was no longer Fuji Film. Rather, the explosive rise of digital imaging forced the company into competition with Nikon, Canon, Leica, and other established camera makers. Even electronics firms such as Sony and Hewlett-Packard jumped into the game. By mid-2004, digital cameras had penetrated 40 percent of U.S. households, and industry analysts were predicting another two years of rapid growth. Given this situation, Kodak had to drastically shift its competitive strategy. To its credit, the company faced up to the new business realities and channeled its strategic resources into digital technology. Only time will reveal how it will fare in the long run.

Situations like Kodak's are common when new technologies turn existing markets on their heads. Business leaders must spot those disruptions in their very early stages and reformulate their strategies accordingly. When they spot them, they cannot bury their heads in the sand.

When faced with a new and disruptive technology, all too many executives feel compelled to invest still further in the technologies that made their companies successful in the first place. For additional historical examples, consider the time when steamships challenged makers of sailing ships, when Thomas Edison's electric lighting systems challenged the gas illumination companies in the late 1800s, and when jet engines challenged piston-driven aircraft engines in the late 1940s. In each case, the companies threatened by these innovations continued to invest in and marginally improve their mature technologies even as the new ones were becoming better and cheaper by the month.

The only antidotes to the invasion of new technologies are the following:

1. **Anticipate them.** New, strategy-wrecking technologies do not appear fully formed. They emerge slowly, often from different sources. In their formative periods, they reveal themselves in scientific papers and are discussed at technical conferences. An alert company—one that continually scans the external environment—can often detect these new technologies long before they have become serious threats. This early detection gives the company time to adapt or get on board. How might your company anticipate emerging technologies? Develop policies that open the windows of your organization to the outer world: sending R&D and marketing personnel to technical conferences, setting up a scanning unit to review technical literature, and so forth.

2. **Imagine "killing" your company.** Ask this question: "What could destroy our business?" Create a team of your company's brightest people and give them the job of developing a business strategy capable of penetrating your organization's markets and stealing its current customers.

Leading Strategic Change

John Maynard Keynes, the famous British economist, was being pestered by a reporter. Why, the reporter asked, had Keynes recommended a shift from his former policy position? "When the facts change, I change my mind," he told the reporter. "What do you do, sir?" Leaders need to be as nimble in their thinking as Lord Keynes.

Holding fast to policies and strategies we've endorsed and supported for years is almost always easier than admitting that it's time to move on to something new. Consider the tragic case of U.S. president Lyndon Johnson, who committed American forces to years of bloody warfare in South Vietnam. Johnson's plan to defeat communist guerrillas and invading forces from the north were based on an untested "domino theory." If South Vietnam fell to the communists, according to that theory, all of Southeast Asia would likewise fall. As would the Philippines, and Japan, and who knows what else. As the toll on U.S. personnel and the nation's treasury mounted and support for the war withered, Johnson stubbornly stayed the course. He clung to his policy despite substantial personal anguish and doubts— and despite growing evidence that the war was going badly. Through the worst of it, his administration told the public that "there is light at the end of the tunnel."

The fact that political and business leaders cling too long to strategies that have failed to achieve their objectives or that have outlived their usefulness should not surprise us. Our culture honors being persistent, pressing forward in the face of adversity, and staying the course when more timid folk are ready to give up. But sometimes, there is no light at the end of the tunnel, and shifting course is the wiser and braver course. That takes real leadership, which is a lot different from simply presiding over the status quo.

As an HR professional, you can—and must—play a vital part in leading strategic change. For one thing, you can demonstrate that you have your own strategic "house" in order by regularly conducting SWOT analyses to identify HR's threats and opportunities as well as strengths and weaknesses—and adjusting your HR strategy accordingly. By making HR a leading example of effective strategic change, you champion larger-scale strategic change in your organization.[4]

Some experts also maintain that to lead strategic change successfully, HR professionals must play four roles:[5]

- **Scout.** Continually assess the business landscape and your company's internal capabilities and weaknesses to identify potential threats and opportunities and determine ways to overcome threats and seize advantage of opportunities. In particular, take stock of your organization's strengths and weaknesses related to people, processes, organizational structure, and technology. Identify the talent your firm will need in the future to support its strategy, and take steps to recruit or develop that talent. Look for change champions throughout your organization who can help develop and drive a new strategy.

- **Chess master.** Determine who the key strategic players are in your organization—those individuals who have the power to define and implement strategy. Decide how best to influence these change champions as well as the executives, managers, and employees in your organization. Develop and deliver communications to support change champions' efforts to lead strategic change. Deploy human resources in ways that support change efforts. And develop strategies for managing stakeholder concerns.

- **Cartographer.** Provide executives and managers with a road map to help them navigate toward strategic change. Educate them on the tools and techniques available to conduct restructuring efforts, mergers, acquisitions, divestitures, and other large-scale strategic-change initiatives. Facilitate two-way communication between leaders and employees about major change efforts, and ensure that everyone understands both the challenges and the benefits offered by a newly defined strategy that must be implemented.

- **Architect.** Considering the strategic changes your company might need to make in order to remain competitive, ask yourself whether you need to alter the following systems and processes for managing workforce performance: performance management methodologies, jobs or job classification systems, organizational structure, compensation and incentive systems, informal recognition systems, and executive- and manager-level training and development programs.

Playing these four roles requires specific attitudes (such as the willingness to open yourself to new business realities) and behaviors (including the ability to take the initiative and apply your powers of influence to effect strategic change). By understanding these roles and their associated attitudes and behaviors, you can equip yourself to partner with other executives and managers in your organization and champion the strategic changes your company must make to leave rivals scrambling.

Summing Up

In this chapter, you learned that:

- Even the most successful strategies do not last forever. Be alert to signals that it's time to rethink or recalibrate your current corporate or HR strategy.

- Financial analysis, the Balanced Scorecard, and market analysis can help you determine how well your strategy and its implementation are working.

- Profitability ratios—particularly return on assets, return on equity, and operating margin—are valuable indicators of the effectiveness of a company's strategy and its implementation.

- The weakness of traditional profitability ratios is that they are backward looking. In addition, these ratios do not directly measure things such as customer satisfaction and organizational learning, which improve profitability in the long run. Many executives find the Balanced Scorecard approach to be a superior methodology for assessing company performance.

- The Balanced Scorecard rates a company on four dimensions: the customer perspective, internal operations, innovation and learning, and financial performance.

- Market analysis should, at a minimum, examine company performance with respect to customer acquisition, customer profitability, customer retention, the success of new products and services, and market share.

- Warning signs that it's time to reexamine your strategy include the appearance of new competitors and the emergence of a new technology.

Leveraging Chapter Insights: Critical Questions

- Review your company's latest income statement and balance sheet. Use the figures on these documents to calculate your company's return on assets, return on equity, and operating margin. What do the resulting figures suggest about the effectiveness of your company's competitive strategy and its implementation?

- Does your company use the Balanced Scorecard methodology? If so, what are the major strategic objectives defined in the corporate-level scorecard's four perspectives (financial, customer, internal process, and innovation and learning)? How well is your company meeting the targets it has defined for each strategic objective? What seem to be the weak areas, and what might your company do to address them?

- Assess the criteria used to conduct a market analysis for your company: customer acquisition, customer profitability, customer retention, the success of new products and services, and market share. What do the results of your assessment suggest about the success of your company's strategy and its implementation?

- In your view, is it time for your company to change its strategy? If so, why? (Do your profitability ratios, Balanced Scorecard results, and market analysis suggest the need for change? Are new competitors cropping up? Are disruptive new technologies emerging?) What steps can you help your organization take so that it can begin shifting course?

CHAPTER THIRTEEN

Developing and Leveraging Your Strategic Mind-set

Next Steps for You and Your HR Department

Key Topics Covered in This Chapter

- *Why it's vital to cultivate a strategic mind-set in HR*

- *How to assess whether you are strategy oriented*

- *How to strengthen your ability to think strategically*

- *How to gauge your HR department's strategic mind-set*

WHEN YOU DEVELOP a strategic mind-set—
aligning HR programs, policies, and practices to
your company's competitive strategy—you gen-
erate important benefits for your organization, your HR department,
and yourself. In this chapter, we'll explore these benefits in greater
detail and discuss ways to assess your ability to think strategically—
and your HR department's ability to support high-level strategy.
We'll also lay out steps you can take to become a more strategic HR
professional and provide a tool you can use to improve your HR department's strategic capability.

The Advantages of a Strategic Mind-set in HR

Why take the time to cultivate a strategic orientation? When you do
so, you help your company achieve its high-level objectives—resulting in rising profits, expanding market share, and more loyal employees and customers. You also ensure that your HR department builds
the credibility and capabilities it needs to get the resources required
to carry out its part of the corporate strategy. According to some
experts, a strategic mind-set enables you to:[1]

- **Drive organizational effectiveness and business strategy.**
  Many key determinants of a company's competitive advantage

depend on effective human capital management. Now more than ever, your company's ability to compete hinges on its power to manage knowledge, change, and capability building—all of which fall under HR's purview. By understanding and communicating the human capital implications of high-level strategic objectives, you help the rest of your executive team formulate a sound competitive strategy.

- **Design valuable systems and practices.** Informed by your company's strategy, you can develop the systems and practices needed to ensure that your organization's employees have the right competencies and motivation to help implement the strategy.

- **Encourage line managers' ownership of strategy.** As you develop systems and practices to support your company's strategy, you involve line managers in the process—thus building their sense of ownership in those systems and practices. The greater their sense of ownership, the more effectively and enthusiastically they can implement the strategic HR practices you've developed.

- **Measure the effectiveness of your HR strategy.** As you develop HR strategies—and define initiatives to support them—you build in metrics for assessing the effectiveness of those strategies and initiatives. Thus you can get the continuous feedback you need to make midcourse corrections and improve your strategies.

- **Help your organization implement strategy.** By enabling your organization to attract, retain, develop, deploy, and motivate the right employees, you help ensure that the company's various units can carry out their part of the corporate strategy—whether it's launching the right brand campaign, adopting a better IT system, serving customers in radical new ways, or some other activity that supports the high-level strategy.

The ultimate payoff for developing a strategic mind-set for your company? Since strategy is all about adapting to and even benefiting from change, having a strategic focus positions you to help your company engineer the changes required to seize advantage of new opportunities, vanquish threats, and leave rivals scrambling.

Finally, a strategic orientation goes a long way toward helping you build a professional reputation as a business partner in your organization. When you demonstrate that you understand corporate strategy and HR's role in supporting it, the other members of your executive team look increasingly to you to provide creative human capital solutions to the company's challenges. One expert defined the individual benefits of thinking strategically as follows:[2]

- Greater job security

- Widespread perception that you're a high-potential player in the organization

- Increased exposure to cross-functional assignments and learning opportunities

- Greater access to resources and budgets

- More opportunities to win promotions

- A less stressful work life, because being strategy minded means anticipating and preparing for surprises

- Visibility to influential higher-ups

How to determine whether you have a strategic mind-set? See assessment tool 13-1 for a checklist that can help you answer this question.

Assessment Tool 13-1
How Strategic Are You?

For each statement below, indicate whether you agree or disagree. Then interpret your score, using the instructions below.

1. I seek to exert a broad impact across my company's business units and regions with the HR strategies I develop.

   Agree   Disagree

2. In developing HR policies, practices, and programs, I focus on my company's future needs.

   Agree   Disagree

3. I create HR systems and initiatives with an eye toward sharpening my organization's competitive advantage.

   Agree   Disagree

4. The HR strategies and programs I develop have the potential to boost my company's revenues or profits.

   Agree   Disagree

5. I can trace a direct link between my HR programs and high-level company objectives.

   Agree   Disagree

6. I regularly participate in strategic planning sessions with other members of the executive team.

   Agree   Disagree

7. I understand how HR systems affect implementation of my company's strategy.

   Agree   Disagree

continued

8. I understand the cultural changes that need to occur in my organization before our competitive strategy can be implemented.

Agree   Disagree

9. I regularly assess the threats and opportunities facing my company, as well as the organization's internal strengths and weaknesses.

Agree   Disagree

10. I regularly assess the threats and opportunities facing my HR department, as well as the department's internal strengths and weaknesses.

Agree   Disagree

11. I get input from business-unit leaders and line managers while developing HR strategies and initiatives.

Agree   Disagree

12. I understand what each part of the organization must do to carry out its part of the corporate strategy, and I know which HR practices and initiatives will help them.

Agree   Disagree

13. In every strategy-related HR initiative I develop, I include a system for measuring the initiative's effectiveness and improving the initiative as needed.

Agree   Disagree

14. I understand how to lead major change initiatives in my organization.

Agree   Disagree

15. I help communicate my company's high-level strategy across the organization's units and down through the ranks.

Agree   Disagree

16. I understand the various types of high-level strategies that companies can develop, and I'm familiar with the unique challenges and opportunities presented by each type.

Agree   Disagree

17. I understand the impact of my company's strategy on our products or services, our bottom line, and our customers and other stakeholders.

Agree   Disagree

Total:

Interpreting your score

If the total number of your "Agree" responses is 14 to 17, you have a strong strategic mind-set. If the total is 1 to 13, you can benefit by strengthening your strategic mind-set. Look again at each statement for which you checked "Disagree." What actions might you take to put yourself in a position to agree with that statement? The following section, "Sharpening Your Strategic Focus," provides additional guidelines.

SOURCES: John Sullivan, *Rethinking Strategic HR: HR's Role in Building a Performance Culture* (Chicago: CCH, 2004), 10; and William J. Rothwell, Robert K. Prescott, and Maria W. Taylor, *Strategic Human Resource Leader: How to Prepare Your Organization for the Six Key Trends Shaping the Future* (Palo Alto, CA: Davies-Black Publishing, 1998).

Sharpening Your Strategic Focus

Strengthening your strategic mind-set is an ongoing process of striving to think and act in new ways. The key thing to keep in mind is that strategic thinking means continually comparing your contributions against your company's major strategic objectives. In other words, you constantly "think like a CEO"—focusing your time and other resources ever more tightly on activities that directly affect those objectives.[3]

One way to develop more of a strategic orientation is to view your HR department as a potential profit center. Indeed, under the leadership of a strategy-minded human resources executive, the HR function has an opportunity to become even more strategically prominent than other business functions. Why? In most companies, people expenditures can reach as high as 60 percent of all variable costs. Thus making your organization's people management practices more effective is likely to exert a positive impact on profits.[4]

When you view your HR department as a potential profit center, you can learn a lot from leaders of other so-called overhead functions—such as logistics and supply chain, marketing or branding, and IT—who have begun aligning their functions' activities with the corporate strategy. By talking with them, you may well discover that, in order to be effective, strategic thinking and acting must permeate a function and an organization. That is, everyone must constantly be aware of the corporate strategy and the ways in which they can support it, and everyone must focus their resources on those activities that exert the most impact on high-level strategy.[5]

In some cases, you can enhance your strategic focus by looking at key facts and trends through a new, more strategic "lens." You can use the resulting perspective to identify the root causes of a performance problem, craft creative solutions, and determine the dollar impact of failing to act. See "HR in Action: From Tactical to Strategic Thinking" for an example.

Experts offer these additional guidelines for enhancing your strategic orientation:[6]

- **Make your organization your priority.** Put your organization's strategic objectives before your department's goals or your personal agenda. With every decision you make, ask yourself whether you're basing that choice on what's best for your company. And whenever you present a proposal, explain how the organization will benefit from implementing your suggestion.

HR in Action: From Tactical to Strategic Thinking

Martha Bowen, an HR manager at Kelleher Associates, had just finished poring over the latest turnover figures for her company when her boss, HR director Janice Kohl, dropped by.

"How's it going, Martha?" Janice asked.

"Fine," Martha responded. "But I'm not sure what to make of these turnover figures. Twenty percent overall—it doesn't tell us much. But when I compare it to the industry average—ten percent—and Callahan Industries, our biggest competitor's rate—seven percent—it looks like we're doing relatively poorly."

"I'd have to agree," Janice said. "What about the voluntary versus involuntary breakdown?"

"Well, for us, turnover is all voluntary," Martha answered, flipping through the report. "Callahan has a five percent involuntary. That means we're not terminating a single employee for cause. Either we've got one hundred percent sterling employees—highly unlikely—or we're not managing performance very well. If Callahan is dropping its deadwood, they're sure to have an edge over us."

"You're right about that," Janice said. "Let's take a closer look at who's leaving us."

"All right." Martha turned to another document. "Everyone who left last year came from a key position or was a top performer. And five percent of those were our best salespeople. Replacing each one is costing us a million dollars a year."

continued

"Combine that with the cost of ramp-up time for new hires . . . ," Janice added.

"And we're talking a loss of fifteen million dollars per year in lowered productivity," Martha finished. "And that doesn't even count the fifty million a year we lost when key accounts left us after their rep defected."

"At least we're not undercounting the cost of turnover," Janice said. "But we do need to get to the root cause of these defections."

"Right," said Martha. "I'll pull together the list of defectors from last year and review their exit interviews to see if I can find a common theme about why they left. If necessary, I'll contact them by phone to get more information."

Within the following weeks, Martha discovered that the main reason top performers had left the company was that they felt they had a poor manager. She had to make a few phone calls to former employees, because several exit-interview files indicated the departing employees had been a bit guarded about their reason for leaving. But on the phone, having logged several months in their new jobs, they proved much more forthcoming. In particular, they complained that their managers at Kelleher had done little to help them identify stretch goals and improve their skills. "Most of us are very achievement oriented," one former high-performing sales rep told Martha. "We get a lot of satisfaction out of raising the bar, and we want bosses who will help us get there."

Martha met with Janice to discuss her findings. "For some reason, we didn't transfer, correct, or terminate these managers—even though their people rated them as weak in their annual assessment process," she told Janice.

"Let's look farther back in our records to find out what happened when we did terminate poor managers," Janice said.

"I knew you'd suggest that," Martha grinned. "And I've got the information. Brace yourself: when we have let a weak manager go, the increased productivity his group generated was *twice* the costs associated with the termination."

"We're going to have to be a lot more proactive about this," Janice noted. "Especially in light of the company's new emphasis on cutting costs and raising productivity."

"Well, we learned a lot from this experience," Martha said. "Let's start practicing prevention instead of just reacting to the numbers. I'll take a look at our manager assessment surveys, to see if we're measuring the right performance criteria."

"And I'll examine our termination policies to find out where we went wrong in failing to remove ineffective managers," Janice added. "We'll also need to look more closely at our professional-development programs, to ensure that we're meeting our best employees' development needs."

Martha's and Janice's effort to think and act more strategically soon paid off. The following year, Kelleher Associates saw a 10 percent drop in its voluntary turnover rate—and a 3 percent rise in involuntary turnover in the managerial ranks. Productivity soared in several units across the company—boosting Kelleher's bottom line 9 percent.

SOURCE: Adapted from John Sullivan, *Rethinking Strategic HR: HR's Role in Building a Performance Culture* (Chicago: CCH, 2004), 16–18.

- **Broaden your view.** Learn as much as you can about your company and the industry in which it operates. If you can, spend time with other executives from a wide range of functions—finance, marketing, operations, and so forth—to find out what their main challenges and concerns are. Become involved in task forces, committees, and cross-functional teams to broaden your perspective beyond HR.

- **Speak the language of numbers.** Provide tangible evidence—in terms of concrete data, facts, and numbers—to back up your strategic proposals. For every new policy, program, or initiative you develop, show how the effort will affect the company's bottom line. Learn to speak the same language of finance that other members of the executive team use.

The following practices can help you further develop your strategic thinking abilities:[7]

- **Use "reverse strategic thinking."** Understand your company's desired outcomes first, then evaluate several possible routes to achieving those outcomes. This practice will help ensure that you select the best possible HR programs and initiatives—not just the first one that occurs to you.

- **Participate in other units' strategic planning.** By taking part in other units' and functions' strategic planning meetings, you gain further insight into how the different parts of your company must work together to support the competitive strategy. You also gather valuable information that can help you develop more effective HR strategies.

- **Sharpen your emotional effectiveness.** To think and act strategically, you need to be willing to take risks, do things differently, and make—and learn from—mistakes. If you find all of this daunting or intimidating, take steps to beef up your emotional resilience: learn to take action despite fear, join a professional association or support group if that's helpful, or develop a relationship with a capable coach who can help guide you. There's nothing wrong with feeling anxious or uncertain about becoming more strategic—everyone else in leadership positions feel the same way. The key is to act thoughtfully and decisively *despite* these emotions.

How Strategic Is Your HR Department?

It's not enough for an HR executive or individual HR professionals within a human resource department to cultivate a strategic mind-set. The HR function overall must also be set up and positioned correctly within the organization to support implementation of the company's competitive strategy. Otherwise, even the highest-quality strategic HR initiatives and ideas won't likely see the light of day. How strategic is *your* HR department—that is, how much of an impact does it exert on corporate strategy? According to some experts, an HR function is strategic if it meets the following criteria:[8]

1. **HR improves employees' productivity**—through programs and services that boost workforce performance in ways that enhance the company's revenues and profits. HR can also show the dollar impact of increased worker productivity.

2. **HR focuses on meeting additional high-level business objectives besides workforce productivity**—such as product quality, customer service, and process efficiency. HR continually adds, cuts back, or eliminates HR programs according to their impact on these corporate-level objectives.

3. **HR leverages tools to improve company performance**—such as differentiation of rewards, penalties for hoarding best-practice information, and prioritization of profitable customers and services.

4. **HR uses metrics to make fact-based decisions**—with an eye toward continually measuring and improving the business impact of HR strategies and initiatives. HR also uses metrics to

proactively identify the company's potential threats and opportunities and generate ideas for leveraging its strengths and addressing its weaknesses.

5. **HR is future focused**—forecasting and anticipating changes in the business environment so HR strategies and initiatives can be adapted in time.

6. **HR makes a coordinated effort**—ensuring that its programs and staff coordinate their efforts to create desired results quickly and to garner the highest internal-customer satisfaction.

7. **HR has a global approach**—ensuring that its programs, policies, and practices have the right impact not only on headquarters but also on the company's global locations.

8. **HR builds a brand**—earning a reputation for the company for being "a great place to work."

9. **HR leverages technology**—using it to develop the right metrics, fact-based decision making, workforce self-service, and globally efficient processes.

How does your human resource department stack up against the preceding criteria for strategic HR? Do you need to make some changes to increase your department's strategic impact? If so, you're not alone: every strategic HR department is a work in progress—as executives work continually to improve. To generate ideas for improving your HR department's strategic capability, try your hand at assessment tool 13-2.

Assessment Tool 13-2
Enhancing Your HR Department's Strategic Impact

Use this worksheet to generate ideas for improving your HR department's ability to help formulate and implement corporate strategy.

Part I: SWOT analysis

1. How regularly does your HR team look beyond your company to identify emerging threats and opportunities? Consider external factors such as workstyle and lifestyle trends, changes in customer preferences, price sensitivity and elasticity of demand, competing companies' moves, and technological change.

2. What steps might you take to improve your team's ability to regularly assess external threats and opportunities? Will you provide opportunities to attend industry conferences? To subscribe to relevant trade journals? To regularly meet with leaders from other units to gain their input?

3. How regularly does your HR team take stock of your company's internal strengths and weaknesses? Consider the company's core competencies (such as innovating, serving customers, and achieving unprecedented operational efficiencies). Also consider your company's financial

continued

strength, the quality of its culture, and the effectiveness of the managerial team.

4. How regularly does your HR team assess your department's internal strengths and weaknesses? Consider the ability to leverage technology, to serve internal customers, to be cost-effective, and other strengths.

5. What might you do to encourage your team to assess internal strengths and weaknesses more regularly? Will you put together an assessment team, made up of individuals from HR and other parts of the company, to use structured brainstorming to identify strengths and weaknesses?

Part II: Types of strategy and strategic moves

6. What type of competitive strategy has your company defined, based on your and other executives' SWOT analyses? Consider low-cost leadership, differentiation, customer relationship, and network effect strategies—as well as combinations of these.

7. What are the corporate strategy's implications for your HR department? For example, what skills and knowledge will your company's workforce need to possess in order to carry out the corporate strategy? What might be the best recruiting sources? How important will employee retention be? What new positions and job responsibilities might need to be defined?

8. What "moves" is your company making to put its competitive strategy into action? For instance, is it trying to gain a market beachhead? Enter a new market through process innovation? Apply "judo strategy"? Differentiate its products from those of competitors? Create and then dominate an entirely new market? Acquire needed capabilities by buying businesses or technologies?

Part III: Aligning HR with corporate strategy

9. How well positioned is your company to carry out the strategy and competitive moves your company has selected? For example, are the right people in the right jobs, and do they have the right skills, knowledge, and attitudes? Do all your company's activities (such as its customer service processes, its use of technology, and so forth) support the strategy? Is your company structured in a way that enables implementation of the high-level strategy—such as rapid communication up and down as well as across parts of the company? Does the company culture and leadership style support the strategy—for

continued

instance, people feel comfortable making mistakes while innovating, and leaders are adept at eliciting creativity from their direct reports?

10. Which HR programs, policies, and practices should your team add, cut, or revise in order to support implementation of the corporate strategy? Your response constitutes your HR strategy. Consider initiatives centering on workforce planning, recruiting, retention, compensation, training and development, and other key HR areas.

11. Is your HR department structured to support implementation of the HR strategy you've defined? For example, do you need a call-center, self-service, e-HR, or some other structure?

12. If your HR department isn't structured effectively to support strategy implementation, what changes do you need to make to align structure? Do you need to adopt a new technology? Centralize or decentralize some HR processes? Make some other changes?

13. How will you make a compelling case for the HR strategy you've defined? Will you use data and statistics to show the potential impact of your strategy on the company's bottom line? Will you anticipate other executives' questions and concerns and prepare responses to them before presenting your proposed strategy?

Part IV: Executing your HR strategy

14. How will you develop an action plan for executing your HR strategy? What goals will you define? What metrics will you select to measure the performance of your plan? What steps will need to be taken to carry out the plan? What resources will you need to carry out the plan? What interlocks—help you need from other units and owe to other units—do you need to accommodate? What financial impact do you expect your plan to have, if carried out as you wish?

15. How will you ensure that the plan for your HR strategy stays on course? Consider progress reviews, informal checks, and contingency plans for addressing the more common causes of implementation failures.

16. How will you ensure that you have the right people working on implementing your HR strategy—and that

continued

you're keeping them motivated? Are you celebrating milestones? Communicating relentlessly about the importance of the plan? Demonstrating your own commitment to the plan through your actions as well as words?

17. What are the most important HR initiatives in your strategic plan? Are they related to workforce planning, recruiting, retention, compensation, training and development, or some other key HR area?

18. How are you evaluating the strategic impact of each initiative? For example, are you regularly monitoring actual performance against the targeted performance you've established for each initiative? And are you using that feedback to make prompt midcourse corrections?

19. What tools are you using to gauge how well your overall HR strategy is working? Do you use an HR scorecard? Are you alert to early-warning signs of strategy derailment? Are you able to lead change efforts if necessary to ensure successful implementation of your strategy?

Summing Up

In this chapter, you learned the following:

- A strategic mind-set in HR offers important benefits on many levels—such as greater profitability for your company, access to needed resources for your HR department, and personal advantages such as more opportunities for career advancement and lower levels of on-the-job stress.

- There are many ways to strengthen your strategic mind-set—including learning from leaders of other strategy-minded support units, educating yourself about your company's key challenges and goals, and gaining a cross-functional perspective of your organization.

- A strategic mind-set isn't enough; you also have to ensure that your HR department is set up to exert a strategic impact. Strategic HR departments have distinctive characteristics—including being future focused, providing their companies with a competitive advantage, leveraging technology, and making fact-based decisions using metrics.

Leveraging Chapter Insights: Critical Questions

- As a result of what you've learned in this chapter, how strong would you say your strategic mind-set is? The strategic mind-set of the rest of your HR team?

- What actions might you take to strengthen your strategic mind-set and that of others on your team?

- Which of the nine criteria for being strategic does your HR department meet? On which criteria does your department fall short?

- What steps might you take to ensure that your HR department meets all nine criteria for exerting a significant strategic impact?

Useful Implementation Tools

The following worksheets are adapted from Harvard ManageMentor®, an online product of Harvard Business School Publishing.

FIGURE A-1

Worksheet for conducting a SWOT analysis

Date of analysis: _____	
What is being analyzed: **e.g., new product development** _____	
Internal analysis *List factors inherent to what is being analyzed.*	
Strengths	**Ideas for building on these strengths**
Weaknesses	**Ideas for reducing these weaknesses**
External analysis *List factors external to what is being analyzed, such as customer needs or marketplace trends.*	
Opportunities	**Ideas for investigating or taking advantage of these opportunities**
Threats	**Ideas for minimizing or overcoming these threats**

Source: Harvard ManageMentor® on Implementing Strategy, adapted with permission.

FIGURE A-2

Work breakdown structure

Develop a work breakdown structure (WBS) to ensure that you do not overlook a significant part of a complex activity or underestimate the time and money needed to complete the work. Use multiple pages as needed.

Describe the overall project:

Major task	Level 1 subtasks	Level 2 subtasks	Level 2 subtask duration

Total duration (hours/weeks/days)

Major task	Level 1 subtasks	Level 2 subtasks	Level 2 subtask duration

Total duration (hours/weeks/days)

Source: Harvard ManageMentor® on Project Management, adapted with permission.

FIGURE A-3

Project progress report

Use this form to help assess progress, present this information to others, and think through next steps.

Project:	Prepared by:
For the period from:	To:

Current status			
Key milestones for this period:			
Achieved (list)		Coming up next (list)	
Key issues or problems:			
Resolved (list)		Need to be resolved (list)	
Key decisions:			
Made (list)	Need to be made (list)	By whom	When
Budget status:			

Implications
List changes in objectives, timeline/delivery dates, project scope, and resource allocation (including people and financial).

Next steps		
List the specific action steps that will be done to help move this project forward successfully. Put a name and date next to each step if possible.		
Step	Person responsible	Date
Comments:		

Source: Harvard ManageMentor® on Project Management, adapted with permission.

Notes

Introduction

1. Carl von Clausewitz, *On War*, vol. 1 (London: Kegan Paul), 177.

2. Edward Mead Earle, ed., *Makers of Modern Strategy* (Princeton, NJ: Princeton University Press, 1943).

3. Michael E. Porter, *Competitive Strategy: Techniques for Analyzing Industries and Competitors* (New York: Free Press, 1980), xxiv.

4. Bruce Henderson, "The Origin of Strategy," *Harvard Business Review*, November–December 1989.

5. Michael E. Porter, "What Is Strategy?" *Harvard Business Review*, November–December 1996, 61–78.

6. Robert J. Grossman, "Must See (People Assets) Inside!" *HR Magazine*, September 2004.

7. Joan Magretta, "Why Business Models Matter," *Harvard Business Review*, May 2002, 86–92.

8. John Sullivan, *Rethinking Strategic HR: HR's Role in Building a Performance Culture* (Chicago: CCH, 2004), 25–28.

9. Ibid., 5–8.

Chapter 1

1. Tony Grundy and Laura Brown, *Value-Based Human Resource Strategy: Developing Your Consultancy Role* (Burlington, MA: Elsevier Butterworth-Heinemann, 2003), chapters 1 and 2.

2. Linda Holbeche, *Aligning Human Resources and Business Strategy* (Burlington, MA: Elsevier Butterworth-Heinemann, 2001), chapter 1.

3. John Sullivan, *Rethinking Strategic HR: HR's Role in Building a Performance Culture* (Chicago: CCH, 2004), 26–28.

4. Holbeche, *Aligning Human Resources and Business Strategy*, 15–17.

5. Wayne Brockbank and Dave Ulrich, *Competencies for the New HR* (Alexandria, VA: SHRM; Ann Arbor, MI: Michigan Business School; and Scottsdale, AZ: Global Consulting Alliance, 2003), chapter 7.

Chapter 2

1. Michael E. Porter, *Competitive Strategy: Techniques for Analyzing Industries and Competitors* (New York: Free Press, 1980), 3.

2. George Day and David J. Reibstein, *Wharton on Dynamic Competitive Strategy* (New York: John Wiley & Sons, Inc., 1997), 23.

3. Michael E. Porter, "How Competitive Forces Shape Strategy," *Harvard Business Review*, March–April 1979, 141.

Chapter 3

1. *The Essentials of Managing Change and Transition* (Boston: Harvard Business School Press, 2005), 42–47.

2. James Surowiecki, *The Wisdom of Crowds* (New York: Doubleday, 2004), xvii.

3. The nine steps are adapted from the Implementing Strategy module of Harvard ManageMentor, an online product of Harvard Business School Publishing.

4. Paul Kearns, *HR Strategy: Business Focused, Individually Centred* (Burlington, MA: Butterworth-Heinemann, 2003), 35–48.

Chapter 4

1. David Bovet and Joseph Martha, *Value Nets* (New York: John Wiley & Sons, Inc., 2000), 30.

2. For more on USAA, see Tom Teal, "Service Comes First: An Interview with USAA's Robert F. McDermott," *Harvard Business Review*, September–October 1991, 116–127.

3. Forrester Research, news release, June 10, 2004, accessed at http://biz.yahoo.com/bw/040610/105021_1.html.

4. Michael E. Porter, "What Is Strategy?" *Harvard Business Review*, November–December 1996, 61–78.

5. The first three entries in this list are adapted from Charles R. Greer, *Strategic Human Resource Management: A General Managerial Approach*, 2nd ed. (Upper Saddle River, NJ: Prentice-Hall, 2001), 136–142.

6. Ibid., 143–144.

Chapter 5

1. Carl von Clausewitz, *On War*, vol. 1 (London: Kegan Paul).

2. David B. Yoffie and Mary Kwak, *Judo Strategy: Turning Your Competitors' Strength to Your Advantage* (Boston: Harvard Business School Press, 2001), 3.

3. Ibid., 23–24.

4. Ibid., 59–60.

5. Ibid., 14.

6. Jim Collins, "The Merger Mystery: Why Companies Cannot Buy Their Way to Greatness," *Time*, November 29, 2004, x.

7. Ibid.

Chapter 6

1. For the complete story, see David Bovey and Joseph Martha, *Value Nets* (New York: John Wiley & Sons, Inc., 2000), 169–182; and "Value Chain Report: Herman Miller Reinvests for Success," *Industry Week Value Chain*, December 12, 2000, http://www.iwvaluechain.com/Columns/columns.asp?/ColumnId-720>.

2. Jeffrey Pfeffer, *The Human Equation* (Boston: Harvard Business School Press, 1998), xvi.

3. Dwight Gertz and Joao Baptista, *Grow to Be Great* (New York: Free Press, 1995), 154–155.

4. David J. Collis and Cynthia A. Montgomery, "Creating Corporate Advantage," *Harvard Business Review*, May–June 1998, 70–83.

5. Michael E. Porter, "What Is Strategy?" *Harvard Business Review*, November–December 1996, 70.

6. Ibid., 73.

7. 3M, "About Us/McKnight Principles," http://www.3M.com, October 5, 2004.

Chapter 7

1. Tony Grundy and Laura Brown, *Value-Based Human Resource Strategy: Developing Your Consultancy Role* (Burlington, MA: Elsevier Butterworth-Heinemann, 2003), 19–21.

2. John Sullivan, *Rethinking Strategic HR: HR's Role in Building a Performance Culture* (Chicago: CCH, 2004), 332–335.

3. Ibid., 45–63.

4. Ibid., 351–356.

Chapter 8

1. This chapter on action plans is adapted from the Implementing Strategy module of Harvard ManageMentor, an online product of Harvard Business School Publishing.

2. This sample HR action plan is adapted from Dale A. Currier, "Increasing Retention Through Selection Testing," in *Retaining Your Best Employees: Nine Case Studies from the Real World of Training*, series ed. Jack J. Phillips, ed. Patricia Pulliam Phillips (Alexandria, VA: ASTD and SHRM, 2002), 99–112.

Chapter 9

1. Sections of this chapter are adapted from the Implementing Strategy module of Harvard ManageMentor, an online product of Harvard Business School Publishing.

2. Larry Bossidy and Ram Charan, *Execution: The Discipline of Getting Things Done* (New York: Crown Business, 2002), 15.

Chapter 10

1. Michael L. Tushman and Charles A. O'Reilly III, *Winning Through Innovation* (Boston: Harvard Business School Press, 1997), 190.

2. John P. Kotter, *Leading Change* (Boston: Harvard Business School Press, 1996).

3. John P. Kotter, "Leading Change: Why Transformation Efforts Fail," *Harvard Business Review*, March–April 1995, 66; and adapted from Rebecca Saunders, "Communicating Change," *Harvard Management Communication Letter*, August 1999.

4. Mark A. Huselid, Brian E. Becker, and Richard W. Beatty, *The Workforce Scorecard: Managing Human Capital to Execute Strategy* (Boston: Harvard Business School Press, 2005), 191, 198–203.

Chapter 11

1. Tony Grundy and Laura Brown, *Value-Based Human Resource Strategy: Developing Your Consultancy Role* (Burlington, MA: Elsevier Butterworth-Heinemann, 2003), 204.

2. Linda Holbeche, *Aligning Human Resources and Business Strategy* (Burlington, MA: Elsevier Butterworth-Heinemann, 2001), 296–297.

3. John Sullivan, *Rethinking Strategic HR: HR's Role in Building a Performance Culture* (Chicago: CCH, 2004), 234.

4. Ibid., 243.

5. Ibid., 244–245.

6. Holbeche, *Aligning Human Resources and Business Strategy*, 289–300.

7. Grundy and Brown, *Value-Based Human Resource Strategy*, 209.

8. Holbeche, *Aligning Human Resources and Business Strategy*, 299–300.

9. Ibid., 168–169.

10. Ibid., 167.

11. Andrea C. Poe, "High-Tech Recruitment: A Competitive Strategy," SHRM white paper, Alexandria, VA, May 2000.

12. The remaining items in this list come from Sullivan, *Rethinking Strategic HR*, 413–414.

13. Paul Kearns, *HR Strategy: Business Focused, Individually Centred* (Burlington, MA: Butterworth-Heinemann, 2003), 187–188.

14. Holbeche, *Aligning Human Resources and Business Strategy*, 176.

15. Ibid., 177–180.

16. Ibid., 180–182.

17. Sullivan, *Rethinking Strategic HR*, 414–416.

18. Ibid., 418.

19. Susan J. Wells, "Merging Compensation Strategies," *HR Magazine*, May 2004.

20. Charlotte Garvey, "Philosophizing Compensation," *HR Magazine*, January 2005.

21. Holbeche, *Aligning Human Resources and Business Strategy*, 189–213.

22. Sullivan, *Rethinking Strategic HR*, 21–22.

23. Ibid., 198.

24. Ibid., 199.

Chapter 12

1. Clayton M. Christensen, "Making Strategy: Learning by Doing," *Harvard Business Review*, November–December 1997, 141.

2. Michael E. Porter, "What Is Strategy?" *Harvard Business Review*, November–December 1996, 61–78.

3. Robert S. Kaplan and David P. Norton, "The Balanced Scorecard: Measures That Drive Performance," *Harvard Business Review*, January–February 1992. For a fuller discussion of the Balanced Scorecard methodology and its implementation, see Robert S. Kaplan and David P. Norton, *The Balanced Scorecard* (Boston: Harvard Business School Press, 1996).

4. Dave Ulrich, *Human Resource Champions: The Next Agenda for Adding Value and Delivering Results* (Boston: Harvard Business School Press, 1997), 187.

5. Cris Hagen, "The Role of Human Resources in Whole Systems Change: HR as Scout, Chess Master, Cartographer, and Architect," *Link & Learn*, September 2003.

Chapter 13

1. Edward E. Lawler III and Susan Alberts Mohrman, *Creating a Strategic Human Resources Organization: An Assessment of Trends and New Directions* (Stanford, CA: Stanford Business Books, 2003), 6–9.

2. John Sullivan, *Rethinking Strategic HR: HR's Role in Building a Performance Culture* (Chicago: CCH, 2004), 6–8.

3. Ibid., 12.

4. Ibid., 13.

5. Ibid., 13–14.

6. Lin Grensing-Pophal, "Getting a 'Seat at the Table': What Does It Really Take?" SHRM white paper, Alexandria, VA, August 2000.

7. Magda Du Preez and Eugene Buccini, "Strategies for Being Seen and Heard at the Executive Table," SHRM white paper, Alexandria, VA, March 2004.

8. Sullivan, *Rethinking Strategic HR*, 72–74.

Glossary

ACTION PLAN   A document that addresses strategic objectives and the steps required to achieve them.

ACTION STEPS   The who, what, and when involved in carrying out a strategic initiative and achieving assigned goals. The sum of these action steps should complete the job.

ALIGNMENT   For a business, a condition in which organizational structures, support systems, processes, human skills, and incentives support strategic goals.

BALANCED SCORECARD   A performance measurement system that includes financial measures and three sets of operational measures that relate directly to customer satisfaction, internal processes, and the company's ability to learn and improve—the activities that drive future financial performance.

BENCHMARKING   An objective method for rating one's own activities against similar activities performed by organizations recognized for best practice. In addition to rating oneself, benchmarking aims to identify opportunities for process improvement.

BUSINESS MODEL   A conceptual description of an enterprise's revenue sources, cost drivers, investment size, and success factors and how they work together.

COMPETITIVE ADVANTAGE   A function of strategy that puts a firm in a better position than rivals to create economic value for customers.

CONTINGENCY PLAN   A course of action prepared in advance of a potential problem; it answers this question:"If X happens, how can we respond in a way that will neutralize or minimize the damage?"

CORE COMPETENCE   A company's expertise or skills in key areas that directly produce superior performance.

CULTURE   A company's values, traditions, and operating style.

DIFFERENTIATION STRATEGY   A strategy in which a company deliberately sets its product or service apart from those of rivals in a qualitative way that customers value.

EXPERIENCE CURVE   A concept that holds that the cost of doing a repetitive task decreases by some percentage each time the cumulative volume of production doubles.

FOCUS STRATEGY   A business strategy built on the goal of serving a targeted market or set of customers extremely well.

HURDLE RATE   The minimum rate of return expected from new projects that require substantial capital investments. It is usually calculated as the enterprise's cost of capital plus some expectation of profit.

IMPLEMENTATION   The concrete measures that turn strategic intent into reality.

INTERLOCK   Points of cross-functional collaboration in pursuit of a goal. These might take the form of a task force team, cooperative individuals in departments who supply resources or advice, and so forth.

JUDO STRATEGY   As conceptualized by authors David Yoffie and Mary Kwak, strategic moves based on the principles of movement, balance, and leverage.

KAIZEN   A philosophy of continuous process improvement that encourages everyone, at every level, to seek out ways to incrementally improve what they are doing.

LEAD USERS   Companies and individuals whose needs are far ahead of typical users'.

MARKET SEGMENTATION   A technique for dividing a large heterogeneous market of customers into smaller segments with homogeneous features.

NETWORK EFFECT   A phenomenon in which the value of a product increases as more products are sold.

NETWORK EFFECT STRATEGY   One based on the network effect.

OPERATING MARGIN   A financial ratio used by many analysts to gauge the profitability of a company's operating activities. It is calculated as earnings before interest and taxes (EBIT) divided by net sales.

OPPORTUNITIES   In SWOT analysis, trends, forces, events, and ideas that a company or unit can capitalize on.

PRICE ELASTICITY OF DEMAND   A quantitative measure of customer price sensitivity.

PROCESS REENGINEERING   An improvement concept that aims for large breakthrough change—either through wholesale change or elimination of existing processes.

RETURN ON ASSETS (ROA)   Relates net income to the company's total asset base and is calculated as net income divided by total assets.

RETURN ON EQUITY (ROE)   Relates net income to the amount invested by shareholders (both initially and through retained earnings). It is a measure of the productivity of the shareholders' stake in the business and is calculated as net income divided by shareholders' equity.

SKUNKWORKS   A team of people brought together in one place to generate an innovative solution or to solve a particular problem. In some cases, skunkworks are sited in remote settings to keep team members focused on their mission, to minimize interference from the rest of the organization, or to maintain secrecy.

STRATEGY   A plan that will differentiate the enterprise and give it a competitive advantage over rivals.

STRENGTHS   In SWOT analysis, capabilities that enable a company or unit to perform well—capabilities that need to be leveraged.

SUBSTITUTE   Any good or service that can fill the role of another. Two goods are considered substitutes whenever an increase in the price of one results in increased purchases of the other.

THREATS   In SWOT analysis, possible events or forces that a company or unit must plan for or mitigate.

WEAKNESSES   In SWOT analysis, characteristics that prohibit a company or unit from performing well and need to be addressed.

WINNER-TAKE-ALL STRATEGY   Same as *network effect strategy.*

WORK BREAKDOWN STRUCTURE   A planning tool that decomposes a project's goals into the many tasks and subtasks required to achieve those goals.

WORKFORCE PLANNING   The process of proactively avoiding talent surpluses or shortages, so that an organization has the right number of people, with the right skills, in the right places, at the right time to carry out its competitive strategy.

For Further Reading

Articles

Brewer, Stephen J. "Aligning Human Capital in Achieving Business Goals and Strategic Objectives." SHRM white paper, September 2000.

Brewer affirms that HR is in a unique position to add strategic value. He lays out six steps for aligning human capital with business objectives and goals: (1) establish business objectives and goals, (2) communicate those objectives and goals, (3) align organizational structures behind the objectives and goals, (4) assess employees' capacity to achieve the defined objectives and goals, (5) fill in gaps between capacity and objectives and goals, and (6) implement action plans, measure progress, and modify as needed.

Christensen, Clayton M. "Making Strategy: Learning by Doing." *Harvard Business Review*, November 1997.

Companies find it difficult to change strategy for many reasons, but one stands out: strategic thinking is not a core managerial competence at most companies. Managers are unable to develop competence in strategic thinking because they do it so rarely. Harvard Business School professor Clayton Christensen helps managers develop a creative strategy and a proficiency in strategic decision making. This article presents a three-stage method executives can use to conceive and implement a creative and coherent strategy themselves. The process forces managers to dig deep in order to understand the forces affecting their business and to link strategic thinking with operational planning, two processes that are often separate but are more effective when connected.

Collis, David J., and Cynthia A. Montgomery. "Creating Corporate Advantage." *Harvard Business Review*, May–June 1998.

What differentiates truly great corporate strategies from the merely adequate? How can executives create tangible advantage for their business that makes the whole more than the sum of the parts?

This article presents a comprehensive framework for value creation in the multibusiness company. It addresses the most fundamental questions of corporate strategy: What businesses should a company be in? How should it coordinate activities across businesses? What role should the corporate office play? How should the corporation measure and control performance?

Collis, David J., and Cynthia A. Montgomery. "Competing on Resources." *Harvard Business Review*, July–August, 1995.

How do you create and sustain a profitable strategy? Many approaches to strategy championed in the past have focused managers' attention inward, urging them to build a unique set of resources and capabilities. In practice, however, notions like core competence have too often become a "feel good" exercise that no one fails.

These authors explain how a company's resources drive its performance in a dynamic competitive environment. They propose a new framework that moves strategic thinking forward in two ways: (1) by laying out a pragmatic and rigorous set of market tests to determine whether a company's resources are truly valuable enough to serve as the basis for strategy, and (2) by integrating this market view of capabilities with earlier insights about competition and industry structure.

Eisenhardt, Kathleen, and Don Sull. "Strategy as Simple Rules." *Harvard Business Review*, January 2001.

The success of Yahoo!, eBay, and other companies that have become adept at morphing to meet the demands of changing markets can't be explained using traditional thinking about competitive strategy. These companies have succeeded by pursuing constantly evolving strategies in market spaces that were considered unattractive according to traditional measures. In this article—the third in a *Harvard Business Review* (HBR) series by Kathleen Eisenhardt and Donald Sull on strategy in the new economy—the authors ask, What are the sources of competitive advantage in high-velocity markets? The secret, they say, is strategy as simple rules. Successful companies know that the greatest opportunities for competitive advantage lie in market confusion, but they recognize the need for a few crucial strategic processes and a few simple rules. In traditional strategy, advantage comes from exploiting resources or stable market positions. In strategy as simple rules, advantage comes from successfully seizing fleeting opportunities. Key strategic processes, such as product innovation, partnering, or spinout creation, place the company where the flow of opportunities is greatest. Simple rules then provide the guidelines within which managers can pursue such opportunities.

Simple rules, which grow out of experience, fall into five broad categories: how-to rules, boundary conditions, priority rules, timing rules, and exit rules. Companies with simple-rules strategies must follow the rules strictly and avoid the temptation to change them too frequently. A consistent strategy helps managers sort through opportunities and gain short-term advantage by exploiting the attractive ones.

Gadiesh, Orit, and James L. Gilbert. "Transforming Corner-Office Strategy into Frontline Action." *Harvard Business Review*, May 2001.

In addition to a strategic plan and companywide meetings, organizations use other channels to communicate their strategies to managers and employees. One of these channels is called a *strategic principle*—a memorable, action-oriented phrase that distills the company's strategy. Here are some examples: Southwest Airlines' "Meet customers' short-haul travel needs at fares competitive with the cost of automobile travel"; AOL's "Consumer connectivity first—anytime, anywhere"; eBay's "Focus on trading communities."

A good strategic principle encourages managers and employees to focus on the corporate strategy and take risks in identifying ways to support the strategy. By communicating your company's strategic principle frequently and consistently, you'll soon have people throughout your organization—as well as customers and competitors—"chanting the rant."

Kaplan, Robert S., and David P. Norton. "Using the Balanced Scorecard as a Strategic Management System." *Harvard Business Review*, January–February 1996.

The Balanced Scorecard has attracted widespread notice as a powerful tool for clarifying and communicating strategy throughout an organization, as well as measuring strategy implementation performance.

In this article, the authors explain how the Balanced Scorecard links companies' short-term activities to long-term objectives through four processes: (1) *translating the vision* by forcing managers to agree on the metrics they'll need to realizes their visions; (2) *communicating and linking* the strategy by "cascading" the top-level scorecard down to the units and then to individuals; at each level, people identify objectives and metrics needed to support the corporate-level scorecard; (3) *linking strategic planning and budgeting* by ensuring that financial budgets support strategic goals; and (4) *encouraging feedback and learning* by enabling managers to reflect on inferences suggested by their scorecard results and adjust their theories about cause-and-effect relationships.

Kent, William. "Human Resources: A Strategic Partner." SHRM white paper, July 2002.

Kent lays out the essential ingredients to strengthening HR's strategic impact. HR leaders, he maintains, must have a genuine desire to move their department into a strategic partner role. In addition, they must understand their company and its needs, link the HR business plan to the overall operation, and develop appropriate metrics to assess their department's strategic performance. Developing a more strategic HR function takes time and effort, Kent agrees. But the payoff is well worth it.

Lauby, Sharlyn. "Human Resource Plans: The Foundation for Organizational Strategic Planning." SHRM white paper, 2003.

Lauby identifies the components of a strategic HR plan and lays out the four phases of planning: (1) formulating a vision, mission, and values for the HR function, (2) conducting a SWOT analysis and defining long-term objectives, (3) establishing short-term objectives supporting the longer-term goals, and (4) regularly reviewing progress against the strategy's intended outcomes.

Porter, Michael E. "How Competitive Forces Shape Strategy." *Harvard Business Review*, March–April 1979.

In this award-winning and highly influential article, Porter contends that many factors determine the nature of competition, including not only rivals but also the economics of particular industries, new entrants, the bargaining power of customers and suppliers, and the threat of substitute services or products. A strategic plan might thus include positioning the company so that its capabilities provide the best defense against competitive forces; influencing the balance of forces through strategic moves; and anticipating shifts in the factors underlying competitive forces.

Porter, Michael E. "What Is Strategy?" *Harvard Business Review*, November–December 1996.

In this classic HBR article, Porter explains that today's dynamic markets and technologies have called into question the sustainability of competitive advantage. Under pressure to improve productivity, quality, and speed, managers have embraced tools such as TQM, benchmarking, and reengineering. Dramatic operational improvements have resulted, but rarely have these gains translated into sustainable profitability. And gradually, the tools have taken the place of strategy. As managers push to improve on all fronts, they move further away from viable competitive positions. Michael Porter argues that operational effectiveness, although necessary to superior performance, is not sufficient, because rivals can easily imitate its techniques. In contrast, the essence of strategy is choosing a uniquely valuable position rooted in systems of activities that are much more difficult to copy.

Porter, Michael E. "Strategy and the Internet." *Harvard Business Review*, March 2001.

> Many pioneers of Internet business, both dot-coms and established companies, have competed in ways that violate nearly every precept of good strategy. Rather than focus on profits, they have chased customers indiscriminately through discounting, channel incentives, and advertising. Rather than concentrate on delivering value that earns an attractive price from customers, they have pursued indirect revenues such as advertising and click-through fees. Rather than make trade-offs, they have rushed to offer every conceivable product or service. It did not have to be this way—and it does not have to be in the future. When it comes to reinforcing a distinctive strategy, Michael Porter argues, the Internet provides a better technological platform than previous generations of IT. Gaining competitive advantage does not require a radically new approach to business; it requires building on the proven principles of effective strategy. Porter argues that, contrary to recent thought, the Internet is not disruptive to most existing industries and established companies. It rarely nullifies important sources of competitive advantage in an industry; it often makes them even more valuable. And as all companies embrace Internet technology, the Internet itself will be neutralized as a source of advantage. Robust competitive advantages will arise instead from traditional strengths such as unique products, proprietary content, and distinctive physical activities. Internet technology may be able to fortify those advantages, but it is unlikely to supplant them.

Raffoni, Melissa. "Three Keys to Effective Execution." *Harvard Management Update*, February 2003.

> Strategy execution gets little intellectual respect. In contrast, strategic planning has all the cachet and gets all the ink. Why? Because it rewards creativity, the most valued of intellectual endeavors. But experienced unit heads know that the most creative, visionary strategic planning is useless if it isn't translated into action. Think simplicity, clarity, focus—and review your progress relentlessly. Execution is what separates the companies that prosper during hard times from the ones that go under. The article includes the sidebar "Books on Execution."

Ripley, David E. "Strategic HR Analysis." SHRM white paper, November 1996.

> Ripley focuses on the art of strategic planning. He explains how to define your company's strategic intent ("What business are we in?" "What is our purpose?" "How do we add value in the marketplace?"). He then offers guidelines for defining your company's strategic position—how it will prepare to take advantage of new opportunities or

vanquish emerging threats. Finally, he explains how to determine the key HR issues associated with strategic intent and position.

Ripley, David E. "Business/HR Alignment." SHRM white paper, November 1996.

The author delves even more deeply into strategic HR planning, showing how to determine the HR contributions required to achieve business goals, how to decide which HR processes and activities to retain or outsource, and how to align current HR programs and policies with business objectives. He concludes with a worksheet that can help you generate ideas for your HR strategy.

Van Zwieten, John. "How Not to Waste Your Investment in Strategy." *Training & Development*, June 1999.

Perhaps you've experienced this in your company: the organization creates a great plan for the future but gets undesirable results when it rolls the plan into action. Managers now lack the confidence to carry out a new plan. Good strategy has apparently been defeated by bad change management.

In this article, Van Zwieten explores six common dilemmas faced by executive and lower-level managers attempting to change strategic direction. He then provides a diagnosis for each dilemma and offers lessons. For example, one dilemma is characterized by divisions that are working at cross-purposes. Such companies, the author explains, likely encourage competition between divisions. The solution? An overarching vision of how divisions can cooperate, including a plan for presenting "one face" to customers.

The article concludes by identifying characteristics of the most successful organizations. These include a well-defined purpose that employees understand, a clear explanation of how the proposed change supports the purpose, shared values that guide the way business is practiced, and a BHAG—a "big, hairy, audacious goal" (as defined by James Collins and Jerry Porras).

Books

Aaker, David A. *Developing Business Strategies*. 6th ed. New York: John Wiley & Sons, Inc., 2001.

This practical textbook gives managers a framework for identifying and selecting appropriate strategies. It provides a thorough discussion of strategic analysis—that is, analysis of the market, customers, and competitors. It then explores various categories of alternative strategic choices, including global.

Andrews, Kenneth R. *The Concept of Corporate Strategy*. Rev. ed. Homewood, IL: Richard D. Irwin, Inc., 1980.

First published in 1971, this is the book that started it all. Andrews defined strategy in terms of what a business could do—that is, in terms of its strengths and weaknesses—and what possibilities were open to it—that is, the outer environment of threats and opportunities. *The Concept of Corporate Strategy* remains one of the classics in modern business literature.

Becker, Brian E., Mark A. Huselid, and Dave Ulrich. *The HR Scorecard: Linking People, Strategy, and Performance.* Boston: Harvard Business School Press, 2001.

This book heralded the emergence of HR as a strategic powerhouse in today's organizations. The authors outline a powerful measurement system that highlights the indisputable value HR provides as a prime source of competitive advantage and a key driver of value creation. The measurement system enables you to embed your HR systems within your company's overall strategy and manage your HR architecture as a strategic asset. The authors also show how to link HR results to measures—such as profitability and shareholder value—that other executives understand and respect.

Bossidy, Larry, and Ram Charan. *Execution: The Discipline of Getting Things Done.* New York: Crown Business, 2002.

These authors, a retired CEO and a business consultant, write that "execution is *the* great unaddressed issue in the business world today. Its absence is the biggest single obstacle to success and the cause of most of the disappointments that are mistakenly attributed to other causes." Yes, a great strategy is insufficient for success; a company must also execute the strategy with skill. This book provides prescriptions for strategy execution.

Day, George, and David J. Reibstein. *Wharton on Dynamic Competitive Strategy.* New York: John Wiley & Sons, Inc., 1997.

For strategists at all company levels, the changing external environment represents a serious challenge. This book aims to help readers rise to that challenge by offering a dynamic and integrative view of competitive strategies. Chapters are written by various management professors of the Wharton School.

Fogg, C. Davis. *Implementing Your Strategic Plan: How to Turn Intent into Effective Action for Sustainable Change.* New York: AMACOM, 1999.

This book lays out the steps required to understand your company's strategy and strategic plan, develop a unit plan, and implement your unit plan. Fogg organizes the book around eighteen keys to successful implementation of a plan. These include establishing accountability; turning strategic priorities into assigned, measurable action plans; fostering creative leadership and mental toughness; removing resistance; allocating resources effectively; empowering employees; and communicating strategy to everyone, all the time.

The book includes a wealth of examples, practical advice, and techniques for turning strategic plans into reality. Though aimed at senior managers, it offers lessons for managers and team leaders at every level of an organization.

Fogg, C. Davis. *Team-Based Strategic Planning: A Complete Guide to Structuring, Facilitating, and Implementing the Process*. New York: AMACOM, 1994.

Fogg focuses on strategic planning in a team environment, exploring six key aspects: (1) structure and customization—designing the planning process to meet the needs of your organization, (2) facilitation—making things happen, from running meetings to documenting decisions, (3) teamwork—building teams and resolving conflicts, (4) leadership—forging the vision and making the plan operational, (5) organizational involvement—gaining commitment at all levels, and (6) information gathering and analysis—benchmarking, competitive analyses, and other valuable techniques.

Examples from actual companies illustrate each step of the process, and case studies reveal what worked and what didn't. The book also includes hands-on tools for mastering the strategic planning process.

Huselid, Mark A., Brian E. Becker, and Richard W. Beatty. *The Workforce Scorecard: Managing Human Capital to Execute Strategy*. Boston: Harvard Business School Press, 2005.

Of all the controllable factors affecting a firm's performance, a workforce that can execute the company's strategy is the most critical. It's also the most underperforming asset in most businesses. The problem isn't that executives don't recognize the importance of human capital. Rather, they lack the tools for measuring—and holding line managers accountable for—the impact their workforce has on strategic success.

Building on the best-selling *HR Scorecard*, the authors take the revolutionary Balanced Scorecard model to its next level of performance management. They introduce a management and metrics system that identifies the behaviors, competencies, and mind-set and culture required for workforce success, and that measures these dimensions' bottom-line impact. A sound Workforce Scorecard identifies the critical few measures that really matter, translates those measures into specific actions and accountabilities, and clarifies what is expected of employees and how they can improve. It also identifies high- and low-performing employees and provides differentiated compensation and benefits systems, determines supporting HR management systems and metrics, and specifies the roles of leadership, the workforce, and HR in strategy execution.

Keen, Christine D. *Effective Strategic Planning: A Handbook for Human Resource Professionals*. Alexandria, VA: Society for Human Resource Management, 1994.

   The author explains why strategic planning is an essential skill for HR professionals and what strategic planning means. She also identifies the components of a strategic plan and describes how to conduct a SWOT analysis. In addition, she provides guidelines for setting strategic objectives, developing an action plan, and evaluating progress. A sample strategic plan for an HR department is included.

Kieffer, David, Haig Nalbantian, Rick Guzzo, and Jay Doherty. *Playing to Your Strengths*. New York: McGraw-Hill Publishing Company, 2003.

   Few executives take the time to examine the alignment between their business strategies and their people practices and policies. These authors explain how misalignment here can jeopardize the success of even the best strategy. Their research describes several companies whose promotion, retention, and rewards practices were inadvertently encouraging employee behaviors contrary to strategic intentions. In one case, a U.S. manufacturer's policy of building general management skills through frequent, short-term job assignments was undermining its higher goals of product quality and bringing new models to market quickly. Analysis indicated that managers who accepted short-term assignments were rewarded with promotions and higher pay, but they failed to build the technical skills needed to advance the company's higher-level strategy.

Lawler, Edward E. III, and Susan Alberts Mohrman. *Creating a Strategic Human Resources Organization: An Assessment of Trends and New Directions*. Stanford, CA: Stanford Business Books, 2003.

   This book explains how changes in the business environment affect human resources and explores the question of how HR can become an even more strategic business partner. The authors provide guidelines for leveraging talent strategies, shared services, outsourcing, IT, and e-HR systems to define effective HR strategies that support the corporate strategy.

Markides, Constantinos C. *All the Right Moves: A Guide to Crafting Breakthrough Strategy*. Boston: Harvard Business School Press, 2000.

   Markides explores the key questions companies must answer to define a strategy: "Who should we target as customers? What products or services should we offer them? How should we do this efficiently? How can we differentiate ourselves from rivals to stake out a unique competitive position?"

   But even the best strategies have a limited life. Companies must continually create new strategic positions—often by breaking the rules of the game. *All the Right Moves* reveals how creative thinking—including examining an issue from a variety of angles and experimenting with new ideas—leads to strategic innovation.

Strategy formulation also requires companies to make tough choices. This book offers concrete advice for thinking through those choices—systematically and successfully.

Pascale, Richard T. *Managing on the Edge: Companies That Use Conflict to Stay Ahead*. New York: Simon & Schuster, 1990.

Pascale, an academic and consultant, is concerned with corporate renewal. He recommends that executives attend to four principles to keep their companies at the top of their games. These are: fit, split, contend, and transcend. *Fit* describes the corporation's internal consistency; *split* refers to the wisdom of reducing big organizations into smaller, more manageable units; *contend* refers to the inevitable organizational contradictions that must be managed. Leaders must also *transcend* the complexity that afflicts every business

Phillips, Jack J., and Adele O. Connell. *Managing Employee Retention: A Strategic Accountability Approach*. Burlington, MA: Elsevier Butterworth-Heinemann, and Alexandria, VA: Society for Human Resource Management, 2003.

This book examines a key lever for formulating and implementing corporate strategy: employee retention. During the past decade, turnover has become a serious problem for many organizations. Managing retention and keeping the turnover rate below target and industry norms is one of the most daunting business challenges. All evidence suggests the challenge will become even tougher in the future.

By managing turnover, HR professionals can add enormous strategic value to their organizations. This practical guide explains how to retain your company's talented employees, how to manage and monitor turnover, and how to develop the ROI of keeping your talent using innovative retention programs. The authors describe a logical process for managing retention—from identifying turnover costs and causes and designing solutions that address the root causes of turnover, to developing tools for tracking turnover and putting alerts in place to prompt intervention.

Phillips, Jack J., series ed., and Patricia Pulliam Phillips, ed. *Retaining Your Best Employees: Nine Case Studies from the Real World of Training*. Alexandria, VA: ASTD and Society for Human Resource Management, 2002.

This volume contains a wealth of case studies of companies that used savvy HR strategies to improve retention of key employees. A helpful complement to Phillips and Connell's *Managing Employee Retention*, this book helps HR practitioners who are struggling to identify the most credible process to manage retention.

Porter, Michael E. *Competitive Strategy: Techniques for Analyzing Industries and Competitors.* New York: Free Press, 1980.

This granddaddy of all strategy books has influenced more business executives around the world than any other. In explaining how to analyze the competitive situation in an industry, the author captures the complexity of industry competition as five underlying forces. He also explains three generic strategies—low-cost, differentiation, and focus—and demonstrates how these can help a firm define its strategic positioning and enhance profitability.

Readers will find Porter's treatment of rival firms very useful. He provides a practical framework for predicting how competitors will respond to one's own strategic moves. The book provides two helpful appendixes: Portfolio Techniques in Competitor Analysis, and How to Conduct an Industry Analysis.

Sullivan, John. *Rethinking Strategic HR: HR's Role in Building a Performance Culture.* Chicago: CCH, 2004.

In this exceptionally clear and readable book, Sullivan explains how to manage HR strategically. He clarifies HR's strategic role and shows how to select an HR strategy. He then examines, one by one, the ten essential criteria a strategic HR department must meet: increasing workforce productivity, having an external focus on affecting business objectives, using performance culture tools, providing the company with a competitive advantage, making fact-based decisions using metrics, being proactive and future focused, coordinating its efforts, having a global approach, building a brand, and leveraging technology.

Yoffie, David and Mary Kwak. *Judo Strategy: Turning Your Competitors' Strength to Your Advantage.* Boston: Harvard Business School Press, 2001.

These authors reveal how a century-old strategy can enable smaller firms to meet and defeat rivals many times their size. At the heart of judo strategy is the premise that sheer size and raw strength are no match for balance, skill, and flexibility. Using examples from companies such as Wal-Mart, Palm, CNET, and others, the authors explain how to translate the three key principles of judo into a winning business strategy: use movement to throw off your opponent's balance; maintain your balance as you respond to attacks; and exploit leverage to magnify your strength. Highly practical tools aid managers in developing their own judo strategies, including identifying competitors' vulnerabilities, staking out unoccupied terrain, and regaining ground after setbacks. A warrior's manual for understanding how judo strategy and defense can strengthen your firm, this powerful book is for both Davids and Goliaths who want to compete and win on the new business battlefield.

Research Reports

Collison, Jessica, and Cassandra Frangos. *Aligning HR with Organization Strategy Survey.* Alexandra, VA: Society for Human Resource Management, and Lincoln, MA: Balanced Scorecard Collaborative, November 2002.

The authors interpret the responses to a survey of 1,310 senior HR professionals who answered questions about how they approach management of human capital, develop and gain approval for HR strategies, review performance relative to strategic goals and initiatives, and other aspects of formulating and executing corporate-level and HR strategies. The survey results reveal the achievements and challenges characterizing the field of strategic HR management. For example, though many organizations have a clear strategic direction, not all of them communicate that direction clearly enough throughout their workforces. And though many employees in the higher levels of organizations understand the strategic direction, many people working in the lower levels have only a partial understanding.

Additional Titles from the Society for Human Resource Management (SHRM)®

Carrig, Ken, and Patrick M. Wright. *Building Profit through Building People: Making Your Workforce the Strongest Link in the Value-Profit Chain*

Collier, T. O., Jr. *Supervisor's Guide to Labor Relations*

Cook, Mary, and Scott Gildner. *Outsourcing Human Resources Functions: How, Why, When, and When Not to Contract for HR Services*

Gardenswartz, Lee, and Anita Rowe. *Diverse Teams at Work*

Grensing-Pophal, Lin, SPHR. *Human Resource Essentials: Your Guide to Starting and Running the HR Function*

Landry, R.J. *The Comprehensive, All-in-One HR Operating Guide.* 539 ready-to-adapt human resources policies, practices, letters, memos, forms . . . and more.

HR Source Book Series

Bliss, Wendy, J.D., SPHR, and Gene Thornton, Esq., PHR. *Employment Termination Source Book*

Deblieux, Mike. *Performance Appraisal Source Book*

Fyock, Cathy, CSP, SPHR. *Hiring Source Book*

Hubbartt, William S., SPHR, CCP. *HIPAA Privacy Source Book*

Lambert, Jonamay, MA, and Selma Myers, MA. *Trainer's Diversity Source Book*

Practical HR Series

Bliss, Wendy, JD, SPHR. *Legal, Effective References: How to Give and Get Them*

Oppenheimer, Amy, JD, and Craig Pratt, MSW, SPHR. *Investigating Workplace Harassment: How to Be Fair, Thorough, and Legal*

Phillips, Jack J., PhD, and Patricia Pulliam Phillips, PhD. *Proving the Value of HR: How and Why to Measure ROI*

Shaw, Seyfarth, LLP. *Understanding the Federal Wage & Hour Laws: What Employers Must Know about FLSA and Its Overtime Regulations*

How to Order from SHRM

SHRM offers a member discount on all books that it publishes or sells. To order this or any other book published by the Society, contact the SHRM-Store.®

Online: www.shrm.org/shrmstore

Phone: 1-800-444-5006 (option #1); or 770-442-8633 (ext. 362); or tdd 703-548-6999

Fax: 770-442-9742

Mail: SHRM Distribution Center, P.O. Box 930132, Atlanta, GA 31193-0132, USA

Index

About the Subject Adviser

For the past eighteen years DAVID J. COLLIS has been a professor at Harvard Business School, where he continues to teach and chair executive education programs. Collis was formerly a professor at Yale University School of Management and Columbia Business School.

About the Series Adviser

WENDY BLISS, J.D., SPHR, has experience as a human resource executive, attorney, senior editor, and professional speaker. Since 1994, she has provided human resource consulting, corporate training, and coaching services nationally through her Colorado Springs–based consulting firm, Bliss & Associates.

Ms. Bliss is the author of *Legal, Effective References: How to Give and Get Them*, the coauthor of *The Employment Termination Source Book: A Collection of Practical Samples*, and a contributor to *Human Resource Essentials*, all published by the Society for Human Resource Management. She has published numerous articles in magazines and periodicals, including *HR Magazine, Employment Management Today, HR Matters,* and the *Denver University Law Review.*

Ms. Bliss received a B.A. degree 'With Highest Distinction' from the University of Kansas and a J.D. degree from the University of Denver College of Law. She is certified as a Senior Professional in Human Resources by the Human Resource Certification Institute. Since 1999, she has conducted human resource certificate programs for the Society for Human Resource Management. Previously, she was an adjunct faculty member at the University of Colorado at Colorado Springs and at the University of Phoenix, where she taught graduate and undergraduate courses in human resource management, employment law, organizational behavior, and business communications. Additionally, Ms. Bliss has served on the board of directors for several professional associations and nonprofit organizations and was a President of the National

Board of Governors for the Society for Human Resource Management's Consultants Forum.

National media, including *ABC News, Time* magazine, the *New York Times,* the Associated Press, the *Washington Post,* USAToday .com, and *HR Magazine,* have looked to Ms. Bliss for expert opinions on workplace issues.

About the Writers

LAUREN KELLER JOHNSON has contributed to numerous volumes in the Business Literacy for HR Professionals series. Based in Harvard, Massachusetts, Keller Johnson writes for a variety of business publications, including the *Harvard Business Review* OnPoint Series, *Harvard Management Update, Contingent Workforce Strategies, Sloan Management Review*, the *Balanced Scorecard Report*, and *Supply Chain Strategy*. She has written numerous modules for Harvard Business School Publishing's online instructional series Harvard ManageMentor, Case in Point, and Stepping Up to Management, as well as online training modules for the Balanced Scorecard Collaborative. She has a master's degree in technical and professional writing from Northeastern University.

RICHARD LUECKE is the writer of several books in the Harvard Business Essentials series. Based in Salem, Massachusetts, Luecke has authored or developed more than thirty books and dozens of articles on a wide range of business subjects. He has an M.B.A. from the University of St. Thomas.

About the Society for Human Resource Management

THE SOCIETY FOR HUMAN RESOURCE MANAGEMENT (SHRM) is the world's largest association devoted to human resource management. Representing more than 170,000 individual members, the Society has a mission to serve the needs of HR professionals by providing the most essential and comprehensive resources available. As an influential voice, the Society has also defined a mission to advance the human resource profession to ensure that HR is recognized as an essential partner in developing and executing organizational strategy. Visit SHRM Online at www.shrm.org.

The Results-Driven Manager

The Results-Driven Manager series collects timely articles from Harvard Management Update and Harvard Management Communication Letter to help senior to middle managers sharpen their skills, increase their effectiveness, and gain a competitive edge. Presented in a concise, accessible format to save managers valuable time, these books offer authoritative insights and techniques for improving job performance and achieving immediate results.

These books are priced at $14.95 U.S.
Price subject to change.

How to Order

Harvard Business School Press publications are available worldwide from your local bookseller or online retailer.
You can also call

1-800-668-6780

Our product consultants are available to help you
8:00 a.m.–6:00 p.m., Monday–Friday, Eastern Time.
Outside the U.S. and Canada, call: 617-783-7450
Please call about special discounts for quantities greater than ten.

You can order online at

www.HBSPress.org